THE PARENT TRAP

THE PARENT TRAP

How to Stop Overloading Parents and
Fix Our Inequality Crisis

NATE G. HILGER

The MIT Press
Cambridge, Massachusetts
London, England

The MIT Press would like to thank the anonymous peer reviewers who provided comments on drafts of this book. The generous work of academic experts is essential for establishing the authority and quality of our publications. We acknowledge with gratitude the contributions of these otherwise uncredited readers.

This book was set in Adobe Garamond Pro by New Best-set Typesetters Ltd. Printed and bound in the United States of America.

Library of Congress Cataloging-in-Publication Data

Names: Hilger, Nate G., author.
Title: The parent trap : how to stop overloading parents and fix our inequality crisis / Nate G. Hilger.
Description: Cambridge, Massachusetts : The MIT Press, 2022. | Includes bibliographical references and index.
Identifiers: LCCN 2021033955 | ISBN 9780262046688 (hardcover)
Subjects: LCSH: Child rearing—United States. | Parent and child—United States. | Child care—United States.
Classification: LCC HQ769 .H5585 2022 | DDC 649/.1—dc23
LC record available at https://lccn.loc.gov/2021033955

10   9   8   7   6   5   4   3   2   1

To my parents, Judith and Christopher, my wife, Bao, and our son, Felix.

Contents

INTRODUCTION

Over the past 20 years, many industries have spent a great deal of money on lobbying to support their economic interests. The US Chamber of Commerce spent $1.5 billion to support business interests. Unions spent $700 million to back labor interests. Real estate, health, pharmaceutical, aviation, and petroleum companies together spent more than $3 billion. The American Association of Retired People (AARP) spent $300 million to support elderly people's interests.[1]

There is one major industry that is not on this list. By many measures, it is the largest industry in the country. Given its failure to lobby, the industry receives little political support. Its many workers toil in isolation, without recognition or compensation. Their backbreaking labor is not counted in any official statistics, as if it were secret or illegitimate. The industry has no centralized organization representing its interests. Relative to its size, it spends almost nothing on research and development to improve operations over time. The industry shuffles along at a fraction of its potential capacity, its participants underutilized, inefficient, overwhelmed.

What is this monumental ghost industry? Parenting.

THE TWO SIDES OF PARENTING

We don't often think of parenting as an "industry" or of parents as "workers," and for good reason. Parents volunteer for the job. They want to do it, and they're more than happy to do it for free. In many ways, parenting is no more a "job" than loving or living. But just because love moves people to do a job for free doesn't mean their work isn't producing something of enormous cultural and economic value. And it is production of that value that can usefully be thought of, in some respects, as a major industry.

Every year American parents provide full-time, overtime, comprehensive child-development services to America's 74 million children. If we value these services at market rate—what it would take to buy the most comparable services we can find for money—they sum to more than $5 trillion of output every year.[2] Valued in this way, parenting emerges as the largest industry in the United States, easily beating out health care in second place at less than $4 trillion. So let's step back for a moment and see what happens if we view parents as members of a (very) important industry. In this capacity, parents have two main kinds of responsibilities.

One of these responsibilities is to *care* for children. Caring is the more personal side of parenting. In this role, parents do their best to love children, protect them, provide for them, bring them joy, and comfort them against life's many slings and arrows. In their caring role, parents also pass along cherished cultural practices, rituals, and faiths to enrich their children's lives.

The second responsibility of parents is to *build skills in children*. This is the more professional side of parenting. In this role, parents manage complex investments in all aspects of children's skill growth. Skills go far beyond "book smarts" such as math and reading. They include general skills such as strength and dexterity, confidence and wit, tenacity and discipline. They also include more specific skills, such as how to play football or tennis, chess or guitar, how to fix a flat tire or build a campfire. These and so many other skills equip children to flourish independently in adulthood.

As a form of wealth, skills are "assets." All assets yield a flow of economic value to their owners over time. Stocks, for example, yield dividends and capital gains. Real estate yields rents. Cars yield transportation services. Skills yield value in the form of higher income, career satisfaction, health, and *fun*.

Despite their diversity, all skills have some key things in common that distinguish them from other kinds of assets. Perhaps the most important and strange feature of skills is that they are *taught* and *learned* rather than bought and sold instantaneously at a fixed price. Learning a skill is a messy process involving different combinations of time, effort, and psychological friction for each individual person.

Compare skills to other kinds of assets, like stocks. Anyone can buy a share of Google stock at the going rate (as of now, $2,349 per share) off the New York Stock Exchange and start earning dividends and capital gains right away. Same for automobiles. Anyone can buy a new, base-model Ford Explorer for about $33,000 and start driving it right away.[3] You get the vehicle fully formed from a dealership, which in turn buys it from a factory that makes thousands of Explorers every year. Skills don't work anything like this. There is no "base model" of literacy or tenacity or guitar skills you can buy at a going rate from a dealership or an exchange. To acquire these skills, you have to find a teacher or a community or a manual, and you have to study, observe, struggle, and practice, all while wondering anxiously if slow progress is normal or troubling and whether the opaque rewards will justify the unpredictable costs. Because skills are taught and learned rather than bought and sold, their acquisition is much more complex and prone to mistakes than the acquisition of other assets.

Throughout history, we have tended to combine the two activities of caring and skill building into one word: *parenting*. But, in reality, due to the unusual nature of skills, caring and skill building are as different as night and day.

Caring is *egalitarian* in that most people can do it successfully. That's not to say we can take it for granted. Some parents abuse or neglect their kids in terrible ways. An online group called Raised by Narcissists has more than 600,000 members. Literature is replete with uncaring parents from *Macbeth* to *Matilda*. But most people do grow into the caring role of parenthood. Many parents, moved by sheer love, develop a certain type of genius when it comes to caring about children.

Building skills, in contrast, is not egalitarian. It is not widely accessible to all parents. Many parents who become experts in the caring department never quite master skill development.

Does reading that make you anxious? Am I accusing some parents of *failure*? Of *inferiority*? No, but it's easy to see why you might feel that way.

We've been programmed to believe that any parents who love their children also have what it takes to build skills, and anyone who says otherwise must be questioning that love. I call this bait and switch the "Parent Trap" because it helps to trap parents in a system that guarantees many of them will fail at preparing their children for success in adulthood.

Why does the Parent Trap persist? Because it has served to protect and legitimize all our society's deepest power hierarchies for generations. Rich and white people's success has had to reflect their superiority, not their greater access to elite skill-building resources in childhood. Women's historical exclusion from professions outside child development has had to reflect male superiority; therefore, child development has had to be deemed simple and instinctual.

In this book, I focus on America, today, at a time when certain kinds of skills have been rising in value for decades.[4] But, in fact, the delegation of child skill growth to parents—isolated individuals often preoccupied with survival and ill equipped to build complex skills—has fueled and rationalized inequality around the world for thousands of years. As the psychologist George Stoddard once wrote, "The chief advantage of kings is not in their lineage; it is in the power, often neglected, to establish from birth upwards the right kind of protection and education."[5] Different skills have brought greater opportunity and wealth throughout history, but their development has been assigned to parents and thereby tacitly reserved for elites. From obtaining literacy and numeracy in medieval Europe to preparing for the national Civil Service Exam in imperial China to building physical and mental strength in feudal societies, some version of this pattern has always applied.[6]

When you feel yourself reacting emotionally to the idea that many kinds of skill building are not accessible to most parents, you are channeling centuries of turmoil and exploitation. You may even sense a glimmer of shame—shame about your own parenting or shame about feeling arrogant or judgmental toward other parents. This shame is how mythologies survive. Our language itself is part of the trick. The trick is to define one word, *parenting*, to convey two glaringly different concepts: *caring* and *skill building*. That way, if we question equal access to one aspect of parenting, we can be accused of questioning equal access to the other. We can be accused of suggesting that many parents don't care about their children.

That is the Parent Trap. In this book, we'll learn how to recognize, avoid, and solve the Parent Trap. We'll transform that anxiety you're feeling into political energy, inspired by hope that an alternate, better reality is possible. The truth is that parents can and should be primarily responsible for caring about children—*and that's it*.

THE POWER OF SKILLS

How we manage skill growth matters because skills are the bedrock of our economy. In 2020, the US economy produced about $20 trillion worth of goods and services. That's everything from soy beans and cell phones to surgeries and surfing lessons. Where does all this valuable stuff come from? Some of it comes from harnessing "capital," such as land, buildings, and machines. But most of it comes from "labor," or human skill—probably about two-thirds of it, or $14 trillion, every year.[7]

Skills drive overall income, but they also drive inequality in that income, alongside other factors including luck, social connections, preferences, and a wide range of institutions and policies from labor unions to minimum wages. In particular, skills play a central role in two of the most worrisome kinds of inequality: the one emerging for children of different classes and the one emerging for children of different races.[8]

Today in America, a child raised by the top 25 percent richest parents will wind up earning about $50,000 more per year than a child raised by the bottom 25 percent poorest parents. Over a lifetime, this rich-kid advantage is like inheriting a trust fund at age 18 worth nearly a million dollars. Black–white income gaps are almost as large, at $36,000 per year. How important are skills, as opposed to other factors such as labor-market discrimination and social connections, in driving these gaps by class and race? One way to answer this question is to compare the incomes of kids from different classes and races who wind up accumulating similar skills in childhood.[9]

Skills, of course, are hard to measure. One very limited measure is the Armed Forces Qualifying Test (AFQT), which is similar to an IQ test.

These kinds of tests measure a narrow subset of skills often referred to as "cognitive" skills, such as basic math, reading comprehension, and pattern recognition. They make no attempt to measure behavioral skills such as self-control, social skills such as confidence, or emotional skills such as resilience. But if rich and poor kids perform equally well on just this one measure of cognitive skill as teenagers, 70 percent of their future income gap disappears. The rich kid still winds up a bit richer, but, then again, the AFQT doesn't capture all of the rich kid's skill advantages.[10]

As we might expect, AFQT scores account for a smaller share of the Black–white income gap—about 50 percent, instead of 70 percent. That is still a lot of racial income inequality to explain with skills captured by one little test, but it's consistent with evidence that discrimination remains a powerful force in American society. Discrimination includes daily insults, such as extra scrutiny while shopping in stores and longer wait times at crosswalks, as well as major setbacks in employment, health care, criminal justice, and so many other systems we all rely on to build economic success. And as we will see, long-term discrimination has also made it harder for people of color to acquire skills.[11]

The AFQT captures something important, but it's just one little test score and cannot possibly capture the full contribution of skill inequality to economic inequality. One way to capture a broader set of skills is to look at whether people attend college and the type of college they attend. Attending a better college has typically required not just higher scores on tests such as the SAT and ACT that are similar to the AFQT but also better grades, teacher recommendations, application essays, and experience in extracurricular pursuits such as sports, music, and activism. Beyond the skills required for admission, better colleges also build additional skills through access to richer educational resources.[12]

One useful way to assess the role of skills more broadly would therefore be to compare incomes of rich and poor children or Black and white children who attended the exact same college, majored in the same discipline, and performed equally well. This comparison has remained elusive because it requires very detailed data on large numbers of children. But in 2017 a team of economists made a good start by leveraging an astonishing new data set that we'll come back to repeatedly in this book. For the first time they were able to compare outcomes of rich and poor kids attending the same exact colleges.[13] Their results showed that, at thousands of colleges around the country, attending the same college at age 19 cut the future income gap between rich and poor kids by about 80 percent. In other words, the careers of college classmates appeared to unfold on a playing field that was, miraculously, *almost level*.

These findings about college, alongside those about test scores, suggest that skills provide the key bridge to economic security in today's American economy. This is clearly true for poor kids, and it's only somewhat less true for Black kids and other racial minorities. And as we'll see, despite the persistence of discrimination, skills play a larger role in explaining racial inequality than these numbers appear to suggest because group skills operate differently from individual skills.

It's hard to overstate the importance of skills in driving economic outcomes. If we could find a way to expand access to skill-development resources, we would increase overall incomes dramatically, *and* we would largely eliminate the most pernicious aspects of inequality in America.

WHO BUILDS SKILLS?

So who *should* be in charge of building all these valuable skills, if not parents? The same kinds of people we put in charge of other complex tasks: professionals. People such as teachers, tutors, counselors, coaches, nurses, and physicians, financed by the general public.

But don't we already do that? Aren't I basically describing *schools*? Schools have teachers, counselors, coaches, and nurses. The Parent Trap thrives on the idea that schools are the primary skill builders. And it's true that the public schools we provide to all children do hire professionals to build skills. *But they build only a small fraction of the skills we need children to develop.*

This is one of the great misunderstandings of our society. Look at it this way: because skills are taught and learned rather than bought and sold, the primary raw ingredient in skill development is *time*. When we add up the total share of hours kids spend in formal public school—from conception to age 18—it turns out to be only *10 percent* of childhood. How is that possible? Public school—the only education everyone gets for free—begins at age five, operates only half of all days each year, and spans only one-third of all hours in each day. That's more time than kids used to get. About 150 years ago, kids spent 3 percent of their childhood in public school. But the current 10 percent still leaves an awful lot of skill building unaccounted for.[14]

Does it really matter that kids *sleep* outside of school? Should we count those hours as part of skill development? Absolutely. Kids who sleep better build more skills, and sleep quality varies dramatically by family environment. Noise, lack of privacy, heat, absence of safety, mold, smoke, air pollution, roaches, and rats remind us that inequality does not magically disappear at night.[15]

The remaining 90 percent of time outside of school is overseen, structured, and managed by *parents*. It is in this 90 percent of time that children must gain physical, social, emotional, and cognitive skills that schools have no choice but to shortchange during the scant instructional hours under their control.

Time is the biggest ingredient in child skill development, but not the only one. There's also money. Public schools spend a lot on kids but not nearly as much as parents do. In addition to direct expenditures, the time parents spend on children has enormous financial value. If we add up these investments, schools account for only 15 percent of spending on children.[16]

THE REAL "SAVAGE INEQUALITIES"

If you think schools are where kids gain skills, it's natural to fixate on inequality in public-school resources. And that's made a lot of sense. For most of American history, rich and white kids have attended schools with much greater resources than poor and minority kids.[17] But if you're really worried about skill gaps among children *today* in America, you should

Table 0.1

Inequality in Schools versus Families

Skill-Building Resource	School Gap	Family Gap
Per Pupil Spending	2%	1,576%
Teacher Skills (% with BA degree)	~ 0%	256%
Teacher Skills (Test Scores)	~ 10%	150%
Instructional Time*	~ 0%	23%
Class Size*	~ 0%	21%

Notes: Gaps represent the percent advantage of rich children over poor children in the specified skill-building resource, where rich and poor are defined approximately as top and bottom parental income quartiles, respectively. The asterisk indicates the difference between children with parents holding college degrees versus those holding only high school degrees rather than different by high and low income, due to data availability. See appendix table A.2 for sources and related gaps by race.

be thinking way beyond inequality in K12 public schools. You should be thinking about inequality in the families we require to do most of the skill building.

Take a look at table 0.1. This table combines a variety of data sources to look at resource gaps between rich and poor kids in two environments: schools and families. Start with the first row, which focuses on education spending. For schools, this is the gap in total budgets. For families, this is the gap in "enrichment" spending on things such as books, computers, tutoring, sports, and summer camps. The gap in per pupil spending in public schools across rich and poor kids is 2 percent, meaning rich kids get about 2 percent more resources than poor kids when they're at school. The per pupil spending gap across rich and poor kids at home is *1,576 percent*.[18]

Huh?? That's right: rich kids get *fifteen times* the enrichment spending of poor kids during that 90 percent of time they spend out of school.

Take the second row: rich and poor kids all learn from teachers with college degrees at school. But rich kids are *256 percent* more likely to learn from teachers at home (parents) with college degrees. The third row: rich kids learn from teachers at home who score *150 percent higher* on a common test of certain kinds of cognitive skills.

The story goes on. At school, on average rich and poor kids get identical instructional time, delivered in classes of equal size. At home, the kids of richer parents get 23 percent more "instructional time" on things such as help with homework, museum visits, and reading out loud. And rich kids get this extra time at home in 21 percent smaller "classes" due to their greater likelihood of living with two parents and fewer siblings. The story is similar for white and Black children:[19] public K12 school-resource gaps today are nonexistent or small compared to vast differences at home between racial groups.[20]

Many people find it shocking that poor and minority children in America today on average attend K12 schools with similar funding. More than shocking, they find it implausible, and it's easy to see why. Many journalists eloquently describe jarring school resource gaps by race and class, and books like *Savage Inequalities* by Jonathan Kozol contrast the kinds of schools attended by rich and poor children in parts of the United States.[21]

In fact, although many examples of school resource gaps do exist and warrant concern, they do not represent the typical situation in American schools today. If that's true, why all the confusion? A few reasons. First, many of these comparisons ignore federal funding, which goes largely to schools serving poor children. This is like calculating personal income without counting tips or bonuses—it's not a complete picture. Once we combine federal, state, and local funding, school resource gaps vanish or even reverse.[22]

Another reason for the confusion is that old perceptions change slowly, and so it's difficult to see that things have gotten much more equal in America's schools. This didn't happen by accident; it resulted from monumental efforts made by legal and political activists. A hundred years ago there really were massive public-school resource gaps by class and race. These days, however, state and federal spending play a larger role than local property-tax revenue and distribute educational resources more progressively.[23]

The final reason for the confusion is that average school resource gaps capture only the typical situation. For any average, there will be many *atypical* situations that can be cherry-picked to confirm any preconceived notion.

As an example, consider one influential article from the *Washington Post* entitled "In 23 States, Richer School Districts Get More Local

Funding Than Poorer Districts." Here the author excludes federal funding from the calculation. She then focuses overtly on only 23 states. Here's an equally accurate, alternative headline: "In 27 States, Poorer School Districts Get More Local Funding Than Richer Districts." In fact, when we include federal aid, 42 states spent more on poor school districts than on rich school districts in 2012. The same pattern holds between schools within districts.[24]

Many readers still find these claims hard to believe. I must be twisting the numbers! So let's get more concrete. Let's examine some outlier school districts with very high and very low per student spending in the United States. What's your guess for the highest-spending districts? Maybe Princeton or Palo Alto? And what's your guess for the lowest-spending districts? Maybe Bedford-Stuyvesant in Brooklyn or the South Side of Chicago?

Not quite. The highest-spending districts are large urban centers such as New York City, Boston, and Baltimore. These cities spend large sums to educate rich and poor children alike. The lowest-spending districts are harder to explain, but they're not poor inner-city neighborhoods. Many of them are in . . . Utah. Why is that? Because Utah has a lot of Mormons, and Mormons have big families. Most education funding still comes from state and local sources. With more children per working adult, Utah schools make do with less funding per student. This funding gap may explain in part why Utah, a rich state, has performed at or below average in academic achievement.[25]

Cypress-Fairbanks and Conroe are two very low-spending districts in Texas. These districts win awards for high academic achievement and serve families with above-average income for the state. Their low spending appears to reflect good management and low costs of living.[26] Several of the lowest-spending districts, such as Capistrano Unified School District, are in California, but these districts don't serve disproportionately poor or minority students. The main factor here is that California education spending overall is low due to decades of bad public-policy mistakes.[27]

The image of low-income, minority children sitting in large classes with badly paid teachers and no resources for books or field trips was accurate for most of American history. Today that image is exceptional, not typical.[28] Although more resources for schools serving poor kids would be useful, this goal should not distract parents from much larger solutions that will be required to close the current skill deficits between rich and poor kids.[29]

Inequality stems not from our public schools but from our neglect of the primary skill builders hiding in plain sight: parents. When we put "family gaps" into perspective, we see that they dwarf K12 school gaps. In fact, they surpass many of the K12 school gaps that distinguished Black and white segregated schools during the "separate but equal" farce under Jim Crow.

Don't get me wrong. I'm not claiming that schools today are equal in all respects. Despite their similar access to funding, lower-income and minority children still experience significant gaps in teacher experience, qualifications, and overall quality. These resource gaps do matter, but they are small in comparison to family gaps. If today's K12 quality gaps are like cracks in a sidewalk, family gaps are like potholes obstructing entire roads. And more importantly, these residual school gaps are largely *caused by* family gaps. Why is that? Because teachers prefer to work with better-prepared, better-supported students. This means communities with parents who are more advantaged at skill building also have a leg up when it comes to hiring and retaining the best teachers.[30]

Overall, children's skill gaps by class and race barely grow during the sliver of time they spend in K12 schools. The large skill gaps by class and race spring up almost entirely before kids enter the public K12 system, when they spend half a decade immersed in radically unequal skill-building environments. After they reach the relative safe haven of K12 schools, skill gaps expand more slowly, and much of this unequal growth occurs *outside of school hours.*[31]

It's pretty simple, really. Kids with fewer resources fall behind during the 90 percent of time we ask parents to manage skill building on their own. That means K12 schools are not the bastions of unequal opportunity we've been led to believe they are. They're actually the smallest and most equalizing part of a much larger skill-building system. Once we grasp that fact, the world turns upside down.

A BETTER WAY

To see our mistake, we need a new perspective. When we talk about building all the skills that allow children to thrive later in life, we can't focus on just one small part of childhood arbitrarily defined as "school." We have to fund and cultivate skill growth during *childhood*.

These opportunities are not mysterious. We're talking about things such as easy, affordable access to high-quality early education, innovative after-school and summer programs, and a richer college and early career support system. New programs would expand the meaning and mandate of "public school" by shifting a larger share of childhood into high-quality skill-building environments that don't require so much parental time, money, or expertise to access or maintain. Parents would not be excluded; they would simply be given breathing room to focus more energy on what they do best, which is to care for their children in the way no one else ever can or will, while managing the rest of their own adult responsibilities as partners, friends, caretakers, creators, and workers. The economic return on many of the proposed investments in skill building would dwarf the return on more conventional investments in things such as business and real estate, and most of these returns would accrue to kids of working- and middle-class parents.

We're not talking about charity. We're talking about cold, hard calculations of collective self-interest. Like it or not, we're all shareholders in each other's children. Your highly skilled kids will invent new technologies, create new works of art, devise new geopolitical strategies, and start new companies that spin off untold value for the rest of us. Someone raised Albert Einstein, Toni Morrison, Franklin Roosevelt, Serena Williams. Those people were parents or other caretakers, putting in work. And if your children get the investments they need to form better-paying careers, we *all* keep a third of that new wealth. It's called tax revenue. Your highly skilled kids pay for our roads, armies, health care, schools, retirements, and everything else governments provide.

So why aren't we already doing more? The investments we need aren't far-fetched. We've already started making them. We began with the free mass public-school movement that America pioneered in the nineteenth and early twentieth centuries. We accelerated this movement during the War on Poverty in the 1960s. Despite what you may have heard, these systems have worked miracles, but they remain radically underdeveloped. We'll see that the obstacles impeding progress are formidable and fascinating, going back to America's original sin of slavery. We'll also see, however, that parents can overcome these obstacles with the kind of political unity that business, labor, and elderly groups have achieved by putting aside petty divisions in favor of much larger shared interests.

PERSONAL NOTE

The origins of this book began more than a decade ago when I and another graduate student, Danny Yagan, now at the University of California at Berkeley, had the good fortune to be recruited by some of the world's leading economists to work on a new project. Raj Chetty at Harvard, Emmanuel Saez at Berkeley, and John Friedman now at Brown were starting a partnership that would eventually turn Americans' tax records at the Internal Revenue Service into the greatest source of (anonymized, hypersecure) information about parents and children the world had ever seen. In that first year, we huddled day and night in a cubicle we referred to as "the bullpen" high up in a drab federal office building in Boston, Massachusetts. Gradually, billions of records spanning hundreds of millions of dynamic and interconnected American households, multiple generations, and dozens of byzantine tax forms metamorphosed into a unified data set. We called it the Databank.

The Databank promised new insights into a wide spectrum of economic questions about business cycles and fiscal policy, unemployment and retirement, career formation and entrepreneurship, and many other domains—all toward a lofty, overarching goal of improving tax administration and tax policy in America. But the single largest breakthrough offered by the Databank centered around how childhood circumstances affect children. Until recently, the vast majority of social science research on children has studied short-term outcomes such as test scores. Of course, the outcomes that matter for tax policy and inequality and that all parents and social scientists actually care about are *long-term* outcomes such as income, employment, health, and longevity. The Databank, along with other so-called Big Data, has provided a bridge to studying long-term outcomes for a much wider range of questions. This means researchers are no longer stuck saying that something about a child's environment, such as a good teacher, increased that child's test score for a year. Instead, researchers can increasingly talk about how a good teacher affected that child's future livelihood as an adult.

After several years of research on the Databank, I went on to work as a professor and to teach a college course called "Inequality of Opportunity in the United States." As I synthesized recent research for my students, I noticed that many of the findings that had emerged over the past 20 or so years seemed to point toward an outsize role for parenting practices in driving economic inequality. This pattern was not widely understood and had important implications for ongoing debates around the roles of private and public resources in raising children. I began drafting a book to explore these ideas and share them with a broader audience.

However, as I shared early drafts of the book with friends and family, I encountered a problem. It was surprisingly hard to convey key research findings about parenting without sounding as if I were "blaming parents." I had no intention to blame parents; I felt nothing but respect and admiration for parents of all backgrounds. My research had led me to believe that parents were doing something much harder and more important than commonly understood. If I was blaming anyone, it was our own society for failing to provide parents with adequate support to do their impossibly hard jobs as well as they wanted to. But despite my intentions, the idea that the book would be dismissed as "blaming parents" continued to haunt me through multiple rounds of revision. In retrospect, I had crashed into the Parent Trap—it was almost prohibitively difficult to talk about the reality of parenting. This experience was a revelation. It crystalized much of what I felt needed to be clarified about parenting to a broader public audience and provided me with a foundational concept for the book.

Finally, as I finished up work on the manuscript, two big changes took place that further tested and deepened my perspective on parenting. One change was global, the other personal.

The global change was the COVID-19 pandemic. All over America, schools closed or became virtual shadows of their former selves. Not only schools but also childcare centers, summer camps, after-school programs, parks, and libraries—everything closed or moved online. In this new world, the thin veneer of equal opportunity melted away. Some kids didn't even have a reliable home internet connection to access online classes, much less parents prepared to tutor them, design lesson plans, and compensate for other fissures in distance learning.[32]

The crisis only increased my sense of urgency around the conclusions in this book. The truth is that child skill development is not only radically unequal during once-in-a-century pandemics but has been radically unequal for centuries and remains so today. By temporarily withdrawing many public and private resources that parents depended on to balance their lives, COVID-19 may have opened more rich parents' eyes to the crushing burdens we impose on families during that 90 percent of time children spend outside our free public-school system: early childhood, afternoons, holidays, summer breaks, and early adulthood.

The personal change was that my wife, Bao, and I became parents. As we plunged into the first few shaky months of parenting, my Google search history revealed a frantic self-education: postpartum edema, baby weight loss, hip dysplasia, breast pump valves, baby gas pain, side sleeping, tummy time, rickets, gripe water, probiotics, lacrimal ducts, childcare centers, pediatricians, birth certificates. It felt like a round-the-clock high-stakes research project with strict deadlines.

Blitzed out on sleep deprivation, I chronically forgot things and bungled routine tasks. I crashed our car into the back of the garage, sliced a petal of skin off our son Felix's fingertip with a nail clipper, and slashed open my hand on the metal clasp of our chaos-tracking clipboard. At one point, my wife asked me what time it was, and I said, "When?" All of this only strengthened my belief that many aspects of what we labeled "parenting" are much more complicated and difficult than commonly acknowledged.

Becoming a parent has also reinforced my sense of urgency. I don't want to see Felix suffer an important setback that could have been prevented with greater scientific knowledge or better access to professional resources. As I watch him sleep, flail his insane little arms, and flash his goofy little smiles, the idea of shortchanging his growth in some important way, seen or unseen, fills me with a dread that surpasses anything I anticipated in my research.

So many parents feel this terrifying kind of love. It is a feeling of hope and generosity. At its best, it transcends our own routine, self-centered quest for personal gratification. The changes I am advocating in this book lean into that feeling, harness that energy, and trace out a way to channel it into building a healthier, stronger, happier, and more prosperous America.

MAIN IDEAS

In this book, we will come to perceive people's economic trajectories in a new way, as a kind of invisible trust fund bequeathed to them by their parents over the course of childhood. This view has the power to reshape both our individual identities and our perception of the inequality that increasingly surrounds us. It can also inspire us to see our own parents, partners, and children differently, as collaborators in a giant construction project with scaffolding shaped by our broader social choices about who is responsible for what.

But this book is not just an intellectual exercise for the curious. My goal is to wake up more people to the political power that parents have yet to claim as citizens and their own untapped potential to instill greater economic security in more children. I hope not only to diagnose the pathological origins of inequality but also to lay out a treatment for these pathologies through voting, activism, lobbying, advocacy, and legislation in order to provide young people with the kinds of resources other better-represented interest groups already receive.

There is no organization like AARP for parents, and there should be. There is no equivalent to Medicare for children's skill growth, and there should be. As a share of total spending, there is virtually no research and development on child skill growth, and there should be. All of these problems can be addressed politically by parents if only they wake up to what they and their children have been missing.

The book lays out evidence and historical context to support several key ideas.

Today in America, skills are the key to economic security and upward mobility. If a child of any background accumulates enough skills to score well on academic tests in adolescence and then attend a good four-year college or well-chosen vocational training program, she has a good chance of achieving economic security in adulthood. Skills are indeed a Great Equalizer in modern America, despite continued prejudice, elitism, and discrimination.

America still relies primarily on parents to build skills in children. The public-school system today plays a smaller role in child skill development than commonly understood.

Professional skill builders, such as teachers and counselors, can dramatically improve child skill growth if given greater access to children's time. Pioneering researchers began to document this pattern well before World War II, but the findings were dismissed and largely forgotten until a series of chance events allowed extraordinary new social experiments to vindicate this earlier work. The implications of these experiments are stark: America could eliminate skill gaps between rich and poor children if it were to rely more on professionals and less on parents to build skills.

The idea of training parents to build skills more effectively on their own has failed to gain traction for more than a century and does not represent a promising path forward today. Even though some parent training programs show impressive results, parents don't sign up for them and don't complete the programs when they do sign up—especially the parents who stand to gain the most from them.

In demanding that parents manage too much child skill development, we ask them to act as pediatricians, nutritionists, college counselors, tutors, real estate agents, and chief executive officers. Comparisons with other occupations illuminate the kinds of life-altering missed opportunities that arise when we ask parents to juggle these often impossible tasks.

Deep economic forces conspire to undermine parental efficiency in child skill development. These forces have been well known to economists for decades or even centuries and arise in many other parts of the economy, but they apply with unusual force in family-based child skill development. We'll see what we can learn about the parental struggle to build skills from unlikely sources including smallpox epidemics, restraining orders, and state lotteries.

The key to effective skill-development programs is to ask less *of parents, not* more. We must shift the skill-development burden from parents to professionals rather than continue to force parents to solve these overwhelming problems on their own with more time, training, effort, or money.

Parental disadvantages in skill development multiply in communities and help to explain why racial income inequality has barely changed even decades after school integration and antidiscrimination laws first took effect. We will learn the real lessons of Asian Americans' success in the face of severe historical discrimination and see what these lessons tell us about the most promising path forward for African Americans, Native Americans, Hispanic Americans, and other historically marginalized groups. The key: much greater structural, community-wide, professional support for child skill growth. We will see that greater public assistance with skill development from pregnancy through early adulthood would eliminate most racial disparities in income and wealth—even if prejudice continued to fester in other respects.

We have failed to invest in skill development, but we can start doing so if parents get organized and advocate for children's best interests. Children cannot vote: they are America's largest disenfranchised minority. Like all other disenfranchised groups historically, children receive fewer resources than they deserve. The solution is parental activism, most likely channeled through a mass-membership, nonprofit "National Association of Parents" modeled on AARP.

Parents have failed to galvanize around shared political interests due to a number of popular fallacies. Some parents believe the required public programs are too expensive, when in fact the absence of these programs is even more expensive. Some parents, fixating on narrow issues such as Ivy League college admissions, believe they and other parents are playing a zero-sum game against each other, when in fact they all are playing a much larger "supersum" game in which other children's success helps their own children succeed. And some parents believe that prior public programs to expand opportunity have failed, when in fact these investments have achieved remarkable success, often "paying for themselves" from the government's perspective. By setting the record straight, this book seeks to motivate more unified political action by parents.

Our story begins in Iowa, where a little more than 100 years ago an obscure pioneer launched a quest to help parents do their jobs better.

1   AN ALTERNATE REALITY

FERMENT

Simply being a child in America used to involve incredible danger. In 1900, one in five children died before starting school. *One in five.* In some cities, it was one in three. This fact of life was obviously a kind of nightmare for parents. Losing a child, one of the worst things that could ever happen to anyone, happened to almost everyone.[1]

It was also around this time, however, that women began to harness political power. Well before securing the right to vote in 1920, women's organizations began to shift national priorities. Women appeared to care about different things than men. In particular, they seemed to view child and maternal health problems as urgent in a way that male-dominated institutions had somehow . . . overlooked.

This early wave of female power led to a number of "firsts." There was the world's first national public agency devoted to children: the US Children's Bureau, founded in 1912 by some of America's most prominent female leaders and reinforced by a vast network of interlocking women's organizations blanketing the country. Julia Lathrop, the bureau's first chief, was the first woman to head any federal agency. The bureau immediately launched a first-of-its-kind study of infant mortality by tracking down the life history of every single baby born in a single city—Johnstown, Pennsylvania—over an entire calendar year, an approach it would repeat in ten other cities around the country over the next decade. As the broader public processed the findings, it confronted a possibility both thrilling and unsettling: maybe our children didn't *have* to die, and maybe their mothers didn't have to die at such high rates, either.

More firsts came along. In 1916, Jeannette Rankin in Montana became the first woman to win a congressional seat, which she used to propose the first federal legislation to improve infant and maternal health care. Her proposal would soon pass as the Sheppard-Towner Maternity and Infancy Act of 1921, the federal government's first effort to assure that people's basic human needs could be satisfied, a category of laws that would become known as "social security."

When the Great Depression hit, the Children's Bureau started to survey families about their employment, income, and other facts of life. President Herbert Hoover assured Americans they could weather the downturn with a little thrift and charity. Grace Abbott, Julia Lathrop's successor as head of the Children's Bureau, consulted her agency's hard data and argued that the president was wrong. Something awful was happening to American families: an epidemic of prolonged unemployment had overwhelmed all existing relief, emptied pantries, stunted growth, and spread disease. Voters agreed with Abbott that Hoover hadn't grasped the situation and replaced him with Franklin Roosevelt. Soon the Children's Bureau was helping Roosevelt assist children and mothers in his sprawling New Deal agenda.

But opponents soon caught up to all these "firsts." Male physicians and heads of competing federal agencies didn't like having their spheres of influence challenged. They said the Children's Bureau was a bastion of communism. They said it was inappropriate to organize a government agency around children rather than around general functions such as health care or pensions. And perhaps most importantly, they said the bureau's efforts threatened their own livelihoods. As one physician representing the American Medical Association explained to a congressional committee, "If you are going to save the lives of all these women and children at public expense, what inducement will there be for young men to study medicine?"[2]

Katherine Lenroot, the third head of the Children's Bureau, tried to preserve its integrity. She warned that children were different from other Americans: they couldn't vote. Without a strong federal agency to advocate for the "whole child" in one place, their interests would be sidelined by concerns for adult voters.

Lenroot failed. Opponents chipped away at the Children's Bureau, dismembered it, and buried its responsibilities deep in the machinery of other agencies that existed almost exclusively to serve adults. This lofty institution described by one historian as "government at its best" and by another as perhaps the most "trusted and loved" government agency in American history today exists as a minor department that bears no resemblance to the grand vision of its founders.[3] As Lenroot predicted, children remain second-class citizens in federal policy making.

Around the same time that women's rising political power created the Children's Bureau, it also created another remarkable institution intended to serve parents and children. This institution was founded by a woman little known outside her local community, much less her state. Compared to the Children's Bureau, the institution she launched was smaller, less glamorous, and more peculiar, but it had one big advantage. Free from the national spotlight, free from pressure to make progress against the most urgent problems of the day, it could focus on wild possibilities. In other words, instead of trying to place a floor underneath children's well-being, this new organization could probe for a *ceiling*.

THE PIONEERS

Later in Cora Bussey Hillis's life, local historians asked her how the institution she created, her life's greatest professional achievement, came into being. She answered with reluctance because, she explained, the institution could be discredited "if it were generally known to have been conceived by a woman."[4]

Hillis was a strategist to her core, and it was her maneuvering that would ultimately crack open the door to an alternate reality where divisions by race and class no longer contoured people's lives. Her work set off generations of researchers who would gradually establish and map out this reality, not as some utopian dream but as a real place we could choose to inhabit.

Hillis was born in the summer of 1858 in Bloomfield, Iowa. Abraham Lincoln and Stephen Douglas would soon begin their debates over the future of slavery just across the border in Illinois; America was gearing up for war against itself. Hillis's father, Cyrus Bussey, was a local business leader who would soon distinguish himself as a decorated brigadier general in the Union army serving under Ulysses S. Grant and later as an Iowa state senator. Hillis's character took shape in a family accustomed to status and influence. Her large eyes and straight, sturdy lips radiated the self-possession of a person amused by her own future triumph. In her journal she wrote, "I feel within myself a power undeveloped which in future years shall command homage for me."

Hillis went on to have a great vision. The vision emerged from two formative experiences. When she was 12, her younger sister Laura came down with a spinal disease. Doctors disagreed about what to do, but they all agreed that Laura would remain permanently bedridden and die young; there was no point in trying to educate her. Cora wasn't convinced. She cared for Laura and homeschooled her at every opportunity. Laura would graduate from high school, start college at age 17, and live a "happy, useful life" until she died at age 34.

The second formative experience was a slower, grinding ordeal familiar to so many parents of her day: Hillis lost three of her five children prematurely. Isaac died of a ruptured appendix. Philip died in a train crash before his meningitis had time to kill him. On New Year's Day of 1907, Hillis's youngest child, Doris, died in an outbreak of scarlet fever that also nearly claimed Hillis's older daughter, Ellen. When Doris died, Hillis couldn't take it anymore. By this time, she had built up a career as a political organizer in the growing women's movement to support mothers' and children's causes. She stopped everything for a year to care for Ellen and battle her own despair.

These two experiences gave Hillis the conviction that parents were on their own, and *it wasn't right*. No one seemed to know anything about how to raise children. Over the years, she came to think this was not a coincidence. Rather, it reflected a bad collective choice not to invest in knowledge about children's problems.

"I got books and magazines," Hillis recalled. "I read everything I could find that wise men had written; I listened to doctors and educators; I waded through oceans of stale textbook theory, written largely, I fancy, by bachelor professors or elderly teachers with no actual contact with youth." She concluded that "all knowledge of the child was theoretical and most advice experimental."

She felt this ignorance most acutely when she compared it to the exploding knowledge about another topic of interest to most Iowa families: *agriculture*. Just as Hillis had found that science had little to offer her own sister and children, farmers around the country had once found science had little to offer their failed harvests and sick livestock. But then the federal government stepped in. Starting with the Hatch Act in 1887, then the Adams Act in 1906 and the Smith-Lever Act of 1914, Americans had chosen to address the "Farm Problem" by investing in scientific research on farming. All over America, including Iowa, agricultural experiment stations had sprung up like beacons of light in the wilderness.

These stations worked miracles. The historian Alice Smuts writes that "experimental research by the stations on animal breeding, nutrition and pathology, soil analysis, crop improvement, and every phase of the dairy industry brought revolutionary changes in American agriculture and enormous benefits to farmers." These investments in research easily paid for themselves many times over in the form of greater income for farmers as well as greater food access for the public.[5]

Hillis saw these miracles and asked a question: Why not "give the normal child the same scientific study by research methods that we give to crops and cattle? Learn how the normal child develops in body, mind, and spirit and gradually evolve a science of child rearing."[6]

For Hillis, this question launched a religious quest. She would "establish an accredited Child Welfare Research Laboratory available to the parenthood of the land." She saw God on her side. She considered the proposed station as "another child," drawing strength from her own suffering to prevent similar tragedy for others.

Founding this laboratory would require new legislation from the state of Iowa. For the rest of her life, Hillis worked like a person possessed by destiny toward this goal. When she first started her work, no researchers, politicians, activists, or anyone else had ever advocated for such a station. The idea struck almost everyone as harebrained. Not even parents wanted it. "Here was I," recalled Hillis, "bidden to preach a new gospel to a state full of mothers, the majority of whom really believed they already knew all there was to be known about child-care."[7]

Within 20 years, she would drive her vision into reality. She began in 1900 by convincing the National Congress of Mothers—an early child-advocacy group that became today's National Parent-Teacher Association (PTA)—to hold its annual convention in Des Moines over 16 other competing cities. She then grew this small seed into an empire of women's and farmers' organizations across the state, reciting over and over her conviction that child development had to follow the scientific path taken by agriculture.

Over the years she approached four different university presidents about founding a Child Research Station modeled after the Agricultural Research Stations. All declined. One suggested Hillis focus instead on helping the university raise funds for a new set of chimes. On a fifth try, she broke through with the State University of Iowa. Hillis insisted that the proposed Child Research Station include a nursery-school laboratory, an idea touched by the mark of genius that would soon be replicated at universities around the country.

The plan would require funding from the Iowa legislature. In December 1914, Hillis took charge of a new lobbying organization formed for this purpose, which contacted nearly a quarter of all voting-age adults in the state. Hillis also recruited all the state's major media outlets. In one newspaper, a cartoon advocating for the bill contrasted a family of farm animals, thriving under data-driven scientific guidance in a cutting-edge state laboratory, with a family of humans trying to console a sick baby with "Old Dr. Bunks Pink Knockout Drops" and a dose of dill pickles.[8]

The bill failed, but Hillis immediately doubled down on a new campaign the following year. When she injured herself in a fall, she continued the campaign by phone from her bed, eventually hobbling on crutches into the Statehouse to impose her full personality on key legislators. Hillis soon zeroed in on a few pivotal holdouts in the Senate. "One was a pessimist, two were old fogies of limited education and narrow outlook. One firmly believed that instinct could teach any mother how to care for her children. . . . Each of the others had some particular bias which it took time to unravel. I never personally spoke to any of these gentlemen, but I know that for ten days thereafter, they had many calls and letters from unexpected sources."

On April 6, 1917, the United States declared war on Germany. One morning, Hillis read in a local paper that most Iowa draftees were failing their physical examinations. Within hours, she sent a letter to every member of the Iowa legislature tying the physical defects of these "rejected patriots" to their parents' overreliance on "inherited tradition" and "instinct" in the absence of scientific guidance. The Child Research Station had now become a "far seeing and patriotic service to the Nation."

This time the bill passed. In the rush to war, barely anyone noticed, but that didn't bother Hillis. She felt she had fulfilled her life's purpose. "For a time I shall feel lost," she wrote. "In putting away some of my material the thought came, this is like putting away the clothes of the child I had lost, so much a part of me has been this work."

For Hillis, serenity was short-lived. She died in a car crash long before the full impact of her work had become clear. At the Iowa Child Welfare Research Station, her life's crowning achievement, things were just getting started.

THE IOWA RESEARCH STATION

What did the Iowa Child Welfare Research Station do? It precipitated a tectonic shift in American assumptions about child development. This shift would move us away from a preoccupation with *nature* toward a quest for better *nurture*. It thereby shifted scientific focus away from breeding, with all its toxic focus on genetic purity, and toward parenting, health care, and schooling.

The Iowa Research Station would initiate a cascade of research establishing that human economic skills—the capabilities workers rely on to produce two-thirds of all annual economic output—could be cultivated with better management and technology, much like we cultivate agriculture and all other industrial output with better management and technology. Because skills form the basis for individual economic security, the new findings suggested that a great deal of inequality represented a choice made by our society to underinvest in child development for certain groups.

Hillis's analogy between parenting and farming was a great marketing pitch in prewar Iowa, and it contained a lot of truth. But, of course, people are not crops or livestock. Among other things, people are much more complex, they cannot be controlled at will, and they take much longer to mature. The station's contributions didn't happen quickly. They didn't happen all that deliberately either. But they did materialize over the next half-century, and they were momentous.

The station's first tremor came when its initial director, Bird Baldwin, learned that his daughter, Patricia, had scored abnormally low on a routine IQ test. At the time, children with very low scores on such tests could be transferred out of normal schools and into a nearby facility for so-called feebleminded children. Instead, Baldwin enrolled his daughter in the station's new experimental preschool that Hillis had fought so hard to include in the plan. After a year in the school, Patricia's test scores shot up. Baldwin thought the preschool had helped his daughter. The experience set him against the prevailing notion among American researchers at the time that human mental capacities were predetermined at birth. Patricia's experience also shaped the outlook of a key researcher at the station, Beth Wellman. Wellman married Baldwin after his first wife died and then assumed custody of Patricia when Baldwin himself died in a freak accident. Like Hillis, Wellman's personal drive as a researcher ultimately pierced through the misogyny and ridicule of complacent male gatekeepers.

Starting in 1928, Wellman worked with the station's second director, George Stoddard, to investigate the impacts of the preschool on students more systematically. By then, they had realized they were sitting on a treasure trove: test score data on hundreds of children that station workers had been diligently recording since 1921.

a)

b)

Figure 1.1

Girls "sorting spools" (*a*) and "working on a test using a battery" (*b*) at the Iowa Child Welfare Research Station Preschool, 1920s. *Source*: Frederick W. Kent Collection, RG 30.0001.001, University of Iowa Libraries, Iowa City. Used with permission of the University of Iowa. These and other photos can be viewed online at http://s-lib012.lib.uiowa.edu/ictcs/icwrs.html and https://digital.lib.uiowa.edu/islandora/object/ui%3Aictcs_7585.

In 1932, Wellman published her analysis evaluating the preschool's impacts on children's cognitive development as measured by these test scores. Without any natural control group of children who did not attend the preschool, Wellman extracted insights in novel and strikingly modern ways. She found that the children's scores tended to increase during the months they spent in the preschool but stagnated during summer breaks between sessions. She found that students enrolled in full-day preschool improved their test scores more quickly than students enrolled in half-day preschool. And she found that all these forces appeared more important for lower-scoring children than for higher-scoring children.

At the time, many people doubted that early childhood test scores contained any meaningful information, but Wellman's work suggested these scores did capture something important about skill growth. More recent studies have validated all of her early findings.[9]

The new facts suggested a simple story: children learned more during the time they spent in the Iowa Research Station preschool than they learned outside the school, especially children whose parents had fewer resources to facilitate learning at home. The preschool appeared to act as a drug that increased children's intellectual development and increased it more at higher dosages for more learning-deprived children.

These results sparked public curiosity as journalists wrote up buzzy stories about "I.Q. Control," but most child-development scholars remained in thrall to the notion of fixed, heritable intelligence. Surely the results had to be driven by some kind of statistical mistake. But then something unusual happened, and the Iowa Station's initial findings became harder to dismiss.

THE ORPHANAGE

In the early 1930s a prominent couple in Davenport, Iowa, adopted a child from the local Soldiers' Home orphanage. As the child grew she displayed signs of severe disability. The parents were upset. They felt the orphanage had misled them and so they sued the Iowa State Board of Control in charge of overseeing orphanages.

The lawsuit was ultimately settled out of court, but it scared state administrators. The state couldn't afford major financial liability every time adopting parents felt they hadn't gotten what they bargained for. The Board of Control reached out to George Stoddard, the new director of the Iowa Research Station, for advice.

Stoddard saw an opportunity and proposed a partnership. The research station would hire a clinical psychologist for the orphanage. This new hire would provide guidance on orphanage policy and, critically, would administer IQ tests and other evaluations of all children in the facility. These tests would establish a kind of due diligence to shield the state from future lawsuits by adopting parents.

Cora Hillis had foreseen this opportunity 20 years earlier. Writing to a colleague, she had argued that "if children are to be thoroughly studied, there must be a selected group of children to study in an environment absolutely under the control of the station. As we are so handicapped for money, it might help solve the problem to secure the cooperation of the Board of Control of State Institutions to let some of its wards be used for experimental purposes."[10]

Hillis's anachronistic language sounds ominous: researchers "using" children in orphanages for "experimental purposes." But the Iowa Station cultivated a tradition different from the insidious human experiments conducted throughout history on inmates, prisoners of war, racial minorities, and other vulnerable groups. In fact, the partnership ushered in reforms that put children's best interests first and helped many of them lead richer, fuller lives.

Stoddard hired a man named Harold Skeels to be the first clinical psychologist at the orphanage. This hire can be regarded either as an act of genius or as another stroke of luck. Skeels had studied under Stoddard and Wellman but was not an established scholar. He was tasked with the seemingly mundane job of evaluating and classifying a few hundred children. But Skeels turned out to be an extraordinary, creative, tenacious researcher who was able to spot surprising patterns and leverage them toward broader discovery. Skeels would become one of the most important researchers of the twentieth century.

The children living at the Soldiers' Home orphanage typically came from difficult circumstances. Their parents tended to be unmarried, with little education and checkered, low-wage employment records. Many of these parents also struggled with substance abuse, crime, and mental illness. The prevailing wisdom at the time indicated these orphans were genetically destined for similar outcomes. Skeels assumed his evaluations would confirm these predictions.

But then he started looking at the data. During his first year, he gave IQ tests to 73 kids who had gotten "lucky" in the sense of being placed with foster parents early, in their first six months of life at the orphanage. Skeels gave these children IQ tests after the children had spent about two years with these foster parents as part of their path toward permanent adoption.

The foster parents had the opposite socioeconomic profile of the children's biological parents. They were married, highly educated, higher income, and recruited by orphanage officials in part on the basis of their prospects for raising healthy children.

When Skeels calculated the average IQ of these orphans, he thought he'd made a mistake. Their IQs were well above average. In fact, their IQs were close to what would be expected of children born to their foster parents, not their biological parents.

He tried to find a mistake but couldn't. The station proposed a follow-up project. Adoption by foster parents seemed to shift a child's skill trajectory, but adoption offered a very limited strategy to accelerate child development because the vast majority of children would never be up for adoption. What if there was a less drastic way to alter these children's lives? What if the kids just attended preschool?

The team was already running a preschool 50 miles away at station headquarters in Iowa City, so they replicated the model at the Soldiers' Home orphanage. They selected 21 children to attend the preschool from 8:00 a.m. to 5:00 p.m. every weekday. They selected another 21 children who resembled the preschool children in age, sex, test scores, and other characteristics. Kids in the control group would spend their days in the understaffed, underresourced orphanage as usual.

It wasn't an ideal experiment because random assignment into treatment and control groups wasn't yet common practice, but it was close. Over time, the station researchers added new children to both groups in a balanced fashion to replace kids who left the orphanage to join foster homes. On average, children in the study attended preschool for about one year.[11]

The first discovery was that these children's institutional upbringing had turned them into rapacious, nihilistic chaos mongers. The children destroyed everything, trusted no one, knew nothing about the outside world, and defaulted to violence. Many of them had no toilet training. The preschool staff, having previously taught children drawn from the Iowa City university neighborhood, were caught off guard. They quickly overhauled the curriculum to focus on basic social, emotional, and physical skills. Over time, as they put this foundation in place, they could focus more on the kinds of cognitive and creative exercises deployed at the university preschool.

Ethel Steward, the lead preschool teacher, recalled the early days of the project:

> [T]he favorite thing [for the children] to do with the fine iron toys . . . was throw them over the railing down the cellar entrance because they made such a good crash on the cement several feet below. What difference to them if they were broken and there was one less thing play with? The children weren't used to playing with anything; they had very little to play with in the cottages, and there were still lots of things left at preschool that weren't yet broken. And what matter what they played with? For the most part they just carried the toys (as many as possible) clutched tightly in their arms to have something to say "Mine" about. This was a mania with these youngsters who owned nothing anywhere outside of preschool. If anyone disputed the "Mine," one toy would do as well as another either to throw or to hit the assailant. It was even impossible to throw the soiled colored paper handkerchiefs into the wastebaskets because the children would take them out and carry them around in pockets or clutched tightly in their hands as a bit of bright something they could call theirs. It did no good to assure the children that the toys belonged to the preschool and would be there today and tomorrow and the

next day, that there would be plenty of opportunity to play with them another time. The children distrusted everyone and did not believe a word of what the teachers said.[12]

Three years later, researchers compared the preschool children with the control group. Rather than fixating on IQ scores, they embraced what today we might call a "whole-child" approach, including cognitive skills, informational awareness, vocabulary and language, motor skills, and social and emotional skills.

They found huge relative gains in many areas. The surprise was how these relative gains took place. The new preschool improved outcomes for the attending children only modestly, but the kids in the control group *deteriorated*. Preschool was protecting children from atrophy caused by the understimulating orphanage conditions that "had previously been regarded as standard." The researchers observed this must be what regular parents accomplished every day—a certain richness of stimulation the orphanage kids didn't receive.

The results shocked orphanage administrators. Going forward, they enrolled all children in half-day preschool and made other changes to invest more heavily in child development. The next question seemed perfectly clear to the researchers: If a basic, improvisational first attempt at educating three- and four-year-olds yielded such dramatic benefits, "what would happen if a really model schooling and adjustment service were applied to experimental groups from infancy to adolescence . . . ?"[13]

BLOWBACK

By the late 1930s, the Iowa researchers were beginning to attract attention not just from curious journalists but also from national power brokers. Henry Wallace, the secretary of agriculture under President Franklin Roosevelt and a key architect of the New Deal, saw the research and considered expanding early childhood education to the masses.

It wasn't the first time America flirted with early education. In the 1820s, more than a century before the Iowa findings, an "infant education" craze had swept through Massachusetts. A Boston newspaper argued that "infants, taken from the most unfavorable situation in which they are ever placed, from the abodes of poverty and vice, are capable of learning at least a hundred times as much . . . and of being a hundred times as happy, by the system adopted in infant schools." *Ladies Magazine* worried that if only poor infants had access to education, "those poor children will assuredly be the richest scholars" when they started elementary school. The system expanded and by 1840 public schools enrolled about 40 percent of three-year-olds in the state—the same share as today, nearly 200 years later.[14]

But then the experts changed their minds. Amariah Brigham, a leading physician, warned that "efforts to develop the minds of young children are very frequently injurious. . . . [I]n attempting to call forth and cultivate the intellectual faculties of children before they are six or seven years of age, serious and lasting injury has been done both to the body and the mind."[15] Such views prevailed, and by the time the Civil War broke out, public schools in Massachusetts had dismantled their early education system.

Why the fickle back and forth? Because there was no scientific evidence either way. There were no randomized controlled trials. There were not even any systematic comparisons between kids who enrolled in early education and similar kids who did not enroll. Without any evidence, attitudes toward children swayed like trees in the wind. Any eloquent spokesperson could start an intellectual movement based on a few anecdotes and a grandiose theory.

In the 1930s, the evidence out of Iowa was making it clear that early education could probably help a great many kids lead better lives—just as advocates of early education in the previous century had claimed.

But once again those insisting that children were born with fixed intelligence fought back. The psychologist Lewis Terman, the godfather of the fixed-IQ position in America, stated incredulously that if the findings of the Iowa Station could be verified, they'd represent "the most important scientific discovery in the last thousand years." Terman's allies and disciples at Stanford waged a proxy war on his behalf. Quinn McNemar, a statistician, raised technical concerns about the Iowa studies while strangely ignoring obvious technical problems in studies reaching opposite conclusions.

Barbara Burke, a Terman protégé, giddily reported that "[Secretary of Agriculture Henry] Wallace is no longer ready to 'buy' IQ's, i.e. to try to manufacture them by given dosages of nursery school."[16]

Skeels and another Iowa Station colleague, Marie Skodak, protested that "calm, impartial weighing of evidence for and against a conclusion signifies the scientific approach. But McNemar has embarked upon the mission of 'demolishing,' 'destroying,' and 'exploding' the conclusions of the Iowa investigators." Beth Wellman, disgusted by the veneer of scientific discourse coming from the opposition, told McNemar to his face that Terman had "poisoned his mind."[17]

Not everyone dismissed the results. Maybe the findings really did represent a major scientific contribution, a once-in-a-thousand-years discovery that could bend the arc of history. A new generation of researchers asked: Can we really alter people's destinies so profoundly?

THE EXPLORERS

Although the Iowa studies were far from perfect, it is doubtful that any evidence, no matter how conclusive, could have penetrated the blanket of cultural bias prevailing before World War II. All of American society—with its overt Jim Crow regime in the South, its hush-hush Jim Crow regime everywhere else, and its semiformal exclusion of women from all of the most elite occupations—was still premised on the idea that white people were born superior to nonwhite people and men were born superior to women. The finding that adult capacities were engineered through investments in children threatened to subvert a core premise of American society.[18]

In terms of social science, the Iowa Station researchers had sketched out the rough outlines of a new continent. As younger researchers emerged from the war, they built on this discovery like explorers carving out paths through uncharted wilderness.

The first explorer in this movement was a psychologist named Samuel Kirk. Kirk grew up on a wheat farm in North Dakota as one of nine children of Lebanese immigrant parents.[19] Early on, he discovered a knack for teaching some of the farm's laborers how to read and later devoted his life to the study of education. In 1939, he saw Harold Skeels of the Iowa Research Station give a lecture at the Milwaukee State Teachers College. Captivated by the findings and a conversation with Skeels after the talk, Kirk would go on to launch the first major postwar study seeking to replicate and extend some of the Iowa group's main findings.[20] The landmark study, published in 1958 after a decade of work, was able to cite only a handful of precedents as inspiration. One was a book called *The Wild Boy of Aveyron* (1802), about the failed recuperation of one boy found naked and mute roaming the forests in south-central France in 1798. The other was the work of Skeels, Skodak, Wellman, and other Iowa researchers from the 1930s.[21]

Kirk's study provided a personalized preschool regimen to a small group of students and tracked both their outcomes and those of a "contrast" group of kids who started out from similar positions. He found preschool had large, persistent benefits for children living in orphanages and smaller but still significant benefits for children living at home. The study retained some of the same weaknesses of the Iowa work. It could not randomly assign children into treatment and control groups, and it largely improvised its curriculum with special accommodations for each child, making the overall intervention hard to describe, refine, or replicate. But it provided the first early confirmation of the Iowa researchers' main claims, and it ushered in a new wave of more rigorous studies.

In 1958, just as Kirk's findings came out, a 27-year-old former marine and education prodigy named David Weikart ditched his PhD program to work as a school psychologist and director of special services in the Ypsilanti, Michigan, public-school system. Two years into the job, he proposed an experiment to assess impacts of preschool on poor kids in Ypsilanti. This was twenty years after the Iowa findings, but opinions hadn't budged. District administrators insisted that local poor kids, who also just so happened to be Black, couldn't be helped because "the test scores just represented the way the children were." Weikart consulted with academic experts. They all assured him that preschool would not only fail to help these children but that it would likely harm them and would therefore be *unethical to attempt*.[22]

Weikart, driven by the Iowa team's findings and his own intuitions as a veteran camp counselor, forged ahead. He found an ally in Charles Eugene "Chief" Beatty, the principal of a local, predominantly Black elementary school. Beatty, a former world-class athlete and the first African American principal of any public school in Michigan, constantly sought out ways to help his students overcome prejudice. Beatty allowed Weikart to use his campus to run the controversial new preschool program and helped build trust among local parents. Ultimately, a group of 58 children out of a total of 123 participants in the experiment were randomly assigned into the preschool program. "Perry Preschool," as it came to be known, provided two and a half hours per day of structured play overseen by professional public-school teachers. Children typically enrolled for two years starting at age three.[23]

Weikart wasn't alone. There was something in the air, maybe driven by the foment around the civil rights movement, some sense that the prevailing wisdom around child development was crooked. At least 12 separate research teams started small early education pilot programs around the United States during the 1960s. Most of these studies, like the one in Perry Preschool, focused primarily on lower-income Black children—the kids many Americans had long been most eager to dismiss.

Nearly all of these researchers found the same thing: the Iowa group had been right. Kids from lower-income families could accelerate skill growth dramatically with access to good professional learning environments.[24] The old dogma that children's skill growth could not be altered with deliberate investments began to crumble. Harold Skeels, whose explosive findings with Beth Wellman and other Iowa colleagues had met ridicule 30 years earlier, found long-overdue recognition.[25]

Most of these new programs, like Perry Preschool, lasted only a few hours a day for children starting at around age three or four. Clearly, they could not replicate the full breadth of private investments typically reserved for children of upper-class parents. Some researchers returned to the question their Iowa predecessors had raised: What if we cranked up the dial on these investments? What if professionals took over skill development from parents not just for a couple of hours a day for kids starting around age three but all day, every day, starting soon after birth?

THE NEXT CORA HILLIS

In 1921, as the Iowa Research Station's first director Bird Baldwin watched his daughter, Patricia, blossom in preschool, another baby girl was born in Brookline, Massachusetts. Like the Iowa Station's founder, Cora Hillis, this girl would be moved by the plight of her own disabled sister. Like Hillis, she would be shocked by the ignorance of so-called experts when it came to child development and parenting and would repeat in her speeches that mothers got "less attention from doctors than cows get from cattle breeders."[26] And like Hillis, she would transmute her dreams into hard legislative reality through hard work, political savvy, and charisma.

But this woman had some advantages over Hillis. In particular, her father was one of the richest men in America, her brother was president of the United States, and her name was Eunice Kennedy.

Eunice's older sister, Rosemary, showed signs of developmental delay from an early age, possibly due to oxygen-deprivation during an awkward delivery at birth. Tragically, when Rosemary was 23, their father, Joseph Kennedy, volunteered her for an experimental medical operation known as a frontal lobotomy, a procedure considered promising at the time but since discredited. The operation backfired. Rosemary lost her ability to walk, to speak more than a few words, or to function beyond the level of a small child. She passed the remaining 63 years of her life cared for by others as an institutional inmate.[27]

Eunice Kennedy had been the sibling closest to Rosemary as a child. Rosemary's plight filled her with guilt and fury. She channeled that burden into a lifelong crusade to prevent and treat intellectual disability in children.

Intellectual disability at that time was no longer referred to as "feeble-mindedness" but rather as "mental retardation." As a description, it was not limited to children with extreme biological disorders but also captured a broad swathe of children who simply hadn't developed healthy levels of cognitive or socioemotional skill during childhood. The quest to prevent intellectual disability was really a broad quest to prevent underdevelopment of skills in children.

When Eunice's brother Jack assumed the presidency in 1961, she was ready to act. She had spent years promoting her cause as head of her family's powerful foundation. President Kennedy told aides to "just give Eunice what she wants."[28]

Cora Hillis had passed one small bill after two tries. Eunice Kennedy passed major legislation on her first try. Within two years, Eunice had prompted the federal government to create multiple new institutions devoted to the scientific study of child development. They included the National Institute for Child Health and Human Development (NICHD)— renamed the Eunice Kennedy Shriver NICHD in 2008—and a network of 12 new research stations at universities around the country.

These institutions were the intergalactic version of the Iowa Child Welfare Research Station. Adjusting for inflation, annual funding for these new endeavors would be *1,000 times* the funding Hillis had obtained for the Iowa Station in 1917.[29]

At 10:00 a.m. on October 31, 1963, President Kennedy described the accomplishment at a press conference in the Cabinet Room at the White House. He predicted, "In a few years, we can look confidently forward to knowing enough about mental retardation to prevent it in most cases." Echoing Lewis Terman's sentiment that unlocking control over human intelligence would be "the most important scientific discovery of the last thousand years," the president called the bill "the most significant effort that the Congress of the United States, of the country—our country—has ever undertaken." He continued, "I think that in the years to come those who have been engaged in this enterprise can feel the greatest source of pride and satisfaction, and they will recognize that there were not many things that they did during their time in office which had more of a lasting imprint on the well-being and happiness of more people."[30] It was President Kennedy's final bill. Three weeks later, he was assassinated.

The new research centers he created lived on, and they thrived, advancing scientific insights that helped parents everywhere raise healthier, higher-skilled children. Innovations included the discovery of fetal alcohol syndrome, infant screening for phenylketonuria and congenital hypothyroidism, folic acid supplements for pregnant women to prevent neural tube defects, back sleeping for babies to prevent sudden infant death syndrome, and new safeguards for premature infants.

These were exactly the kinds of practical insights Cora Hillis and Eunice Kennedy had envisioned. However, most of these conditions affected only a small share of children. Infant screening produced miracles, preventing what had previously been devastating lifetime setbacks—for one in every 300 births. Folic acid supplements prevented debilitating neural tube defects—for less than one in every 3,000 births. The biggest impact of these more biological interventions probably arose out of greater public awareness of fetal alcohol syndrome, which still may affect up to one in 20 births today. These discoveries were important, but they weren't altering the daily fabric of childhood and parenting on a massive scale.[31]

Fortunately, these discoveries weren't the only legacy of Eunice Kennedy's new research juggernaut. The most important discovery would look more like the kind of holy grail that Kennedy had dreamed of and Terman had mocked as implausible. It would take more time. It wouldn't call for a new pill, supplement, or procedure. It would call for a more revolutionary change in how we build skills day by day, hour by hour, from the moment children come into existence.

TRAILERS ON THE EDGE OF CAMPUS

Today nearly 15 percent of American children wind up in what is known as "special education." These children struggle to keep up with schoolwork in standard school environments, and in some cases they can disrupt the education of others around them. Many additional children with these problems are not in special education. Of the 3.7 million or so children born every year in America, something like a million of them fit this description.[32]

The vast majority of these children don't have any distinct biological ailment. If there were a way to build enough skills in these children to make school a better experience, both for them and for the classmates and teachers they interact with, then we would no longer be tinkering around the edges. We'd be accelerating human skill development on a grand scale.

In 1966, a pair of psychology professors at the University of North Carolina cofounded one of the 12 new university research centers funded by Eunice Kennedy's new federal agency. They named it the Frank Porter Graham Child Development Institute. Frank Porter Graham was a beloved president of the University of North Carolina who ushered in a new wave of research on links between racism and poverty in the South. He was also an advocate for workers' rights, an architect of Social Security, a US senator, and, according to one famous adversary at the time, a "sweet little son of a bitch."[33]

The founders of this new child-development institute were Hal and Nancy Robinson, and they took a different approach from the 11 sibling institutes scattered around the country. Instead of trying to alleviate intellectual disability after it had emerged, they would focus on preventing it from emerging in the first place. In particular, they would focus not on medical and biological origins of these disabilities but on social and economic origins.

They decided to set up an experimental childcare center for parents in the local community, much like the Iowa Research Station had done in 1921. But their center would be different in a key way: it would start with infants.

At the time, childcare for infants was still a fringe idea. The psychologist Frances Campbell was hired early on for her expertise in testing infant cognitive development. She recalls the childcare began as a chaotic program, improvised in "trailers on the edge of campus." Researchers were terrified that grouping infants together would breed infectious disease, so at first the staff wore hazmat gear and changed the children into sterilized clothing every morning on arrival. After a while, they realized the babies were doing fine, getting a few little bugs sooner than they might have otherwise, but nothing terrible. People started to relax.[34]

This early program had not coalesced around any grand strategic vision. The children came from all walks of life rather than some target group most likely to benefit from care. Not much thought went into the curriculum; they just tried vaguely to make good use of time. Most importantly, there was no control group, no random assignment, and therefore no scientific way to assess whether the program was having any impact on the children. It was the skeleton of an idea without the flesh and blood of science.

But then in 1969 Hal and Nancy Robinson got recruited away by another university. They were replaced by a new lead researcher, Craig Ramey, and he did things differently.[35]

THE ARCHITECT

Craig Ramey is a tall, jovial, dough-faced man from West Virginia with a dignified expression and a baritone voice reminiscent of Johnny Cash. As a child, he grew up discussing Shakespeare, Milton, and great philosophers over the kitchen table with parents who had dropped out of school after eighth grade. His interests include sailing, skiing, classic cars, and French architecture. But the bon vivant exterior belies an almost elegiac idealism, a worship of scientific rigor, and a longstanding personal quest to unravel the origins of human skill development.

Ramey was steeped in the Iowa Research Station's findings by Wellman, Skeels, and Skodak, the early preschool experiments by Kirk and Weikart, and studies on early development in animals, from ducks and owls to monkeys and rats. Since graduate school he had dreamed of conducting an experiment—a real experiment with proper random assignment— that would transform learning environments for disadvantaged kids. The program he had in mind would not target kids already showing developmental delays at age three or four, but *infants* who hadn't yet had time to fall behind. And it would not last a few hours a day; it would last *all day*. Maybe this new form of education, he thought, could replicate the equalizing effects provided by adoption into more-advantaged families. How much of the full rich-kid experience could he transport out of the family, into a classroom?

The new Frank Porter Graham childcare program was his opportunity, and he seized it. He got off to a rocky start. During his recruitment, the institute had assured him it had already obtained funding for the project, but that wasn't quite true. After he arrived, the center's first grant application to the new NICHD fell through. Ramey was shocked. For a while, he thought taking the job may have been a massive professional mistake. It took him a year, but he recovered. "That cost me two bottles of scotch. At the time the new building under construction was not finished. I rewrote the proposal on a card table in the trailer where the [old nursery school] used to be located. I worked around the clock to revise it, and that one was funded." Even after that, Francis Campbell remembers a constant struggle to maintain funding and Ramey recalls multiple times when the project "came within days of running out of money."[36]

With startup funding secured, he set about formalizing the center's haphazard infant care program into a laser beam focused on testing the core hypothesis that the right kind of early education could prevent intellectual disability. The new program would enroll only children with lower-education, lower-income parents and thus children who were statistically most at risk of missing out on key skill-building investments. In Chapel Hill, that description wound up meaning Black children, reflecting demographic clustering in part but also the fact that local low-income white parents were unwilling to place their babies into a racially integrated setting.

Ramey made some other key changes. He assured that the experimental and control groups were close to identical, on average, by using random assignment. He hired early learning experts Joseph Sparling and Isabelle Lewis to design and document a curriculum. A formal curriculum would make it crystal clear exactly what the experimental group had received that the control group had not received, so the results could be replicated and extended later. To aid the recruitment of families into the study and to demonstrate the team's goodwill, he made sure all study participants would benefit. All 120 of the children recruited into the study would receive excellent medical care, a full supply of free infant formula and diapers, and social services for help in claiming public benefits. But of these children, only half were randomly selected to get the all-day, year-round preschool program starting just a few months after birth. That was the fulcrum.[37]

They named the study "the Carolina Abecedarian Project." The word *Abecedarian* (pronounced "A-B-C-darian" as if reciting the alphabet) refers to a person who is just starting to learn something. It is also an ancient poetic form frequently used for religious compositions. The most famous Abecedarian is Psalm 119 in the Bible, which consists of 22 stanzas, one for each letter of the Hebrew alphabet and offers an ecstatic celebration of learning.

> Make me to understand the way of thy precepts: so shall I talk of thy wondrous works.
> My soul melteth for heaviness: strengthen thou me according unto thy word.
>
> (Psalms 119:27–28, KJV)

Campbell recalls her first conversation with Ramey when he recruited her to work in the new program. He gave her a condensed version of Psalm 119: "We're gonna get these infants, enrich their environment, and boost their cognitive achievement." She didn't think it would work, especially with Black kids. As she puts it today with impressive clarity, "Well, let me be honest. I'm from the South. Grew up in Alametz County, all white. My father was a farmer and not a successful farmer. I was never around Black people; I went to a segregated school. . . . I had this definite sense of white superiority; I just took that for granted."

Creating the program posed a big question that will sound familiar to parents the world over: What should we do all day with these kids? They had eight hours a day, Monday through Friday, 50 weeks a year, for five years. That's 10,000 hours of time.

In fact, it was more than 10,000 hours because they also started a transportation logistics system to bring the kids to and from the center. Every minute from the moment the kids entered the car to the moment they were dropped back off at home would be used in service of building skills. "The curriculum activities," they would write, "are adjusted to inside or outside, play, dressing, eating, etc., so that when it is functioning properly, the curriculum permeates the whole day."[38]

Sparling and Lewis were responsible for these 10,000 hours. They had to invent a curriculum for babies.

LEARNING GAMES

What Sparling and Lewis produced, the Carolina Infant Curriculum, may someday be regarded as a landmark innovation of the twentieth century. They started with their belief that children learned through spontaneous play, such as touching and licking and staring at objects or garbling and squirming in reaction to events. But they believed adults could guide spontaneous play to speed up learning beyond what would take place by chance. They settled on the idea of "Learning Games."[39]

Each Learning Game would be a self-contained, structured interaction between a child and an adult. The games had to fit a few criteria. They had to be very low cost. A game could use a towel or a cardboard box, for example, but not any fancy toys or electronics. The games had to be simple enough for almost any adult to master. And the games, with enough repetition, had to change a child's behavior in a way that could be predicted, observed, and measured.

To fill 10,000 hours of time, they would need a lot of games. Sparling and Lewis wrote down five areas of inspiration: what parents and kids valued, expert opinions, facts, child skills they wanted to develop (language, motor, social/emotional, and cognitive/perceptive), and warning signs that children were going off track. They pasted hundreds of word fragments from these domains on a giant kaleidoscopic wall chart in a windowless room with a big table. Every day they would go into this room together, stick pins into a few pieces of information, and try to build a Learning Game around those few ideas. "Let's let the Wall talk to us," they would say. Once they formed an idea for a new Learning Game, they would write up a one-page sheet with instructions and a Polaroid photograph modeling the interaction. Sparling, always a careful observer, loved photography. He even reached out to Polaroid, described their project, and received a pile of free film.[40]

Over the next few years, Sparling and Lewis would produce about 500 Learning Games, then whittled this number down to 200 keepers through classroom practice. Each of these 200 games had been battle tested and refined into a well-oiled skill-building machine.

━━━━━━━━━━━ **HOW** ━━━━━━━━━━━━━━━━━━━━━━━━━━━━━━━━━━━━━━

✻ ADULT: Hold the baby to your shoulder. Keep your hand near his head but *let him support his own head for a few seconds*. Do this often when you pick him up. *Sit or stand so he sees something pretty over your shoulder*. Talk to him and stroke him as you hold him. Another person could stand behind you and talk to him.

✻ INFANT: The baby will hold his head steady for a moment then it will drop back to your shoulder. He will soon be able to hold it up longer and longer.

✻ EQUIPMENT Picture or any colorful object.

━━━━━━━━━━━ **WHY** ━━━━━━━━━━━━━━━━━━━━━━━━━━━━━━━━━━━━━━

✻ GOAL: To give him something to look at so he will want to hold his own head up.

✻ USES: The baby needs to be able to hold his head steady before he can learn to sit alone.

Figure 1.2

A prototype Learning Game. *Source*: From Joseph Sparling's personal collection.

In the Learning Game "What's Gone," the teacher sits with a toddler and places, say, a blue frog, a red car, and a striped box on the floor between them. The teacher then names the objects out loud, asks the child to close her eyes, and hides one of the items behind her back. At first, children struggle to identify the missing item. But they catch on with practice, and they delight in their growing mastery. Sparling adores this game. "The notion of paying attention at the beginning, keeping that information over a period of time, and then using it later, is a really important principle of learning, at least school-type learning. This walks the child through that process in a playful way."

Taken together, the curriculum differs dramatically from what most parents would do with their infants and toddlers. In "Conversational Reading," teachers start out ignoring the plot of books and following children's lead, "wrapping language" around whatever grabs the child's attention. In applying a principle of "language priority" to block play, teachers set up two identical sets of blocks, one for the child and one for the parent, then mirror and describe what the child does. In "Enriched Caregiving," teachers talk children through daily tasks such as changing diapers and eating lunch, saturating the day with words, grammar, and concepts. Through all this activity, the program tracks each child's hour-by-hour progress with video cameras and teacher note-taking protocols. The data record big milestones, such as first steps, as well as smaller advances, such as the moment a child first inspects her own hands. Teachers then use the data to identify skill gaps and deploy specific Learning Games.

None of this is rocket science. But, then again, wheels and paper aren't "rocket science," either. The Abecedarian program was like an assembly line for human beings—an exquisitely engineered, individualized, five-year-long assembly line. But if it was an assembly line, it was a very happy assembly line. Ramey remembers one clear, sunny morning around 1975 when a carload of kids, then three or four years old, arrived at the center. "They were smiling and running enthusiastically into this ugly 1960s low, bitter principle [sic] Frank Porter Graham Center, this very uninspired building. . . . [T]hey were very enthusiastic, happy, and eager, and I thought, 'This is a sign things are going well.'" Years later one of the kids, then an adult, told Ramey she couldn't wait to get there in the morning; she knew she would have a good time all day.

Meanwhile, while 60 kids spent their days moving along this magnificent assembly line, 60 other kids had not drawn the lucky number. They were in the control group. Most of these kids did not attend any educational program at all, especially during their first three years of life. They lived at home with their parents, or they were cared for by relatives or friends or neighbors. The children who did attend childcare centers wound up in programs that spent less than half as much per child as Abecedarian, with only half as many teachers per child.[41]

One hundred twenty kids were born into poverty in Chapel Hill, North Carolina. Due to random chance, 60 of them wound up on the Abecedarian assembly line for 10,000 hours. The other 60 spent that same 10,000 hours at home with their families or in childcare programs unlikely to make similar investments in their skill growth.

What happened?

THE TRANSFORMATION

What happened is that Abecedarian worked even better than expected. At the time, the project researchers had to start with IQ scores. Craig Ramey was not fixated on IQ. Much like the Iowa Station researchers, he focused the project on a wide range of child skills measured in a variety of ways. But among other developmental psychologists at the time, IQ was the yardstick for success. As Campbell recalls, "The bottom line for the Abecedarian study when I started was that IQ test."

Campbell remembers seeing the data come in as statisticians coded all her painstaking measurements into punch cards that fed into IBM mainframe computers. "There's a two-month score. We have a three-month Bailey [IQ test] on almost everyone. [The treatment and control groups] were right on top of each other. By six months, they had begun to diverge a little bit. The treated group was scoring a little higher. Things looked a little floppy at nine months, so I decided I didn't believe it. . . . They were diverging a little bit by 12 months, and they had diverged wildly by 18 months."

In David Weikart's part-time Perry Preschool experiment for children ages three and four in Ypsilanti, Michigan, kids had also shown big early IQ gains, but these impacts faded out completely by age 10. A similar finding had also been observed for children in the new public-preschool program known as Head Start: early positive impacts on test scores that dissipated within a few years. Today, decades later, we know fade-out of early test score impacts did not mean these programs had failed to improve long-term outcomes in adulthood, but at the time almost everyone assumed that was the case.[42]

Time kept passing, and Abecedarian kept measuring every child in both groups. "I thought [the impact of Abecedarian on IQ scores] might go away because it had in other studies," recalls Campbell. "When I found it had not . . . the effect size was holding up, we can still see it at 12 years old. Still saw it at 15. We still saw it when they were 21. That's when we hit the big time, big press conference in Washington, made the evening news. [The kids] were doing better."

And time still kept passing, and they continued tracking every child in both groups. By now, it's clear that 10,000 hours of turbo-charged early education jolted these children toward middle-class adult careers. Compared to the control group, the participants were dramatically more likely to graduate high school and college. By age 30, they earned $12,700 more per year at work. That's a third of the Black–white income gap. And remember the main Abecedarian program lasted only through age five, or less than a third of childhood. You can even tell which group of kids attended Abecedarian by looking closely at their blood cells: by their thirties, members of the fortunate group were at lower risk of cardiovascular and metabolic disease.[43]

One of the children involved in the study wound up committing murder. That one child was in the control group—he didn't get the early education. This may have been a fluke. But a similar tragic finding arose in the Perry Preschool experiment, and other early education programs have also reduced crime. Needless to say, even small reductions in violent crime have enormous value.[44]

As the results piled up, Ramey was ecstatic. The study was a unique contribution to knowledge. He had created an educational experience that began shortly after birth, lasted all day every day for many years, built on a clear and replicable curriculum with no "secret ingredient," and used strict random assignment to overwhelm almost any conceivable scientific objection. He'd basically realized his dream, and there was nothing else like it in human history.

But for all its virtues, Abecedarian was still just 120 kids in a pilot program managed by one small team of ambitious researchers in one particular city. Had Ramey provided a new general insight into human potential, or had he gotten lucky? Could the approach work on a larger scale, managed by a more diverse range of people and in a more diverse range of environments? Could it work for a whole country?

That's when Ruby Hearn got involved.

THE BUILDER

Ruby Puryear Hearn was born in Winston-Salem, North Carolina, in April 1940. "I just turned eighty," she noted in her jovial tone when we spoke over the phone in the summer of 2020. "I'm still trying to convince myself that is the case." Her mother taught at the historically Black Morehouse College, and her father spent most of his career working on public-policy issues at the Urban League. She grew up middle class, but she was always reminded of her race. "I went to segregated schools and lived in a segregated city."[45]

Today, as she observes protests against police brutality, she remembers her visceral childhood fear of white police in particular. "My mother told me, if a policeman tried to stop me, go to the nearest house and say 'Mother, Mother'" to fool the officer into thinking she was not alone. "Police were not viewed as anyone who would be helpful to you. Interesting now they're talking about public safety. Police were not viewed as a source of safety."

Prejudice shaped her career choices and her identity. "I wanted to be in an objective field where people couldn't discriminate against me because I could show two plus two equals four, and it doesn't matter if you're Black, blue, or green. . . . At that time Black people were considered inferior and constantly challenged to show you were as smart as any other person."

Her instincts quickly proved useful when she began college at Skidmore in New York. "I had a bizarre experience in college. For my first two years I was the only Black person on campus. I had a teacher in one of my science classes who didn't like me. The other kids in the class knew he didn't like me. He mismarked my paper, and I pushed to get it corrected, and he wouldn't do it. So I went to the dean, and I was right, and he was wrong. So that did underscore my belief in the protection that comes from being in an objective field."

Hearn graduated at 20 with highest honors and a double major in biology and chemistry, then earned a PhD in biophysics at Yale with a dissertation titled "Thermodynamic Parameters in the RNase-S System."

"I had originally intended to spend my career in a lab, working on problems affecting children's health." But she struggled to square the demands of her research with raising two children and found a position at a philanthropy called the Robert Wood Johnson Foundation, or RWJ. At that time, RWJ was the largest private organization working on health-care issues in the country. She was responsible for developing and overseeing their investments in maternal and child health.

In the 1980s, two trends converged in a way that gave Hearn an idea. First, improvements in ventilation machines, incubators, and infant-monitoring technologies had increased survival rates among premature, low-birthweight babies. RWJ had recently completed a study trying to broaden access to these technologies. But although low-birthweight infants increasingly survived, they tended to suffer severe skill deficits. Second, Abecedarian had announced its early education program's massive positive impacts on lower-income children's skill growth.

As Hearn and her colleagues anticipated the struggles lying ahead for all these tiny, premature infants now given a chance at life, "we wanted to know whether there was anything we could do." Hearn decided to persuade RWJ to invest in a new project to see if Abecedarian-style early education could improve outcomes for low-birthweight babies.

Up to that time, RWJ had conducted only "demonstration projects" showing that smaller programs such as Abecedarian could be scaled up successfully. Demonstration projects were not experiments but were a good way to learn about scaling-up smaller programs. Because there was no experimental control group in such projects, they could produce only suggestive insights.

For Hearn, that wasn't good enough. Her experience with discrimination had led her to prefer irrefutable evidence, not suggestive insights. So she fought for RWJ to do the new project as a proper experiment, with random assignment of low-birthweight babies into treatment and control groups. Some kids would get better health care and Abecedarian-style education; other kids would only get better health care.

But Ruby Hearn had a lot more resources behind her than Craig Ramey had with Abecedarian. Instead of an experiment with 120 kids in one city, the RWJ project would be an experiment with nearly 1,000 kids in eight diverse cities around the country. The megaexperiment would be called the Infant Health and Development Program, or IHDP, and would ultimately cost more than $100 million.[46]

Hearn recruited Craig Ramey to lead program implementation on the strength of his experience in creating Abecedarian. Hearn also brought in luminaries from medicine, statistics, developmental psychology, and other disciplines to design the intervention. To avoid any hint of bias, the program would be evaluated by a separate, independent set of researchers who had nothing to do with program design or on-the-ground implementation with babies, parents, and teachers. As Donna Bryant, a lead IHDP administrator, summarized it, "The whole show was split so everything was pristine." If Hearn's big bet on IHDP had any flaws, she had assembled the ideal team to discover them.[47]

Everyone who worked on IHDP still marvels at the scope of the project. Ramey considers IHDP "the most complicated [randomized controlled trial] that has been conducted I think anywhere in the world. . . . We didn't cut any corners. It's the way human science about important issues should be conducted."

At some point in late 1988 or early 1989, the full research team from all eight cities gathered at Stanford University to see the results up through the children's third birthday. No one managing the program had been permitted to see any results up to that point. The psychologist Jeanne Brooks-Gunn, an early contributor, remembers the meeting vividly. "It was so exciting, it was nerve wracking, 'Oh my God I hope we had some effect on the kids!'"[48]

When Helena Kraemer, the IHDP's lead statistician, revealed the findings, people gasped. The IHDP had produced a near-perfect replication of the earlier Carolina Abecedarian Project. Abecedarian had required normal-weight babies, and the results for the more normal-weight babies in IHDP looked just like those in Abecedarian. Impacts were enormous at all eight sites, with one exception: oddly smaller impacts in Boston.[49]

Later researchers, exploiting IHDP's large sample and immaculate design, were able to calculate the likely consequences if such a program were scaled up nationally. They found the impacts would be so large and so much larger for the lowest-income kids that it would more or less *eliminate* inequality in early cognitive skill development for as long as the program lasted. Because skill gaps account for the majority of income gaps by class and race in adulthood, the program appeared to set kids up for lifelong economic success.

IHDP, like Abecedarian, appeared to provide most of the key missing investments that lower-income parents couldn't pull off on their own during their children's early years. Positive impacts mostly persisted after the program ended at age three and through age five when the kids started school. Then, gradually, the renewed onslaught of disadvantage and missing investments began eroding the gains. The kids were like little airplanes, no longer receiving sufficient fuel to fly at cruising altitude.[50]

Ruby Hearn and the extraordinary team she assembled had conjured up an experiment even more impressive than Abecedarian, one of the greatest social experiments the world had ever seen. It was now clear the big impacts of Abecedarian-style early education were not a fluke but a natural phenomenon, as real as the impacts of aspirin or penicillin. Hearn had sought better ways to help low-birthweight infants. Almost incidentally, as a by-product of her program design, she had given the final turn to a key that unlocked a door to a miraculous alternate reality that the Children's Bureau's work had barely hinted at and that Iowa Station researchers had only begun to sketch out half a century earlier. In this alternate reality, children began their lives building skills with professional educators rather than relying entirely on parents to do all the heavy lifting. As a result, poor children gained just as many skills as rich children, as if divisions by economic class had evaporated. Apparently, this alternate reality was a real place.

Since the days of Perry, Abecedarian, and IHDP, mounting evidence has confirmed the vast potential of early education to narrow skill gaps. Programs such as Head Start and public preschool expanded far beyond experimental research into large-scale efforts overseen by democratic governments in cities, states, and federal agencies across America. Inch by inch, the door to the alternate reality began to crack open. The problem was that most parents still had no idea this door existed—or that they and their children were living squarely on the wrong side of it.[51]

TREASURE HUNT

What does all the work that parents put into child development really accomplish?

This is a hard question with a long history and only recently a clear answer. The main problem is that it's difficult to distinguish impacts of parental skill building from the genetic influences children inherit from their biological parents. This is closely related to the classic question of nature versus nurture or, in more modern terms, the importance of pre-birth versus postbirth factors in human development.

Fortunately, there is a naturally occurring workaround. The solution to finding the answer is to focus on *adopted* children, who don't get any genes directly from the adopting parents who raise them. For example, if kids adopted by rich parents wind up doing better than kids adopted by poor parents, we might attribute the difference to greater skill-building investments orchestrated by rich parents.[1]

This simple idea, however, is devilishly hard to execute in practice. Many adopted children are placed with relatives, who after all *do* share some of their genes. In other cases, adoption agencies place kids with parents based on some combination of what the birth parents want for their child, what kind of child the adopting parents want, and what the agency believes most likely to benefit the child. This means some kinds of adopting parents may be matched with infants who already have greater advantages. For example, wealthier adopting parents may get matched with healthier children or with children who have more highly educated birth parents. If we can't be sure kids are matched with parents at random, it's hard to draw conclusions about what exactly caused some adopted kids to do better than others.

As if these difficulties weren't enough, it's also hard—or used to be hard—to keep track of adopted children as they grow up. Harold Skeels and Marie Skodak from the Iowa Child Welfare Research Station tried to do it. In 1966, they observed: "There exist today hundreds of comprehensive studies in the behavioral and biological sciences, which if followed up and reevaluated after the lapse of a major interval of time could produce extremely valuable data. . . . Many research workers have undoubtedly been intrigued by such a possibility, but may have abandoned the idea because the venture seemed too complicated, too expensive, or unlikely to be fruitful because of the erosion of time."[2]

Undaunted, Skeels and Skodak decided to search for 125 children involved in major adoption studies they had begun in the 1930s. They had already tracked these children through adolescence in 1949 when they drove 12,000 miles across the United States and Canada in a period of ten weeks. (That's like driving halfway around the earth.) Now in the 1960s they tried to track down these children one more time to see how they were faring as adults in their thirties.

They found all the kids, but their efforts explain why no one had accomplished anything like this previously. One adopted girl they found was born under the name Katherine Tilson. Skeels and Skodak found out that Katherine's adoptive parents were dead and that she had married a man named Frank Adams. So they consulted a directory in Washington (in person) and then pursued a lead in Florida (in person), where they discovered Katherine's aunt living in a nearby house. This aunt told them the family had moved to Tucson, Arizona. Off they went to Tucson (in person). Here's their research diary for Tucson:

March 1962. Using a city map of Tucson and the address supplied by the aunt, tried unsuccessfully to locate the residence, since Frank Adams was not in the city telephone directory. Failing to find any house corresponding to the address, I went back to the post office and obtained a map which showed the approximate location of the cabins, in one of which they were supposed to be residing. Also found an elementary school in the area which might be helpful if one of the boys was old enough to go to school. Armed with the new information, made an unsuccessful house-to-house inquiry at each of several motels and courts in the indicated area. Went to the school, but found no Adams boy registered. The principal, however, named another elementary school in the vicinity. This school was also another dead end. Here, however, the principal suggested checking with the utility company, as most people in the area have their own gas or electric meters. This check finally located the Frank Adams family at an entirely new address. Interviewed Katherine and had an opportunity to observe her two boys.[3]

That is one case. One hundred twenty-four to go!

It's no wonder that no one had been able to measure the true value of parental skill-building behaviors for most of human history. The intermingling of parental skill building with parental genes, the deliberate placement of children with adopting parents, and the challenges of finding adopted kids later in life have created a kind of Temple of Doom, concealing the answer to this question from even the most determined researchers.

Until 2002, when something amazing happened.

A BREAKTHROUGH

Bruce Sacerdote is an outrageously good-natured professor of economics at Dartmouth University with bright green eyes and a boyish grin. He conveys the sunny, preppy, almost shaggy vibe of a person who has succeeded at doing something he enjoys for a long time. He grew up middle class in Massachusetts, then attended Dartmouth, where he joined a fraternity, wrote a thesis about the boating industry (he still loves boating), and graduated second in his class. After getting a PhD at Harvard, he returned to Dartmouth, where he has taught ever since.

He first got interested in adoption after reading Judith Harris's famous book *The Nurture Assumption* (1998), in which—like other influential scholars such as Robert Plomin, Steven Pinker, and Charles Murray—she concludes parents make almost no difference to their children's life outcomes. Sacerdote remembers thinking, "Can that really be true?" The closer he looked, the less confident he felt that Harris's evidence could really support her claims.[4]

As Sacerdote started looking into available data sets on adopted children, he found they were almost useless. Many kids were adopted by relatives—clearly not a useful way to measure the impacts of parental skill building separate from the influence of genes, since relatives by definition also share genes. Even the kids adopted by nonrelatives appeared to be matched to their adoptive parents in highly nonrandom ways that could easily wind up reviving the key problematic link between parental characteristics and children's genes.

Sacerdote started cold-calling adoption agencies to learn more about how they placed children with parents. At some point, he came across the Holt Adoption Agency. Holt is one of the oldest and largest international adoption agencies in the world. Harry and Bertha Holt began facilitating adoption of Korean babies during the 1950s in the aftermath of the Korean War. When Sacerdote got Holt administrators on the phone, they told him something incredible. For many years, they had been assigning babies to parents literally *at random*. Moreover, the 7,700 kids who had been matched to parents as babies were now adults in their twenties and thirties. If Sacerdote could find a way to learn how the kids were doing, he would have a truly blockbuster data set.

The National Science Foundation agreed and gave him funding to survey these families with the Holt Agency's help. In the end, he reached out to 3,500 families and received 1,200 responses. Like so many other researchers, Sacerdote had no way of contacting the adopted children directly, so he surveyed the adopting parents about their children's outcomes. The survey yielded data on the children's later adult earnings, education, health (obesity, alcoholism), and many other outcomes. The data set captures an experiment that social scientists, philosophers, and biologists had been dreaming about for centuries.[5]

His findings overturned what still remained the bizarre conventional wisdom among psychologists: the idea that parents barely matter apart from their genetic contributions. In fact, Sacerdote found that parenting matters enormously. Children adopted by *moderately* more-advantageous parents wound up accumulating more skills and earning more in adulthood. We're not talking about radically more-advantageous parents—just moderately. On average, the adoptees assigned to these parents completed nearly a full additional year of schooling, were about 20 percentage points more likely to graduate from college, and had about 25 percent higher household income as adults.[6]

What would these impacts mean? Economists estimate that a typical American worker starting her career can expect to earn income over her lifetime that is financially equivalent to a $1 million stock of wealth. That means parents who bestow moderately more advantage on their children endow each of them with the earnings equivalent of an additional $250,000 of wealth. We can think about this contribution like an invisible trust fund inherited in the form of skills, which children then apply to elevate their income consistently throughout their professional lives. For parents raising two children, that's half a million dollars.[7]

And, in fact, the implications of Sacerdote's findings are even more remarkable for reasons Sacerdote didn't fully appreciate at the time. It turns out the true impacts of parents are even larger than those implied by Sacerdote's results—likely *much* larger.

THE RESTRICTED RANGE PROBLEM

Sacerdote's research design solved the two big problems that had previously held back efforts to measure the impacts of parents. The Holt Adoption Agency's random assignment of babies to parents severed the link between parenting practices and children's genes. And the mail survey of the adoptive parents about their children, placed decades in the past by one central agency, at least partly solved the problem of long-term follow-up.

But the study still had some problems. These problems basically guaranteed that his estimates dramatically underestimated the true importance of parents.

The first problem is that adopting parents get a late start with the children they adopt. Children in the study typically joined their adopting parents before their second birthday, but that's still a lot of time. Nutrition, drugs and alcohol, stress, disease, pollution, and other conditions all start to affect long-term human development during pregnancy and infancy. That leaves adopting parents with less influence over children's life outcomes than biological parents. All studies that focus on comparisons among adopted children therefore tend to understate the impacts of nonadopting parents.[8]

The second problem with Sacerdote's study is less obvious and more important: *adopting parents are much more similar to each other than biological parents.* This is called the "restricted range problem" because the range of parental characteristics prevailing among adopting parents is "restricted" compared to the range of characteristics among the general population of all parents.[9] In Sacerdote's study, for example, the adopting parents are alike in a very obvious way: they are nearly *four times* more likely to have graduated from college than other parents in their generation.[10]

Why are adopting parents so oddly similar to each other? Because adoption is highly selective. If having a child were like joining the Navy, adopting a child would be sort of like joining the Navy SEALS. First, there's the fee. At Holt, the going rate to adopt a child is $30,000; at other agencies it's often higher. People applying to adopt children have to demonstrate steady employment or independent wealth, navigate reams of paperwork, pass criminal-background checks, and undergo invasive home inspections. Drug problems, domestic abuse, and child abuse are deal breakers. In the past, women also had to be over a certain age and have a stable marital history. When I spoke with an administrator at the Gladney Center, another leading adoption agency, she mentioned additional deal breakers: any evidence of problems with sex or porn addiction, a house that contains a lot of guns, rooms that aren't clean enough, a history of being abused by others, or health problems such as cancer that are in remission but not yet 100 percent resolved. All of these requirements screen out parents who are more likely to struggle with aspects of skill building in children.[11]

Around the world, these kinds of filters result in a population of adopting parents that looks radically more advantaged than the much larger population of biological parents. A study in Sweden found a quarter of biological fathers had been arrested at some point in their lives, whereas a sample of 862 adopting fathers contained exactly zero arrests. In the general population, child abuse is disturbingly common; among adopted children it is almost nonexistent.[12]

Sacerdote's estimates, like so many other estimates based on comparisons among adopted children, are therefore based on artificially compressed differences among the few parents who make it through the adoption gauntlet. How much does this compression matter? We can't be sure, but the best work on the restricted range problem suggests that the impacts of parents as measured in a study like Sacerdote's are probably biased downward by one-half or two-thirds. In that case, his results would suggest very big impacts indeed—so big that even modest differences in skill-building obstacles encountered by parents could easily account for a large share of the skill gaps observed between children of different classes and races. In other words, adoption studies are perfectly consistent with the idea that unequal parental access to skill-building resources is the keystone propping up social and economic hierarchies.[13]

And we know restricted range isn't just a theoretical problem because not *all* adoption studies suffer from it. In the 1970s, for example, a former nuclear physicist named Michel Schiff led a monumental quest to find rare cases where one sibling had been adopted by highly educated professionals, and the other sibling had remained with less-educated, lower-income birth parents. Inspired by Marie Skodak and Harold Skeels from the Iowa Research Station, Schiff's team followed their dictum to rely on "flexibility, ingenuity, and tenacity" to obtain information about children later in life. They eventually found 43 such cases in France. Of these 43, they tracked down 32—and even then only in adolescence, not in adulthood. It took years. They almost gave up.

They found that adoption by highly advantaged parents made all the difference. The adopted children's school failure rates—a key signal of skill-accumulation problems—plummeted. These kids now failed school at rates that were almost identical to the rate for kids born and raised by their biological parents in highly advantaged families. It was as if genes played almost no role in the faster skill growth of advantaged children; their parents just invested in their skill growth more effectively. The findings are highly consistent with Sacerdote's results after adjusting for the restricted range problem. They are also consistent with the finding of large impacts of adoption, and of adoption by higher-income and more-educated parents, in data covering the entire population of Sweden.[14]

The implications of adoption studies, properly understood, are galling. By relying so heavily on parents to build skills, our society guarantees the persistence of economic class across generations. We enshrine an economic caste system.[15]

What do these studies mean for individual parents? For parents whose work, managerial skill, and personal and financial sacrifice improve child development, it means major economic contributions to society. The increase in children's future income captures only a small part of this contribution, but it helps to convey the magnitudes. Parents with two children who achieve moderately greater success in child skill development generate more than a million dollars in new wealth. The thing about income is that it's *taxed*. That means about a third of this new wealth, more than $330,000, winds up in public treasuries as tax revenue. Next time you talk to a parent doing her best to develop skills in her children, thank her for giving you and your fellow Americans enough wealth to build two new classrooms in your local school, to pay an Army soldier's salary for a decade, or to cover the full cost of chemotherapy for two cancer patients.[16]

For parents *not* set up for skill-building success, these numbers mean something else: your children are being robbed. The Parent Trap is America's attempt to shame you into silence while liquidating your children's economic future.

Adoption studies prove that some parents are doing *something* to build skills in their children much more effectively than other parents. But what exactly are they doing? How can so many parents unwittingly forego investments that might otherwise increase their children's future wealth by *hundreds of thousands* of dollars?

A BETTER MICROSCOPE

To understand how so many parents miss out on key investments in child skill growth, we need to consult other kinds of research. Just as it can be useful to think about parenting as an industry, it's useful to think about the skill-building aspect of parenting as a *job* that draws on elements of many other jobs. This approach lets us learn from recent insights into the nature of these other jobs and then take those insights back to understand what kinds of behaviors are driving the big impacts found in adoption studies.

Much of this research builds on new Big Data resources such as the IRS Databank, the data set based on IRS tax records pioneered by economists Raj Chetty, John Friedman, and Emmanuel Saez, described in the introduction. The Databank links adult workers' life outcomes (college, income, home ownership, marriage, retirement savings, and more) to their parents' income, and it covers all 300 million Americans. Data sets of this quality, breadth, and size act like microscopes that enable skilled researchers to describe previously invisible patterns, and in some cases to distill exact cause and effect from the swirling ocean of nebulous correlations. The Databank is *10,000 times larger* than the main data sets that earlier studies had relied on to link children with their parental backgrounds. Actual microscopes, the kind scientists look through to study fruit flies and bacteria, have also improved by a factor of about 10,000, but that took 150 years.[17]

Iowa Station researchers had recognized that if past social science experiments could be "followed up and reevaluated after the lapse of a major interval of time," they could produce major new insights into child skill development—that is, if only the process weren't so outrageously burdensome.

The Databank and other "administrative" data sets are solving this problem around the world. Suddenly, children involved in any American social science experiment since World War II can, in theory, be linked to their tax records in adulthood.[18] This possibility applies to all the studies we've discussed so far: Sam Kirk's preschool program, David Weikart's Perry Preschool, Craig Ramey's Abecedarian early education regime, Ruby

Hearn's Infant Health and Development Program, the Holt Adoption Agency's randomized placement of children with different families, and many more. All it would require is access to the original data, some government approvals, and a little computer programming to match the kids into the Databank.

In 2011, our research team used the Databank in this way for the first time. The study we chose to follow up on was a landmark educational experiment called Project STAR. Researchers had originally designed Project STAR to measure the value of smaller school class sizes. Starting in 1985, researchers partnered with 79 public schools in Tennessee to randomly assign more than 11,000 children entering kindergarten into either smaller or larger classes. As part of this process, the study also randomly assigned children to different teachers. So in addition to measuring the importance of attending smaller classes, STAR could also help us measure the importance of individual teachers. That second feature turned out to yield the more interesting set of findings.[19]

After a few months of work, we had matched more than 95 percent of the kids who had been involved in Project STAR to their adult tax records in the Databank. In a few months, we did what previously would have required many years spent piecing together a sprawling geosocial jigsaw puzzle, and we got much higher-quality data.

We could now see the STAR children's incomes up through age 27. We found that receiving a moderately better kindergarten teacher, defined in this case by the teacher's impact on kindergarten test scores, raised each child's future wealth by $16,000.[20] For the 20 kids in each classroom, that's $320,000 of new wealth every year. The study confirmed what many teachers all over America had long felt but had no way to prove: when they did their jobs well, they generated enormous social value—more value than many prestigious professional jobs in, say, finance and law that paid three or four times as much as teaching.

This study, along with subsequent blockbuster studies on middle school teachers in New York and preschool access in Boston, proved that education programs could have long-term impacts on college and earnings even when their short-term impacts on test scores appeared to "fade out" within a few years. This finding was a big deal because many programs, including the federal government's most high-profile investment in early education, Head Start, had been written off by opponents based on fade-out.[21]

These new studies provided a way to map short-term impacts on test scores into long-term impacts on earnings. Most studies of child-development programs can estimate only short-term impacts on things such as test scores. Suddenly, researchers could use insights provided by the Databank to make a well-founded guess about the economic value implied by programs' short-term impacts. In other words, the better microscope allowed researchers to glimpse tiny seeds of distant future impacts embedded in contemporary results.[22]

As we'll see, insights from the Databank and other emerging data sets, statistical techniques, and sociological investigations have gradually given us a new window into the challenges besetting parents as they try to build skills in children. The picture that emerges is clear. Skill building entails taking on a portfolio of complex managerial problems that many parents are too isolated and overwhelmed to master, and the mistakes that result have enormous long-term ramifications. This reality has always existed but has been hidden from plain sight for thousands of years. The new findings are finally pulling back the curtain on why the best adoption studies find that parents are so pivotal, what it is that parents really do, and how badly we throw them to the wolves.

NEIGHBORHOOD ROULETTE

Let's start with where parents wind up living. At every income level, parents have options, and these options matter. In this process, parents have to evaluate homes, neighborhoods, and schools in much the same way as *real estate agents.*

Business owners are used to this problem. Here is how one successful restaurant owner scouted out his options.

> The research I did was from trusted family and friends. . . . Ybor City [in Tampa] . . . was attractive for some reasons. But then [trusted local contacts]

would tell us that it was a weekend place, and it was young, and there's not a lot of money down there, and on the weekdays it's kind of dead. . . . [We] would also go out and eat lunch and dinner two or three days in a row in all of these areas that we were looking at, to just kind of get a feel for what kinds of people were eating in those places, and how busy they were at different times.[23]

In a 300-page book of interviews with successful small business owners, the word *location* is used 100 times.[24] For larger companies such as Starbucks and Costco, location is more science than art. At these companies, teams of professional analysts scrutinize local traffic patterns, labor markets, and customer profiles to pinpoint the most profitable locations.

Now, consider this. In 60 top parenting books found on Amazon and the *New York Times* bestseller lists, there is no advice about where parents should raise their children.[25]

In 2012, the sociologist Annette Lareau and her team talked to dozens of parents about how they chose their neighborhoods and schools. What she found echoes the silence on the bookshelves. A few of the savviest parents acted like business owners in their location research. Dolores Carlton, a PhD student and mother of two, was one example. She realized her neighborhood school had weak test score data, and she confirmed in multiple visits that the school did not appear well run. She tried unsuccessfully to transfer her daughter to another school. She then started gathering information from other parents, looking for an edge. "You always wanna see what the next parent's plan is because they might have considered something or found out about something you don't know yet."

But she didn't take people's opinions at face value. "As you hear about a school that you hadn't heard of before, you check it out, and if you continue hearing about it or if there's something on the website—I think I went to the state's website to check test scores—if there's something that really stands out to you as extraordinary about the school . . . I started organizing a formal list. . . . It emerged from this informal mental list." The list became a data set: "Oh, I had a lot of stuff! I had bookmarks in my Web browser. . . . There was a section for the school websites. There was a section for state resources, you know, places to find test scores and things about funding. . . . And then I had a spreadsheet where I listed all the schools that I planned to apply to, and I prioritized them according to 'what's my top choice?' And then I had kind of different columns—like, Had I submitted the application? What materials are they asking for? What's the due date?—so I can stay organized." The data set guided her investigations as she visited four public and one private school in her city. Her daughter wound up winning an admission lottery to attend her top-choice charter school.[26]

Dolores Carlton was unusual among the 46 parents with whom Lareau's team spoke. Few parents did this kind of research when choosing where to live. The following recollections were typical:

> We didn't really look up any test scores or anything like that before we moved here. . . . I just feel like it's just so much that I'm maybe assuming about the schools. Some of my decisions are not like I've carefully researched.

> I'm embarrassed to say it was like we didn't even think about schools. We just didn't in our, you know, our mindset at all. You know, had we taken into account schools, we would not have bought a house there.

> You know, I'm a scientist, I know how to check things out, and the fact is I really didn't do it.[27]

These challenges facing parents as real estate agents go far beyond finding school performance data and they take a heavy toll, especially among lower-income parents such as those eligible for housing assistance. We know how big this toll is thanks to extraordinary social experiments that have randomized thousands of families into more- and less-advantageous kinds of neighborhoods and to the powers of the Databank.[28]

The most recent experiment was Creating Moves to Opportunity (CMTO), based on its landmark predecessor Moving to Opportunity (MTO). In the 1990s, MTO provided thousands of families around the United States with housing vouchers, but some of these families could use the vouchers only if they moved to higher-income neighborhoods. CMTO, in contrast, let parents move wherever they wanted but gave them more precise information about where children like theirs were most likely to thrive later in life. CMTO also helped parents search for apartments, engage with landlords, and pay small fees that got in the way of sealing a deal. CMTO basically provided the support that people might hope to get from a close friend or relative.

It's telling how parents reacted to CMTO. Jackie, a former therapist with a nine-year-old son, recalled: "A light bulb went on . . . it was this whole flood of relief . . . it was just the supportive nature of having lots of conversations with [the search assistance team] about, that they could call the landlords, that they—just about all the different programs. And, you know, helping pay the deposit was immense. That saved me, because I don't know how I would have done that. Yeah, just, you know, personally, mentally, emotionally, and financially, in every way, they were support-ive . . . they just sort of swooped in."

Another parent, echoing the sentiments Lareau heard in her interviews with higher-income families, reflected that CMTO had reminded her of "things you need to think about like school district, grocery stores, public transportation. . . . And you don't think about it—you don't think about how something so simple [as where you live] is so important."[29]

The Databank allowed researchers to follow up on the kids that MTO had shifted into better neighborhoods decades in the past and to predict the long-term future impacts on kids shifted into better neighborhoods by CMTO. In both cases, the affected children increased their lifetime wealth by hundreds of thousands of dollars or the financial equivalent of a $100,000 trust fund received in early childhood.

Reflecting on their findings in CMTO, the researchers note: "Parents who participated in CMTO were juggling a number of things alongside their housing searches—including childcare, multiple jobs, the fallout from domestic violence, and anxiety about becoming homeless. The many moving parts of the search process—from online searches to the landlord calls, apartment visits, security deposit paperwork, background checks, applications, inspections, and voucher payment paperwork—were often overwhelming for parents. It also took precious time away from their children."[30]

It's no wonder parents on their own struggle with choosing a good location to raise children, even when they have access to subsidies or "advice" or "data." They're a little . . . preoccupied.

It might feel stressful to think about all these children's future wealth disintegrating as their parents choose where to live without enough support. But keep it together because these children have some questions for you about a math problem.

HOMEWORK

"[I]t was a battle every night when she was doing her homework," recalls Ms. Corsaro of the year her daughter started taking advanced math in fourth grade. "[My daughter would say,] 'I don't understand this' and 'It's so hard.' And math is definitely my weakest subject, so I wasn't much help there. And there was one time, in fourth grade, I was helping her with it, and I was like: 'Oh! It's all coming back to me.' And then she went in, and she got everything wrong. And I said: 'I am not helping you with math anymore.'"[31]

"I was never good at math," posted another parent online. "My son is struggling too. I am a single mom and I feel stupid I can't help him figure this out. I am afraid of what he will think of me when he figures out I don't know what I'm doing."[32]

Many parents feel this way when it comes to their kids' homework, but not all of them. When journalist Karl Greenfeld tried to do his teenage daughter's homework for a week, he found "the math is easier than I thought. We are simplifying equations, which involves reducing $(-18m^2n)^2 \times (-(1/6)mn^2)$ to $-54m^5n^4$, which I get the hang of again after Esmee's good instructions. I breeze through those 11 equations in about 40 minutes and even correct Esmee when she gets one wrong."[33]

This enormous variation in parents' own academic skills has big implications for kids because we also demand that parents try to be *tutors*. During normal times, parents in America spend an average of *six hours* per week helping—or trying to help—their kids with schoolwork. Six hours per week is more time than K12 math and English teachers get with children.

Parents who can't provide these services themselves have to buy them for thousands of dollars, beg school administrators for extra help, track down scarce nonprofit options—or watch their kids fall behind.[34]

How much does this matter? In 2015, an experiment in Chicago provided high-quality tutoring services to a random subset of 2,700 high school students. They found that good tutoring improved children's academic outcomes even more than good teaching, which makes sense given tutors can focus all their energy on just a few students rather than managing an entire classroom. We can use results from the Databank to map these impacts on test scores into likely impacts on adult earnings. This exercise suggests that good tutoring by parents for six hours a week, every week, year after year of childhood could raise children's future earnings by as much as $300,000.[35]

This is like winning an educational lottery. So why don't parenting books talk about this? Why do they focus on sleep training, breastfeeding, and discipline techniques when so many kids could benefit so dramatically from basic tutoring?

One reason is that no one knew about these long-term impacts until new resources such as the Databank gave us the information required to make a good guess. But the darker reason is that there's simply nothing most parents can do about this problem on their own. Tutoring is hard or expensive. This is an ugly facet of inequality in our parent-centric skill-building system that makes excellent educational investments a privilege for the elite.

But studying is just one aspect of mastering educational opportunity in America. And many other aspects are even harder for parents than helping a child solve polynomial equations.

THE FAFSA IS HOW MANY PAGES?

In America, graduating from high school is not always easy, but it doesn't require a lot of weird tricks or insider information. That's one reason why 80 percent of kids pull it off. But after twelfth grade, things change. In comparison to graduating from high school, graduating from a four-year college is like running a marathon through a swamp.

First, kids often have to take an entrance exam such as the SAT or ACT. Some kids don't take the test because the testing center is far away, or they miss the registration deadline, or some other life constraint gets in the way. Many of these kids would score well and go on to college if only the test were free and compulsory, but in most states it's not.[36]

Often, just taking the test is not enough. Kids also have to take it early so they can take it *again* if they have a bad day the first time. Once they're done taking the test, they have to send score reports to any number of colleges. They can send only a few reports for free; after that, they have to pay a fee or wade through red tape to get a fee waiver.[37]

In recent years, many colleges have begun to make SAT or ACT test scores optional in their application process. This may benefit students who would struggle to navigate the testing process, but in another sense it only increases the rewards to mastering the process. Now the optimal strategy is to take the test, take it early, retake it if needed, and *then* decide whether and where to report scores. High test scores still confer advantages to students who submit them.[38]

Then students apply to colleges. There are thousands of colleges, all allegedly as different as snowflakes. Many people, understandably, don't know much about this marketplace. Some kids think "liberal arts" colleges are only for communists (liberal) who like to paint pictures (arts). This is like confusing eggplants with eggs. Other kids think for-profit colleges are better than local public community colleges, which is often wrong— they're just more expensive. Many colleges have unique applications requiring multiple essays, teacher recommendations, test scores, and transcripts. Each application requires a fee or more red tape to obtain a fee waiver.[39]

Separately but simultaneously, families who can't afford the full (ridiculous) sticker price, that is, almost all families, apply for financial aid. They start with the Free Application for Federal Student Aid (FAFSA), which guards scholarships confusingly referred to as "Pell Grants" and requires 10 pages of sensitive information (most of which the government already has but doesn't bother to recycle). Many families who stand to gain immense benefits fail to complete this form. Students who need help can also beg for aid from states, local governments, charitable organizations, and every individual college they apply to. This means more paperwork, more essays, more interviews—all before knowing with certainty what they can afford or whether they can afford anything at all.[40]

Among all these real opportunities tied up in red tape, families also fend off fake opportunities engineered by scam artists. These threats complicate matters by putting families on guard. For example, many families struggle to believe an important fact that sounds for all the world like a scam but isn't. Some of the best colleges, boasting great teachers, small classes, and extravagant job networks, have sticker prices such as $75,000 per year but wind up costing low-income families *less* than other colleges, even local community colleges and penny-pinching for-profit colleges. It's as if, for some inscrutable reason, Louis Vuitton decided to charge low-income families lower prices than Old Navy.[41]

All of this is so baffling that the public K12 school system hires people whose full-time job is to help families navigate the process. These people are called *guidance counselors,* and their efforts do improve children's college outcomes significantly. But schools don't hire that many of them, so each one serves more than *300* kids. Not exactly special attention.[42]

So now maybe we've gotten our children into college. Congratulations! Unfortunately, that's just the beginning. Once kids actually enroll, they're on their own. Choosing whether to study cultural anthropology or mechanical engineering, deciding between Linear Algebra G131a or Differential Equations IIb, interacting with professors and teaching assistants in lectures that contain hundreds of students, buying stacks of expensive books every term, and then ultimately building résumés, applying for internships and jobs, practicing for interviews, or taking more exams for additional graduate schools that are just as baffling as colleges—kids take on all of this with barely any professional guidance provided by the public.

Unless, of course, their parents can help. And so parents are also *guidance counselors.*

In practice, our system relies on parents to help children work through all these logistics. Parents help children write polished humble-bragging college application essays about their most traumatic or triumphant or poetically bittersweet experiences. Parents badger children to sign up and study for tests, request teacher recommendations, and send out high school transcripts and financial aid applications just in time to meet unique deadlines set by different colleges. Parents propel adolescents through choice overload, procrastination, fear of rejection, myopia, all while children's normal high school coursework and sports and part-time jobs and existential crises continue as usual. And then we rely on parents to support children in college, even if for some parents "college" may as well be the International Space Station.[43]

How significant is the damage when parents can't guide kids through this swamp? Parents have huge impacts on college outcomes, and children who get college degrees earn much greater incomes in adulthood. You might think this is a fluke, that colleges attract children who would wind up being more productive anyway, but you would be wrong. Multiple studies have now rejected that theory. For example, people who barely miss out on attending their most convenient four-year universities because they scored just below a key admissions cutoff on their SAT wind up earning about $300,000 less over their lifetime than people who scored just above the cutoff. In other words, children whose parents aren't college-swamp masters once again stand to forfeit hundreds of thousands of dollars from their invisible trust fund.[44]

By now we're starting to grasp the true portfolio of jobs we impose on parents: where to live, how to help their children learn and study, how to help their children get a good college degree and land a good job, all the while fighting through processes that seem engineered to frustrate and bewilder outsiders.

But it's not just educational investments we ask parents to manage. It's also activities so basic—almost passive—that we don't always perceive their significance or their profound connection to how skills are built in children: activities such as, say, deciding how to react when a child seems out of breath a little too often.

Child health is a primary skill just like academic achievement, and parents manage it right away when children are still in the womb. In this way, parents also act as *pediatricians*.

Nancy Sander, mother of four in Fairfax, Virginia, remembers struggling to control her daughter Brooke's asthma: "What I remember most about attacks is watching her straining to lean forward to cough, her eyes bugging out of her head. But she didn't seem to be frightened; she seemed to just want air."[45]

Asthma is a chronic disease that affects about 8 percent of American children. Without proper management, asthma can be a scary, debilitating burden that interrupts children's schooling and prevents them from playing sports or pursuing a full social life. When well managed, however, asthma can be reduced to a minor inconvenience.

Unfortunately, managing asthma is not a simple task. For a long time, life for Nancy and Brooke was "a blur of ER visits, doctor appointments, hospitalizations and medical bills."[46] Nancy struggled to try to understand the disease in her spare time while also taking care of her three other children.

Finally, when Brooke was five, they got in touch with an allergy doctor named Martha White at Georgetown University Hospital. They learned to follow a treatment plan involving special medications and symptom-tracking tools. Brooke learned how to measure her own airflow every morning, adjust her medication accordingly, and then continue monitoring her airflow to report additional problems promptly. The new protocol ended their routine trips to emergency rooms.

Nancy figured out the right investments to protect her daughter's health. But Nancy was not a typical parent. She would go on to partner with Dr. White to cofound the Allergy & Asthma Network Mothers of Asthmatics (AANMA), an organization she would lead as president for the next 28 years.

For many other parents, managing a child's asthma remains a daunting challenge, despite the work of organizations such as AANMA. Children juggle "quick-relief" medications, such as short-acting beta agonists and anticholinergics, with "long-term control" medications taken as inhalants, such as corticosteroids and Cromolyn sodium, or as pills, such as Leukotriene modifiers. Parents also have to identify and remove the dozens of potential "triggers," from dust mites to roaches and rodents, pet dander, pollens, molds, smoke, smog, perfume, and gasoline. Parents also must monitor how and when their child exercises, taking into account the weather and the child's specific asthma profile.[47]

Asthma is just one health problem. Other common chronic diseases include bronchitis, diabetes, hay fever, epilepsy, hearing and vision disorders, and deformities such as clubfoot and cleft palate. Each of these conditions entails its own little labyrinth of protocols and procedures. Parents also have to manage mental health problems ranging from anorexia to schizophrenia; environmental threats such as lead and smoke exposure; and habits related to sleep, exercise, and diet.

Researchers have surveyed parents to gauge how much they know about child health. They find big misunderstandings overall and big disparities across income and education groups. Many parents struggle to interpret nutrition labels, drug prescriptions, and treatment regimes. When the Surgeon General warned in 1964 that smoking by a woman while pregnant damages infant health, it took decades for less-educated mothers to get the message. Many parents miss key facts about lead poisoning: that even small amounts of lead are dangerous, that boiling water does not remove lead, and that renters are entitled to lead-related disclosures from landlords before signing a lease. Many parents have distorted views about child injury risks and rely heavily on vigilance and reminders rather than on more effective techniques.[48]

And so it's not surprising that children with less-advantaged parents gradually accumulate large health deficits during childhood. That's not the parents' fault. They just get lost in all these little labyrinths.[49]

By the time low-income kids reach adulthood, their average health is so much worse than their higher-income peers that they wind up falling behind by nearly a full category: from "excellent" to "very good," from "very good" to "good," or from "good" to "fair." It's not a subtle difference.

We don't yet know the exact income loss accruing to children due to this health deficit, but it's likely to be large because we know what happens when adults are hospitalized: their incomes plummet. Being hospitalized in adulthood reduces the value of future expected income by $100,000 to $200,000. In this respect, it's similar to being laid off. And hospitalization is just one channel that affects income. Less-healthy children also face greater challenges in school due to absences and attention problems, and as adults they face career obstacles due to the need for more sick days and to on-the-job fatigue.[50]

Pediatricians spend *11 years* or more after high school preparing to manage children's health care. They have hard jobs. No wonder many parents struggle in this area.

At least, when it comes to these medical aspects of child health, most parents get occasional access to physicians. In other, equally fundamental aspects of child health, parents get virtually no help at all. When this happens, problems can reach epidemic proportions before we even notice something is wrong.

EAT YOUR VEGETABLES

In managing what their children eat and drink, parents also act as *nutritionists*.

This is striking because childhood obesity has gone haywire over the past 40 years. Today nearly one in five children is obese. Obese children, like children afflicted with unmanaged chronic disease and environmental toxins, can suffer earnings losses later in life. Obesity reduces the lifetime earnings of women in particular by about $100,000. Obesity reduces earnings by reducing health and productivity but also by triggering discrimination.[51]

On top of reducing earnings, obesity also increases health-care spending by $3,500 per adult per year, accounting for a quarter of all health-care costs in America or 5 percent of the entire formal economy. People afflicted with obesity don't pay these bills; everyone pays them in the form of higher insurance premiums and public-health programs such as Medicare.

Why do so many parents who clearly cherish their children's health wind up raising obese children? Why is this nutrition problem apparently so much harder for lower-income and less-educated parents?[52]

You might think the issue is one of access to healthy food. It's not. Many parents, acting on a lifetime of acquired habits and tastes, choose unhealthy food over healthy food even when new neighborhood grocery stores dramatically expand local access to healthy food.[53]

You might think it's about income, that many parents can't afford fresh produce and whole grains. It's not about income. Studies find that income windfalls and greater food affordability do not improve dietary health or reduce childhood obesity.[54]

So here's a thought: what if nutrition is just complicated and challenging, like other aspects of health? Researchers in Australia, which has an obesity rate nearly as high as America's, looked into this idea. They sat down with dozens of parents struggling to control their children's obesity and talked to them about their roles as child nutritionists. The parents knew apples and oatmeal were healthier than Coke and Oreos, but they disagreed with nutrition experts in other ways. They thought it made perfect sense to give their children junk food "treats" not only occasionally but every single day. They saw no problem with using unhealthy food as a reward to encourage better behavior despite the addictive dose–response associations such rewards can burn into children's psyches. Many parents believed inaccurately that most obese children ultimately outgrow their weight problems. They worried their children might starve if they didn't get to eat all the junk food they demanded, despite evidence that repetitive, persistent exposure to new foods can alter children's preferences and that manipulating portion sizes and meal compositions can trick children into adopting healthier diets.[55]

All of these parental beliefs are plausible and understandable. In some cases, they are also consistent with wishful thinking. And, unfortunately, they are also wrong.

Managing children's nutrition, like health care in general, is very challenging. This challenge has exploded with the proliferation of cheap, unhealthy, delicious, and highly addictive foods and drinks. But if child skill building is starting to sound overwhelming, go grab another Oreo because we're not done yet.

WELCOME TO THE C-SUITE

In 2013, five economists published results from a major experiment. On the surface, the study had nothing to do with parenting.[56]

In the experiment, the economists worked with a leading management-consulting firm to introduce modern management practices to a randomly selected sample of textile companies in India. Many of the new management techniques sound like common sense on steroids: *Keep the plant floor clean to reduce accidents. Keep yarn inventory at some target level. Fix the sewing machines and record reasons for failure to learn from mistakes.*

Within a year, plants showed dramatic efficiency gains. Defects plummeted, inventories declined, and profits increased by $350,000 per year at each firm. The firms began spreading the new gospel of good management to factories outside the experiment. Higher profits persisted years after the experiment ended.

The results raised an intriguing question. If the gains from these management practices were so large, why hadn't they been adopted earlier? Why did business owners need eggheads from other countries to show up with advice?

To answer these questions the economists used an advanced technical method known as "talking to people." It turned out some owners had never heard of modern management techniques, while other owners didn't believe they would work. No wonder the process of change, though successful, had proven arduous. Take the case of routine quality checks: "The owner frequently argued that quality was so good they did not need to record quality defects. This view was mistaken, however, because, although these plants' quality was often relatively good compared to other low-quality Indian textile plants, it was poor by international standards." Owners often persisted in their bad management practices until confronted with vivid proof that new approaches worked better.

The owners often had strong prior beliefs about the efficacy of a practice, and it took time to change these. This was often done using pilot changes on a few machines in the plant or with evidence from other plants in the experiment. For example, the consultants typically started by persuading the managers to undertake preventive maintenance on a set of trial machines, and once it was proven successful, it was rolled out to the rest of the factory. As the consultants demonstrated the positive effect of these initial practice changes, the owners increasingly trusted them and adopted more of the recommendations, like performance incentives for managers.[57]

But this just raised another question. Why hadn't local consulting firms already approached these owners with promises of higher profit and used similar demonstrations as proof?

One obstacle was the intermingling of good and bad advice. "Indian firms are bombarded with solicitations from businesses offering to save them money on everything from telephone bills to yarn supplies, and thus are unlikely to be receptive." Just like parents trying to sort out financial aid for college, managers struggle to distinguish scams from opportunities.

The other obstacle? Managers were overconfident, stubborn, and uninformed. And due to India's high import tariffs on textiles, these men (they were all men) had never faced a reality check from competition with better-managed global rivals.

Nick Bloom, one of the authors of the study and a pioneer in research on the importance of management practices to firm performance, remembers a conversation with the worst manager in the entire sample. "This manager had adopted less than 20% of the basic management practices. But he was supremely confident. He told us his plant was fantastically well-managed and he didn't really need the help. He mentioned that three years earlier some [business school] students had run a similar evaluation of his plant and given him a whole set of recommendations. We asked him what they had recommended, and he told us he had no idea, he'd never read the report—it was lying up on a shelf collecting dust."[58]

Research by Bloom and others has uncovered how bad management practices can persist. In global surveys, managers estimate that their own firms are managed better than 70 percent of all other firms, which is obviously impossible. Managers' self-confidence is unrelated to more objective measures of actual managerial quality. All around the world, it turns out three kinds of managers are most likely to avoid basic mistakes: highly educated people; people hired as professionals rather than founding or inheriting their companies; and people facing do-or-die levels of competition.[59]

What do all these findings from Indian textile plants and global management surveys mean for parents?

We've seen that skill building combines many hard jobs. In fact, the more we dig into what skill building actually entails, the more it feels like asking parents to manage a full-scale business enterprise. In other words, it's as if parents were ultimately tasked with being CEOs.

The trouble is that all parents lack at least two of the three characteristics that keep CEOs on track. Obviously, parents aren't hired professionally to build skills—they volunteer and hire themselves. And, obviously, parents don't face do-or-die competition—their role as skill builder is permanent, even if they struggle to master the craft. The third characteristic is a good education, but many parents also haven't had that opportunity in their own lives. So if we're really depending on parents to be CEOs of a complex business enterprise, every sign points toward big delusions, big mistakes, and big missed opportunities to set children up for economic success.

If we want to escape the Parent Trap, we have to talk about these facts in the right way. It is wrong to say these parents are "failing." Most people are great parents, and they know it. Four out of five parents consider themselves "a really good parent," and 90 percent grade their own parenting as an A or B. Even when researchers ask kids to grade their parents, rather than asking parents to grade themselves, three-quarters of kids give their parents an A or B. *These high marks are likely spot on when it comes to caring about children.* Most parents succeed in this regard, and *we rightly celebrate that triumph.* Caring is the rightful and inescapable responsibility of parents. The most common problems, however, arise not in caring but in the more clinical work of skill building. There, parents either apply their own professional skills to manage complex investments, or manage the complex outsourcing of these investments to hired help—or fumble the investments and forfeit a large share of their children's future income.[60]

On the other hand, the experiment with Indian textile plants demonstrated that CEOs can seriously improve their management practices when given the right training. Is that also true for parents trying to build skills in children?

3 TEACHING OLD PARENTS NEW TRICKS

LOTS OF FLOPS

A hundred years ago, the same people who helped finance the ground-breaking research at the Iowa Child Research Station also financed a movement to train parents in child skill development.

A man named Lawrence Frank, an orchestrator of the movement from his perch as director of the Laura Spelman Rockefeller Foundation, saw gaps in parental skill building as the "most tangible obstacle to rapid progress in child care." He concluded that the "crux of the problem" would be to "persuade or compel adults to give up traditional beliefs and established habits for procedures established by science."[1]

Philanthropists and academics worked up a frenzy of new initiatives. They financed parent-education staff and outreach at the new research centers. They founded new organizations such as the National Council of Parent Education and the Child Study Association of America. They created *Parents* magazine.

Apart from *Parents* magazine, it all fizzled. There were two problems.

First, there wasn't yet any rigorous scientific research on how to build skills in children. Second, most parents had no interest in the little knowledge that did exist. The historian Hamilton Cravens, diagnosing the collapse of this movement, observed that "parent education was limited in its appeal chiefly to middle-class white parents with above-average education, so that it was, for all practical purposes, preaching to the converted."[2]

Since then, we've made progress on the first problem. There's a lot of good information about how to build more skills in children, as we've already seen in health care, nutrition, neighborhood choice, K12 schooling, and college. Psychologists who study parent–child relationships have also built up a strong body of knowledge that can help many parents manage their children's skill growth more effectively.

And a small parent-education movement has survived, trying to disseminate useful information to the masses. There are three general kinds of programs: home visiting, one-on-one parent counseling, and group counseling. Many of these programs have yielded disappointing results. Many more remain untested, like drugs never put through clinical trials. But a few exemplar programs have been tested rigorously and repeatedly and found effective.

What do the most successful programs have in common? They ask parents to make large investments under the guidance of highly trained experts. In other words, they treat learning how to build skills in children like gaining an advanced professional capability, not like a side project anyone can master in her spare time.

HOME VISITING

After David Weikart founded Perry Preschool and Craig Ramey founded Abecedarian, both men landed on a similar idea for their next projects: "home-visiting" programs. These programs would seek to train parents in child skill development and thereby transfer the magic of the classroom into the living room. They developed extensive training materials, hired and trained staff to do the visits, spent a lot of time and money, and generated a great deal of excitement. In the end, both men found the same thing: zero impact on children's skill development. "We were stunned," recalled Weikart. "We were at a loss to explain our findings."[3]

In 2010, the Affordable Care Act of 2010 financed a new wave of investment in similar home-visiting programs, such as Healthy Families America, Home Instruction Program for Preschool Youngsters (HIPPY), and Parents as Teachers. In 2019, researchers released a landmark evaluation of these programs through the children's first 15 months of life. Had they found a way to break through the wall that blocked Weikart and Ramey?

Not exactly. Most child and parent outcomes were zero or too small to detect with any confidence. Analogous impacts for the Abecedarian early education program were about *40 times* larger on cognitive skills and 10 times larger on behavioral skills. The overall pattern of these new programs' impacts did suggest some benefits, and more time has to pass before we get the full picture. But it's clear that home-visiting programs today are still nothing like the door to an entirely alternate reality presaged by high-quality early education programs taught by professionals.[4]

Among home-visiting programs, however, there is one exemplar that stands above the others.

David Olds graduated from college in 1970 and landed his first job as a teacher at the Union Square Day Care Center in the basement of a church in West Baltimore.[5] Day after day, Olds encountered children exhibiting major obstacles to skill growth as a result of troubled home environments. One boy could barely speak due to birth defects acquired in utero as his mother struggled with alcoholism and drug addiction. Another boy couldn't settle down during nap time, having developed a reflexive fear that his mother would beat him if he wet himself.

Olds began trying to mold the day care into a more ambitious educational experience. He imported the new preschool curriculum that David Weikart had just developed for Perry Preschool in Michigan. Seeing the origins of so many problems in children's home lives outside the school, Olds started inviting parents into the center during nap times to discuss potential solutions. He quickly noticed a pattern: the parents most in need of assistance were least likely to accept his invitations.

He decided to return to school and think about how he might reach children earlier in life, before debilitating problems hemmed in their fates. After obtaining a PhD in developmental psychology, he started work on a new program. The program would send professional nurses to the homes of low-income, first-time mothers, often teenage girls with little support from their partners. Olds reasoned that first-time mothers might be more open to advice about parenting techniques and that nurses could bring the credibility required to build trust with these new parents. He also decided the nurses would begin visiting mothers during pregnancy. That way they could start building the relationship before the stress of caring for a new infant kicked in.

Olds was building on an earlier idea. Josephine Baker, the first American woman to earn a PhD in public health, had pioneered large-scale nurse home-visiting programs as head of the nation's first Bureau of Child Hygiene in New York City in 1908. Searching for ways to reduce the city's appalling infant-mortality rate, Baker hired nurses to visit new mothers in low-income, overcrowded neighborhoods to teach healthier feeding and bathing techniques. Baker gathered data suggesting the program had saved more than 1,000 infants' lives in its first year of operation, then oversaw its expansion across New York City.[6]

Olds thought a more structured, longer-term version of Baker's nurse home-visiting program might go beyond improving basic health and nutrition into broader kinds of child skill development. He started planning an experimental test of the program in Elmira, a working-class city in upstate New York.

The program came to be called the Nurse-Family Partnership, or NFP. NFP nurses provide parents with health screenings and referrals; advocacy to secure public benefits such as the Supplemental Nutrition Assistance Program (SNAP, previously known as Food Stamps); training in child skill development; and guidance on stress management, family planning, employment, and other challenges. An assigned nurse builds a relationship with each mother over the course of more than 30 home visits spanning two and a half years from pregnancy through the child's second birthday.

Among home-visiting programs, the main distinguishing feature of NFP is its reliance on registered nurses. Becoming a registered nurse requires 1,800 hours of postsecondary training. Then NFP requires an additional 70 hours of training on top of that. To put this in perspective, NFP home visitors have more training than the highest level of commercial helicopter pilots.[7]

In an extraordinary sequence of large-scale, randomized controlled trials over the next 30 years, Olds found that NFP could deliver significant benefits for children and mothers first in Elmira with white low-income families, then in Memphis with Black low-income families, then in Denver with Hispanic low-income families.[8]

In the Denver study, Olds tested whether the program could replace nurses with lower-cost "paraprofessionals." He found the diluted program no longer had any impact. This finding helped to resolve the puzzle of zero impacts encountered by prior researchers such as David Weikart and Craig Ramey, who had relied on paraprofessionals to do their home visits. Apparently, facilitating greater skill growth in low-income children was so complicated that it required home visitors with advanced postsecondary degrees.

Wendy O'Shea has worked in NFP as a registered nurse in Harrisburg City, Pennsylvania, for more than a decade. I asked her what kinds of issues she tends to work on with parents. She told me that nurses often help parents navigate America's byzantine health-care system. "Even I find it difficult after working for 26 years in health care," she admitted. Some mothers, for example, still haven't met with an obstetrician by late in their pregnancy. "If there's no OB, why hasn't a family gotten an OB? Maybe they don't have a primary care physician, they're not connected into health care, they're not sure how to go about it. Who do they call? They did a Google search and lots of doctors came up, but who to call?"[9]

Beyond health care, NFP nurses also help out with things such as how to babyproof a child's environment in temporary housing, how to quit smoking or drinking too much, how to squeeze the most nutrition out of a limited food budget, and how to build language skills in children by reading to them early, even during pregnancy ("Really?" one parent asked. "The baby can hear me?").

The nurses also teach parents how to handle frustration. "We know sometimes a baby will cry," O'Shea explained.

> [The mothers] have their toolbox—does the diaper need a change, is he hungry, hot, cold. They have gone through the checklist and the baby is still crying. We talk to moms about how if they are starting to feel a trigger that they're getting frustrated with the baby, it's really important and ok and good

parenting to lay the child down in a safe place and walk away for a couple minutes and take a couple deep breaths. . . . Just taking a moment to center themselves, and maybe they need to call somebody and talk to someone. Letting them know that that's good parenting, not any kind of failure.

O'Shea brims with admiration for the mothers she serves. "These are amazing moms. These mothers are navigating situations that are so complex. . . . I'm honestly not sure how great a mom I would be in those situations. . . . They want to do right by their kids. The challenge is to help get them there."

O'Shea has seen up close just how deeply parents in tough situations master the art of caring for their children, and she rightly considers that caring element the mark of a good parent. At the same time, she recognizes that these excellent parents often need help with child skill development.

Today, NFP serves more than 60,000 American families every year.[10] That's about one in ten low-income, first-time mothers giving birth annually.[11] NFP has shown that low-income, first-time parents can learn to build skills in children more effectively, but it's not easy, and there's no gimmick—just a fine-tuned, heavyweight investment managed by highly skilled trainers over multiple years.

PARENT MANAGEMENT TRAINING

We're starting to see how parents are expected to act as real estate agents, tutors, guidance counselors, pediatricians, nutritionists, CEOs, and so many other professional roles. In general, they have not sought out and not received training in these broad skill-building areas. Most parents don't even consider the need for the kinds of general training in child skill development provided by a program such as the Nurse-Family Partnership.

Among parents who seek out such training on their own, they have tended to pursue training in a parental skill-building role we might call "child psychologist." Child psychologists specialize in building and repairing behavioral skills such as anger management, communication, and conflict resolution.

The outsize role of behavioral skills in parent training programs likely reflects the outsize impact of these skills on families' day-to-day quality of life. If children fall behind in math, reading, health, college readiness, social dexterity, and most other skills, parents may never quite feel an immediate sense of urgency, but alarm bells go off loud and clear when children scream, hit people, or harm themselves.

About 20 percent of children develop clinical psychiatric disorders of some sort. These disorders include, for example, oppositional defiant and conduct disorders, attention-deficit/hyperactivity disorder, severe forms of depression and anxiety, and substance abuse. A prevalence rate this high suggests at least 14 million American children could potentially benefit from some form of psychiatric treatment every year.[12]

Psychologists have developed a rich set of programs to help parents keep these children's skill growth on track. "Parent Management Training," as the most widespread type of program has come to be known, goes back to the late 1950s when a revolution swept over psychology. At that time, most psychologists viewed behavioral problems as symptoms of deeper biological ailments such as brain damage or as manifestations of repressed emotions boiling up from personal trauma. The role of the psychologist came down to diagnosing and curing these biological issues or providing a space in which past traumas could be surfaced, confronted, and resolved. This view was known as the "medical" model of behavioral disorders, and it is most closely associated with Sigmund Freud.[13]

In the 1950s, however, the Freudian foundation began to crack. In 1952, the psychologist Hans Eysenck gathered some rough data on rates of recovery among patients who received psychotherapy and compared them with recovery rates among patients who had similar conditions but did not receive psychotherapy. There was *no* difference. Eysenck concluded that psychotherapy as practiced at that time was pointless. A few years later, the psychologist Eugene Levitt replicated Eysenck's analysis and found that psychotherapy also seemed to have no impact on children. Some psychologists took these findings to heart and began searching for better ways to treat behavioral disorders.[14]

The new approach that emerged was not, in fact, new at all; it had just fallen out of fashion in America, much like early childhood education. The approach went by many names, including the "psychological model" of behavioral disorders (in contrast to the "medical model"), "learning theory," "behavior-modification theory," and the "behavioral approach." It built off a simple premise: most behavioral problems do not have any deep, mysterious root causes. As Eysenck put it, "Learning theory . . . regards neurotic symptoms as simple learned habits; there is no neurosis underlying the symptom, but merely the symptom itself. Get rid of the symptom and you have eliminated the neurosis."[15]

Some evidence suggested that psychologists had already practiced the behavioral approach in the early 1800s with better results than those achieved by psychotherapy in the mid-1900s, and a wide range of behavior-modification techniques had already been documented by World War II. The behavioral approach was also popular among regular people trying to solve everyday problems. In the 1930s, the psychologists Arthur Jersild and Frances Holmes interviewed hundreds of parents about how they handled their children's phobias concerning everything from dark rooms and imaginary animals to vacuum cleaners and running water. Most parents tried things that didn't work: explanations, reassurances, temporarily removing or concealing the object, ridicule, or forcing children into terrified confrontations. However, a few parents developed techniques that did seem to work. These parents introduced children to the feared object by degrees or helped children build skills to cope with their fear through games, tricks, practice, and praise. Future psychological research would refine these techniques and validate them in randomized controlled trials.

In the medical approach, psychologists assumed that altering someone's problematic behavior directly would fail. The alleged root cause—injury or trauma—would continue festering, inevitably producing a new problematic behavior to replace the old one. This idea was known as "symptom substitution." The new wave of psychologists, however, found little evidence that symptom substitution actually took place when they modified people's behavior. And when a new undesirable behavior did arise, it could also be treated directly until a more favorable behavior materialized.[16]

If most behavioral problems could be treated directly, then new behavioral modification techniques held enormous social value, much like new medicines. By the 1960s, decades of work by pioneering experimental psychologists such as Ivan Pavlov, Edward Thorndike, John Watson, and B. F. Skinner had yielded a rich tool kit.[17] These studies focused on the many subtle ways a person's environment could *reinforce* behavior and how various kinds of reinforcement could be fine-tuned to provide treatments that delivered spectacular effects.

A famous case study published in 1959 by the psychologist Carl Williams illustrates the approach. Williams described his work with a family trying to stop a toddler from throwing "tyrant-like" tantrums at bedtime. The child would scream until an adult sat with him in the room and would scream if the adult tried to read or do anything that removed attention from the child. The family turned to Williams in desperation.

Here are two things Williams did not do: he did not search for a deep emotional trauma buried in the child's past, and he did not assume some ailment was afflicting the child's brain or body. Williams thought the parents were simply reinforcing the child's behavior by rewarding the tantrums with attention. He suggested a simple technique: ignore the tantrums. He then measured the child's progress.

The first night the child cried for 45 minutes. The crying then declined in fits and starts until the tenth night, when the child "no longer whimpered, fussed, or cried when the parent left the room. Rather, he smiled as they left. The parents felt that he made happy sounds until he dropped off to sleep."[18] Then the child had a bad night, and an aunt once again attended to his crying. The tantrums began anew, and the parents had to start the process over again. The second "extinction" followed the same trend as the first one. Stark evidence like this suggested that parents could often mold children's behavior much more readily than they realized.

Psychologists continued expanding and refining the art of behavior modification, using laboratory experiments and clinical practice to design better systems for managing child skill development.[19] Ignoring certain kinds of pathological behaviors "extinguished" them in a wide range of cases beyond this one toddler's bedtime tantrums and often worked

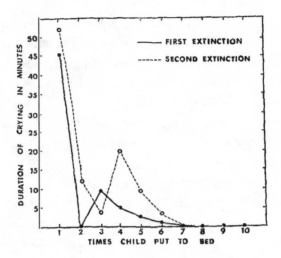

Figure 3.1
Length of crying in two extinction series as a function of successive occasions of being put to bed. *Source*: Carl D. Williams, "The Elimination of Tantrum Behavior by Extinction Procedures," *Journal of Abnormal and Social Psychology* 59, no. 2 (1959): 269.

miracles compared to the reprimands, criticism, and punishments that many parents turned to on their own. Parents learned to reward children's good behavior *immediately* rather than later in the day or, even worse, in some undefined future. They learned to use rewards consistently, so that children began to associate better behavior with better consequences, not just in theory but in their bones. Parents learned to reward small, *incremental* improvements in behavior and to reward them enthusiastically even when they felt children could do better.

Parents learned to pay closer attention to children's good behavior, to "catch" children doing things right, and to expand the menu of rewards. They could use praise, such as a simple "great job taking out the trash," and they could improve their intonation, facial expressions, and physical gestures to convey warmth and optimism.

The psychologists Marion Forgatch and Gerald Patterson, two pioneers in Parent Management Training, would teach parents new ways to perform even the most mundane daily tasks, such as directing a child to hang up her jacket in the closet: "(1) identify the goal behavior (what they want the child to do, such as hang up the jacket); (2) calm oneself; (3) get the child's attention (with proximity and physical or eye contact) and state the child's name in a neutral manner; (4) state the goal behavior (what is wanted rather than not wanted) with no extraneous words; (5) add the word 'please'; and (6) stand and hold in a neutral manner for 10 seconds after giving the directive." Forgatch and Patterson observed that during the role-playing exercises used to practice these techniques, "laughter tends to characterize much of the session, and parents often later comment that they hadn't realized how much of their own behavior plays a role in their child's reactions."[20]

In addition to "social rewards" such as praise, some psychologists taught parents how to leverage "tangible rewards" in the form of points that could later be exchanged for privileges at predefined prices, for example 10 points to play video games for an hour or 5 points to eat pancakes for dinner. Keeping track of points forced parents to recognize positive behaviors that had previously gotten lost in the barrage of frustrating interactions. These miniature economic systems, or "token economies," didn't have to be improvised by every parent starting from scratch. They could be optimized by psychologists based on research and experience with hundreds of families to deliver rapid, flexible, consistent, positive—and therefore maximally effective—reinforcement of children's advantageous behavior. Contrary to many parents' initial (reasonable) concerns, psychologists found that children did not become dependent on these rewards to maintain good behavior. Instead, good behavior tended to create new self-reinforcing conditions such as greater trust, more routine praise, and better communication that rendered the tangible rewards obsolete over time.

Parents learned they could even engineer semiartificial kinds of good behavior in their children for the sole purpose of rewarding and reinforcing the behavior more frequently. One ingenious technique involved "practice trials," or *simulations*, of difficult interactions. By inviting a child to play a game, parents could induce opportunities for practice and reinforcement in lower-stakes environments. This is exactly how pilots use flight simulators: to practice landing on icy runways or navigating thunderstorms without having to crash real airplanes.

Alan Kazdin, director of the Yale Parenting Center and a leading expert in Parent Management Training, explained how these practice trials work at his clinic.

> I say [to the small child named Billy], "We're going to play a game. . . . I'm going to tell you you can't do something, but you really can. And you can have a tantrum and you can get mad, but this time you're not going to hit mommy, and you're not going to go on the floor. And it's only a game, but if you can do that, I'm going to give you two points on this little chart."
>
> [After the fake tantrum], the child is probably smiling a little bit and the mom says with great effusiveness, "That was fabulous! I can't believe you did that!"
>
> . . . You do the game maybe a little bit more, but what happens now is that the likelihood of these tantrums outside of the game being good tantrums, really increases. [The change] usually takes about one to three weeks.[21]

Parent Management Training suggests that many parents are indeed like the Indian textile plant managers from the experiment discussed in chapter 2, in that they could dramatically improve their skill-building productivity if they adopted different techniques. Behavior-modification tools amount to good-management principles such as "*Keep the plant floor clean to reduce accidents*" and "*Keep inventory at some target level*," but in this case applied to raising kids.

Overall, the evidence points in this direction. Many of today's leading Parent Management Training programs report large positive impacts on children in randomized controlled trials. The most prominent programs include the Parent Management Training Oregon Model, Parent-Child Interaction Therapy, Incredible Years, and the Positive Parenting Program (Triple P). Unfortunately, many of the studies involve just a few dozen families. A notorious problem with small experiments is that researchers may not publish results until they confirm their motivating hypothesis, especially when they can cherry-pick the results they like best among different child outcomes.[22] Some program developers have gone on to create for-profit companies to market and distribute their programs, thereby compounding the bias toward favorable evidence. As we've seen with the Nurse-Family Partnership and the Infant Health and Development

Program, however, these concerns regarding bias can be addressed with large-scale field experiments analyzed by reputable, independent researchers. For now, even accounting for all these issues, the evidence on Parent Management Training is promising.[23]

So in some ways the old dream of training parents to improve child skill development lives on even if programs cover only a tiny subset of child skills in practice. One thing the most successful programs have in common—for both home visiting and Parent Management Training—is that they treat child skill development like a complex, unintuitive enterprise and respond to this challenge by providing parents with deeply researched, expert-guided, extended assistance. In other words, they treat child skill development more like flying a helicopter than driving a car.

But is training parents really a promising approach to addressing our country's monumental skill gaps? Maybe. There's just one very big problem.

EMPTY SEATS

The main problem with parent training programs—home visits, one-on-one counseling, and group counseling—is not that they never work but that most parents aren't interested in them. That was true 100 years ago, and it's true today.

Many parent home-visiting programs are chronically undersubscribed, even when freely available. Of the few parents who do sign up, some never show up for a single session, and most others drop out long before program completion. In a recent overview of home-visiting programs, the developmental psychologists Ariel Kalil and Rebecca Ryan conclude that "it's just too difficult to deliver the programs as intended."[24]

Even the most successful home-visiting program, the Nurse-Family Partnership, suffers from chronically high drop-out rates. Drop-out rates are especially high for young, single, less-educated mothers whose children are most likely to suffer skill deficits. Interviews suggest a simple explanation: these parents are too busy to participate consistently in a structured, time-consuming, invasive program. As one mother put it, "I was doing so much. I was going to school, trying to work. I couldn't keep appointments. . . . And I was a new mom, first time mom. It was just too much."[25]

Parent Management Training programs have the same problem. In Colorado, the nonprofit Invest in Kids provides one of the largest Incredible Years training programs in the country, offering free classes with meals and complementary childcare to parents across the state. Yet even after a decade of expansion, less than one in every 500 eligible parents participates.[26] The parents most likely to need additional support are least likely to seek out these programs and least likely to continue participating in the programs once they start. A recent review of these programs noted "an overrepresentation of white, well-educated, and middle-class parents," just like early parent training advocates discovered 100 years ago.[27]

A big part of the Incredible Years program is its library of "vignettes," short videos that depict parent–child interactions that illustrate more- and less-effective ways parents can develop behavioral skills in children. Each session of the program asks parents to watch some of these videos and then engage in role-playing exercises and discussions. I watched some of the videos, and I am confident they would not receive high scores on Rotten Tomatoes. They reminded me of sexual-harassment training videos we've all yawned our way through at work or the cheesy dramatizations of drug addiction and teen pregnancy that schools foist on teenagers. Even if watching Incredible Years videos were useful, it's not exactly how I'd want to spend my limited free time as a parent.

But perhaps the vast majority of parents who ignore these opportunities are making a mistake. Maybe if more parents made time (lots of time) to attend parent training programs, they could prevent the kinds of skill-building problems that undermine their children's future wealth and well-being.

To get a deeper sense, I decided to attend a parent training program myself. I wanted to find a program that attracted a broader set of parents, not just the small subset of mostly white, middle-class go-getters who voluntarily seek out parenting classes. I wondered: Is there any training program that parents *have* to attend, whether they want to or not?

As it turned out, there was.

THE PARENT PROJECT

It was 1987, and Chaffee High School in Ontario, California, had a discipline problem. They had expelled about 16 kids in ninth grade, their first year of high school—way more than usual for a class of only a few hundred students. But homeschooling wasn't working out well for these troublemakers, who were "pillaging and plundering" the neighborhood. The parents begged the school to readmit their children, and the school agreed under one condition: the kids had to enroll in an experimental counseling program. They hired a psychologist named Roger Morgan to run the program.[28]

"At that time I'd been working with children as a psychologist for 12 years," Dr. Morgan recalls. "I thought of myself as an expert. It was a humbling experience. Nothing these students were doing was on track for graduation. They had been failing every class, getting into trouble every day."

Dr. Morgan figured they simply weren't interested in doing what all the nagging adults thought they should do. But on the first day he asked the children, "How many of you want to graduate from high school?"

To Dr. Morgan's surprise, all 16 children raised their hands immediately. "There were zero behavioral clues. No studying, no listening, no effort. They wanted the diploma. They had the insight; they knew it was important. But the insight made absolutely no difference. They didn't want to do the work to get it. There was no relationship between insight and behavior. All of the 'insight-oriented' stuff I had learned in graduate school didn't seem to apply. These kids needed Mom and Dad to hold their hands and really move them toward their goal." Around the same time, a police officer named Ralph "Bud" Fry had switched into community programs in nearby Pomona. To Fry, it seemed as if "every third call to our unit was a parent saying my kid is strung out on meth or using heroine, how do I get my child back?" So the unit started offering four-session classes for parents trying to manage their children's drug problems. Fry was expecting to teach parents all about drug addiction, withdrawal, and overdosing, but that wasn't what happened. "The parents started asking questions that had nothing do with substance abuse. 'My kid just ran away, what do I do?'

'My kid just beat me up, what do I do?' 'My kid has stopped going to school, what do I do?'"

At some point, Fry and Morgan crossed paths and started to collaborate on a new program to help these families in crisis situations. "With all the questions the parents were asking, we decided to can the program and just start answering their questions."

And so the Parent Project was born. The Parent Project's flagship program is a class for parents dealing with "strong-willed" teenagers. Parents attend for two to three hours a week for 12 weeks. Many criminal justice agencies around the country sponsor Parent Project classes as a way to reduce costly, repetitive arrests of minors. The key feature of this arrangement, for my purposes, is that courts often *require* parents to attend. In part due to this mandate, over the past 30 years more than *half a million* parents have graduated from the program. It is the largest court-mandated juvenile diversion program in America and probably the only parent training program to achieve this kind of scale in American history.

After chatting with Dr. Morgan, I decided to see the Parent Project for myself. How much could parents learn about the intricacies of child skill development in a 12-week class that most of them didn't seek out voluntarily?

FIRE HOSE

Over the next three months, I watched 25 parents from all walks of life work through struggles with children who had run away from home, assaulted family members, developed substance-abuse problems, been expelled from school, and threatened or attempted suicide.[29]

As I'd hoped, the mandatory nature of the program resulted in a very diverse set of participants. There were people of many races and accents, single parents and married couples, younger parents radiating swagger and older parents and grandparents trying quietly to stay awake. Weeknight outfits ranged from business casual to denim-blue work shirts to baggy sports jerseys and cowboy hats. There were barbers and taco truck owners, basketball coaches and chemists, neck tattoos and nose piercings. The class felt like a small, tumultuous snapshot of America.

Two good-natured former police officers, Felicia and Frank, taught the course. Both had personal experience with their own strong-willed teenage children as well as with the many troubled kids they came across in law enforcement. Parent Project courses follow the lesson plans laid out in a program handbook titled *Changing Destructive Adolescent Behavior*. The course employs a set of behavior-modification techniques that are reminiscent of other leading Parent Management Training programs. The main difference is that the Parent Project relies more heavily on lectures and discussion and less on role playing or modeling of skill-building techniques.

The first lesson of the Parent Project is deceptively simple: *Tell your children you love them*. Not once in a while but every day. Not just in your actions but in words. Directly. Out loud.

Many parents believe their children already know they love them. They think their actions make it clear. The Parent Project asserts that many children do not get the message. They need to hear it directly, out loud, again and again.

Felicia testified that many parents aren't used to this crystal clarity because it's not how they were raised. For these parents, it can feel unnatural to say "I love you" out loud to their children. Felicia told the class that the first time she ever said "I love you" to her father, she was 17 years old at a hospital, and her father had just suffered a stroke.

All parents in the class received homework after the first three-hour session: tell your children "I love you" out loud at least one time every day.

One mother wearing a t-shirt with the word "Whatever" printed on it predicted her child would ignore her. "*Come on*, Mom, I know you're just doing this cuz that class told you to." Felicia and Frank replied immediately in unison: "That's fine. Do it anyway."

Closely related to "I love you" are "positive strokes." Parents are encouraged to find opportunities—somewhere in the vortex of arguments and manipulation and rebellion—to *approve* of their children. The handbook provides examples so parents get the idea.

Thank you for cleaning your room; I'm proud of you for doing that.

Frank described one mother who struggled to think of anything her daughter was doing that warranted praise. But the daughter would get up in the morning, get dressed, and get in the car to go to school, so the mother started telling her daughter she was proud of her for doing that.

Many parents struggled with the idea of positive strokes. "[My kids] cleaned their room, yeah," said one mother, "but they haven't solved the bigger problem, their grades are still bad, so why should I let them have fun . . . ?" Why praise children for achieving small wins but neglecting much bigger priorities? The Parent Project insists that positive strokes are necessary for a simple reason: children must feel in their bones that parents *want* them to succeed.

Another critical teaching of the Parent Project: *Stop mistaking your child for a reasonable person.* As Felicia told the parents, "*You* are your child's frontal lobe." The program asks parents to give up on changing children's behavior with logic, reasoning, and explanations. Strong-willed children's behavior does not reflect careful reasoning; it is impetuous and experimental. Instead of persuasion, parents are encouraged to set up clear, short-term, *material* consequences that consistently reward good behavior and punish bad behavior.

If you've ever owned a dog, you may recognize this emphasis on consistency and repetition. The resemblance is not lost on Dr. Morgan. "I know a dog trainer," he says. "She was helping me out with my dog, and I was talking to her about her kid going through a rough patch, and we were giving each other a lot of the same tips."[30]

The Parent Project teaches parents exactly how to implement these rewards and punishments. For rewards, they suggest using the word *absolutely.*

"*Absolutely*, you can go to the concert with your friends if you clean your room."

"*Absolutely*, you can go skateboarding with Felix if you finish your math homework."

Felicia asked one father to use this approach in a sentence. He said, "Absolutely, if you clean your room, you have a chance to go to the movie with your friends."

Felicia stopped and smiled. "Did you hear what you said there?," she asked. The father had inserted "have a chance." That one phrase undermined the entire premise of guaranteed rewards, and thereby the prospect of consistency and predictability. The father winced—he couldn't bear the idea of *guaranteeing* something to his unpredictable child.

The course taught parents that they cannot *control* teenagers, but they can influence teenagers by controlling *things*. The program proposes a novel strategy called TEASPOT: "Take Everything Away for a Short Period of Time." If a child breaks an important rule, she loses access to *things*: cell phone, computer, car, television, tablet. The loss can last from a few minutes to a few days.

Some parents viewed TEASPOT as too lax. "If my kid really screwed up, why should she get everything back in a couple days?" The instructors explained that strong-willed children operate on short timeframes. Anything beyond a few days makes children feel as if they are on "death row." And if you feel as if you're on death row, well, you have nothing to lose from more bad behavior.

Other parents found TEASPOT too crude. They felt more comfortable with verbal communication: yelling, expressing disappointment or anger. The instructors suggested that reasoning only produces more frustration. Blunt material consequences may feel draconian, but they increase harmony by avoiding bitter disputes.

"Our whole culture is oriented towards words and persuasion," Dr. Morgan told me. "We feel taking everything away from a child is mean and harsh, but really if I explain myself to death and then get frustrated and yell at my kid, that's a lot meaner."

Another Parent Project insight is to ignore children's "bad attitude" and focus entirely on *actions* such as attending school, completing homework, and abstaining from drugs and alcohol. Ignoring undesirable behavior, as we saw in Carl Williams's "extinction" of the toddler's bedtime tantrums, is a classic behavioral modification strategy. Many parents strongly resisted this suggestion. These parents viewed grudging or snarky compliance by children as an act of disrespect warranting punishment. Their reactions seemed to mix an admirable desire to instill cooperative skills in children with personal grievance at having their authority questioned. As one young father explained, "If I raise my voice, you do *not* talk back to me."

Felicia and Frank persisted: ignore the kid's stupid attitude, focus on his actions. Frank acknowledged the challenge. "Guys, out there I know it's hard, but you have to let go of 'attitude.' Let it go. If my son stops smoking pot but has a 'bad attitude,' I don't care because I'm *winning*."

The Parent Project counsels parents *not* to challenge their children who are threatening to run away or harm themselves. One father reacted emotionally to this advice. "This whole page [of the Parent Project manual] is my daughter, the whole thing. She cut her wrist with a razor because I took her cell phone away. I noticed it the next morning and took her to the hospital. She said, 'I'm gonna leave.' My fault, I did, I challenged her, 'Go ahead! I'm doing everything I can; if it's not enough, then get out of here!' She went to school, got high, got sent home, and ran away later that day."

Many parents had trouble swallowing their pride in these difficult situations. They felt they were bestowing all their hard-won insights upon children, working long hours to provide food and shelter and medical care, but their children were going out of their way to throw all these gifts in the trash.

All parents can relate to this tension; it is one of the oldest challenges faced by parents everywhere, described in literature from Plato to *Siddhartha*. The Parent Project tries to help parents react to these situations more clinically. Parents are the adults in the relationship, and they must work hard to replace their own emotional reactions with calm, strategic techniques.

I sat in on Parent Project classes and read the handbook week after week for three months. Like the other Parent Management Training programs I'd read about, the class presented a rich set of ideas and practices. It was often inspiring.

But I couldn't help but notice how *complicated* it all sounded. Alongside the broad overarching themes of love, calmness, and consistency, the class offered up a steady stream of other reasonable but nonobvious ideas. Here's a sampling:

- Parents should implement a TEASPOT when children fail to complete homework but should not require children to make up past homework so delays don't pile up.
- Parents should warn that if children violate a major rule, "the consequences will be severe," but they should not always state a specific punishment in order to maintain flexibility and avoid losing credibility when children find loopholes.
- Parents should increase punishment severity only by taking away more things, *not* by lengthening the duration of the restriction. The basic TEASPOT can be augmented with the "Extended List," including hair products, makeup, toiletries, favorite clothes, hats, shoes, junk food, and even bedroom doors and furniture.

And then there were the "action plans": the six-step action template for dealing with drugs and gangs; the seven-step action plan for monitoring children's online activity, social media, communications, video games, and music; the four-step action plan to ensure children complete their homework; the other seven-step action plan for dealing with runaway children.

There was advice to provide a structured daily routine for children that incorporated school, friends, family, homework, chores, and free time. Many tactics involved a recipe for "active monitoring" premised on a "who, what, when, where, why" framework. Parents were advised to require that children enter all their social media login credentials and all their latest friends' addresses and phone numbers into family databases.

All of these action plans and recommendations made sense, but they added up to a pretty daunting set of tasks. In fact, the recommendations sounded an awful lot like, well, a *job*. Deploying all these strategies would require sophisticated prioritization, people and project management, data collection and storage, communication, leadership, contracting and procurement of third-party services, structured performance feedback, and motivation tempered with emotional distance. Adults with career experience will recognize these skills from job descriptions, performance evaluations, and promotion guidelines. Substantial economic skills would be crucial to implementing these recommendations with fidelity. In fact, parents who could master all these skills might wind up accelerating their career growth.

It was no surprise that many parents had trouble absorbing all the lessons. Some parents were unable to attend all the sessions, despite being required to do so by a court of law. As I participated in group exercises during class, it became clear that many parents struggled to register and process all the information.

A final key goal of the Parent Project is to encourage bonding among the parents who take the class. "Parents are also like children," explained Dr. Morgan. "We also need reinforcement, support, and positive strokes. If people just learn things and then go off to do them in isolation, nothing will stick." So in the last six classes, parents brought food for potlucks and spent more time sharing their own stories about trying to use what they had learned in the first six classes.

Participating showed me how big an investment this kind of class required. Every Wednesday, I would hop on a train to commute to a public high school campus for another two to three hours of . . . work. Beyond the fatigue, it was disconcerting to find myself back in an institutional environment. I sat in a rigid blue plastic chair with cold metal legs and watched social cliques converge around different personalities and styles. I listened to the teachers explain what I was doing wrong with my (at that time hypothetical) children. I muddled through what often felt like forced interactions with classmates during sometimes fun, sometimes painfully awkward group exercises. It wasn't the most enjoyable evening of the week.

And compared to the other parents, I had it easy. I didn't *have* to be there. I didn't have a child in serious trouble. I was just a guy conducting research for a book. The experience made it easy to see why these programs had failed to catch on more widely after 100 years of nudging by academics and rich people with big ideas. Many parents' day-to-day lives already involve a tough slog. Parent training programs offer . . . another slog.

But then again most investments require a slog. Saving money, going to school, watching your diet—none of these things are a breeze. The key question is: Does this particular slog pay off?

UNKNOWNS

Anecdotal evidence suggests the Parent Project may help parents get children's skill growth back on track. Several parents in the class told me they found it useful. Some told me they now understood better not to yell at their children or provoke them when frustrated. They said they imposed short-term, calmer TEASPOT-style punishments instead of longer-term, messier restrictions. They worked hard to be consistent, to praise their children even during rough patches, and to recite the three magic words *I love you* every day.

But many of these families began the class at a low point, suggesting that improvement in their situation might occur even without the classes. This phenomenon is known as "reversion to the mean," capturing the pattern that abnormal conditions often "revert" back toward normality over time even without any special intervention. Reversion to the mean can be accounted for only by comparing rates of improvement to families in a control group who start out in equally dire straits but don't participate in the program. So there's still no clear evidence the Parent Project achieves its goals even after taking up 30 solid hours of time from each one of half a million parents.[31]

The program founders want this evidence. They have been trying to conduct randomized controlled trials for years, but projects keep falling through. In 2004, they set up a study in Ohio, but the juvenile court judges who had agreed to participate ultimately refused to randomize parents into a control group excluded from Parent Project services.

"Ninety-eight percent of the programs that are research based are prevention models, not intervention models," Bud Fry explained when I asked about this. "Doing [a randomized controlled trial] with parents who are not in crisis is so much easier. Which parent of the meth-addicted kid are you going to have wait 10 weeks to take the course? Every parent we work with is in crisis."

I saw how that made sense in any individual case, but it adds up to major gaps in knowledge over time. It's like saying we don't have time to test if new chemotherapy drugs actually cure cancer because cancer patients need urgent help right away. This approach assures that program efficacy remains bottled up in folklore and personal convictions rather than proven, shared, and replicated in science. It falls right into the trap that people such as Cora Hillis, Craig Ramey, and Ruby Hearn have been so desperate to avoid.

As I finished work on this book, the Parent Project obtained preliminary results from its first successful randomized controlled trial, conducted by independent researchers with 59 participating parents. The study suggests promising positive impacts after 10 weeks of participation, when parents have just completed their last mandatory session. The study is a major milestone for this program. However, the authors acknowledge a number of important limitations. Most importantly, all child outcomes used in the study were reported by parents to their course instructors, who were also probation officers. Probation officers have immense legal influence over parents' lives. For obvious reasons, it may be hard for parents to report progress honestly in these circumstances. Future research can build on this foundation by collecting better data on children's outcomes from independent sources such as schools and courts, and possibly by leveraging the natural experiments that arise from random assignment of cases to judges rather than having to orchestrate randomized controlled trials.[32]

Even if we ultimately discover the Parent Project does have big impacts, attending this class reinforced my sense that we'll probably never be able to address America's main child-development problems by offering more and better training programs to parents. The classes intrude too heavily into parents' busy lives, the material is too demanding and complicated, and the learning process is too exhausting. And the same factors that have typically made parent training and home-visiting programs more effective—better-trained facilitators and longer duration—also make the programs more expensive and burdensome for parents.

At the very least, these programs will have to become much more fun to attract large-scale, voluntary participation. Less than half of mothers and less than a quarter of fathers report consulting any books, magazines, or online sources at all for parenting advice. It will be like pulling teeth to enroll this large majority of advice-wary parents in 10, 20, 30, or more hours of scheduled parent training programs, no matter how effective the programs are for those parents who manage to attend them.[33]

These considerations raise a different question. It seems clear that many parents could dramatically improve their skill-building practices. The stakes are high: a life-altering fortune in future earnings, a bridge from poverty to freedom for the people whom parents care more about than anyone else in the world. But somehow that future payoff doesn't seem to be enough: parents continue making costly mistakes on a massive scale. Why is that? Why can't all these loving, devoted parents achieve their goals?

As it turns out, economists have some good answers to that question. Parents building skills in children suffer the same kinds of deep, structural problems that drag down efficiency in other parts of our economy, from manufacturing to insurance to transportation. The problems are familiar. They're just *worse*.

DEEP BREATH

At this point, you may find yourself feeling that I am being too hard on parents.

Guess what? That feeling is the Parent Trap. That feeling is the backlash of a great delusion resisting scrutiny in order to preserve itself in your mind. All I have done is describe the realities of skill building. I feel nothing but admiration for all the parents out there who struggle with skill building despite their profound excellence in caring. So many parents do their very best to help the children they love, which is all any of us can do.

And if you look closely, you may find that uncomfortable feeling in the back of your mind is actually *you* being hard on parents. Perhaps you have bought into the idea that parents who can't build all the skills their children need are somehow failing, somehow worthy of judgment or blame, even as we start to recognize that child skill development is outrageously difficult, time-consuming, and expensive.

We all acknowledge that most parents can't fly helicopters or build their own microwaves or remove a child's gallbladder—at least not without the extensive training and practice that few adults have the bandwidth or inclination to complete in their spare time while also managing kids, jobs, homes, cars, relationships, health, pets, bills, and all the rest of it. For that matter, we all acknowledge that most parents can't leave their children large financial bequests. So why should we feel squeamish acknowledging that many parents cannot possibly build such a large share of the skills their children need for success, which is simply a bequest in the form of skills instead of financial assets?

Try saying this to yourself: "Many parents can't do some very hard stuff their kids need to thrive as adults, *and that's ok*. We just need professionals to do it on their behalf."

Does that feel too hard on parents? Or does it feel like a big relief?

4 WHY PARENTS CAN'T BUILD SKILLS ON THEIR OWN

FIVE KEY CHALLENGES

So now we're learning how to talk about the reality of parenting and working our way out of the Parent Trap. Caring is a vital ingredient in child development, and it's also accessible to regular people moved by love and generosity. Skill building is also critical, but it's *not* accessible to all people and the difficulty of skill building is just one of the problems that hold parents back. Put simply, if you wanted to design a job to *maximize* managerial mistakes and *minimize* productivity, that job would look an awful lot like parenting as we construct it today.

There are five key structural challenges facing all parents that we must recognize in order to help children thrive. They fall under the banners *complexity, learning, information, borrowing constraints*, and *spillovers*.

Once we understand these challenges, we'll see why asking individual parents or even private markets to solve the child skill-development problem is like trying to grow crops in a forest fire.

COMPLEXITY

If you haven't noticed, I really like helicopters and apparently analogies with helicopters. I once read *The Art and Science of Flying Helicopters* by Shawn Coyle. I learned all about autorotation, retreating blade stalls, collective pitch control. It was fascinating. I understood some of it and I might be able to pass a written test on the basics of helicopter flight. But I sure as hell can't fly a helicopter.

This observation brings us to the first problem that limits skill building by parents: *complexity*. We've seen that child skill development is a much more complex task than we've been led to believe. We saw the elaborate protocols and fine-tuned Learning Games invented by Abecedarian to provide developmentally appropriate, early childhood education starting from birth. We saw the multitude of challenges involved in managing children's health, nutrition, neighborhoods, schools, and colleges. We saw the intricate psychological techniques and action plans within action plans recommended to parents managing children's behavioral problems.

Complexity implies that even if parents did have an instruction manual, sometimes they wouldn't be able to follow it. In other parts of the economy, we allocate complex tasks to people with advanced training and experience—people like professional helicopter pilots.

In child skill development, these helicopter pilots are professional teachers, tutors, counselors, nurses, doctors, and social workers. It should be assumed that all parents need extensive assistance from professionals to make proper investments in their children's future. Asking parents to do too much on their own or to find and purchase all these services independently guarantees that millions of children won't get the skill-building investments they need to contribute fully as adults.

The Parent Trap makes it hard for Americans to talk about this fact: we've been duped into thinking any parents can build child skills if they put their minds to it and that needing more help is a personal failing. But parents shouldn't feel ashamed of being unable to build all the skills their children need, any more than they should feel ashamed they can't fly helicopters. *That's what helicopter pilots are for.*

LEARNING

The second problem holding parents back is a lack of *learning*. Learning happens in two ways: practice and feedback.

Professional teachers, unlike parents, get a lot of practice and feedback. A middle school teacher might teach 100 kids of similar ages *every year*. They see these children's performance on homework, quizzes, exams, essays, research projects, group conversations, presentations, and state test scores. Most teachers also receive feedback from peers and managers.[1] As teachers manage classrooms for children of similar ages, covering similar material, year after year for hundreds or even thousands of students, they get better at their jobs, and their new students learn more quickly than their former students.[2]

How many times do parents raise children? On average, parents have about two kids—so, twice. They figure out early education—twice. They figure out where to live and what schools to attend at each grade—twice. They figure out how college works or not—twice.

We might think parents get a lot of practice simply because we focus on day-to-day activities such as changing diapers or getting kids to bed. Parents do get to improve in these areas, but this fact obscures the bigger picture. For most key choices in child skill growth, parents get almost no practice. Each child is a fresh odyssey through a different uncharted wilderness, and parents have exactly one shot to get it right.

How much feedback do parents receive on their skill-building techniques from credible, independent third parties? In many cases, almost none. Are their kids learning enough? Are they as healthy as they can be? Are they building the right physical, cognitive, social, and emotional skills? Finger to the wind.

Public schools are supposed to provide parents with feedback on child skill growth starting when children are five. How's that working out? Well, about 90 percent of parents report their children are meeting grade-level standards in reading and math. Unfortunately, more than half these parents are wrong. Only 40 percent of kids perform at grade level. Many parents also hold overoptimistic beliefs about their children's absences and missed assignments.[3]

Why are parents so overconfident about their children's academic performance? Why don't schools clue them in? Learning Heroes, a nonprofit organization that studies parental beliefs, has uncovered one culprit: *report cards*.

Many parents infer children's academic progress from seeing As and Bs on report cards. What most parents don't realize is that report cards

Scaled Score: 475

The Scaled Score is the overall score that your child received on the STAR Early Literacy assessment. It is calculated based on both the difficulty of the questions and the number of correct responses. Scaled Scores in STAR Early Literacy range from 300 to 900 and span the grades Pre-K through 3.

Lisa obtained a Scaled Score of 475. Scaled Scores relate to three developmental stages: Emergent Reader (300 - 674), Transitional Reader (675-774), and Probable Reader (775 - 900). A Scaled Score of 475 means that Lisa is at the Emergent Reader stage.

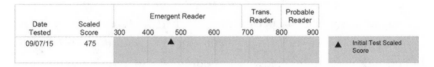

Figure 4.1

A typical test score report: Is this child doing well or not? *Source*: Renaissance Learning, "Parent's Guide to STAR Assessments: Questions and Answers," 2015.

don't capture academic achievement—they mix in effort, improvement, and other factors unrelated to hard mastery of grade-level academic skills. On top of all this, grades and teachers' overall perceptions of children's learning are highly relative. A sophomore receiving a B– in English at a high-achieving school may struggle to articulate well-reasoned closing arguments in a mock trial of Hamlet. A sophomore receiving the same grade at a lower-achieving school may struggle to read the newspaper.[4]

To really understand their children's skill growth, parents would have to assess how hard their classes are, decode grading policies, demand brutally honest feedback from teachers, and parse cryptic test score reports.

Under these circumstances of high stress and weak feedback, it's understandable that parents fall prey to wishful thinking. Cora Hillis had marveled that the majority of mothers "really believed they already knew all there was to be known about child-care," and things are no different today: many parents seem strangely optimistic about their children's education, health, and future prospects. In interviews about their parenting strategies, parents admitted to the sociologist Sharon Hays, "I think I look for the things that I agree with," and "I believe what feels good to me."[5]

Parental overconfidence can take an even more pernicious form known as the "Dunning-Kruger effect": the phenomenon that less-informed people often wind up being *especially* confident in their choices because, after all, they have no idea things can be done better.

The Dunning-Kruger effect creates another kind of trap: the people who would benefit most from external support are the least likely to seek out that support voluntarily. Under limited learning and feedback, these kinds of cognitive biases can lock in false beliefs, allowing misinformation to shape decisions indefinitely. Many more parents would carefully monitor children's performance, help their children with homework, hire tutors, or request help from schools if they learned the darker truth about their children's academic progress with all its long-term social and economic implications.[6]

Why are schools allowing confusion to prevail, at least when it comes to academic progress? Many teachers confess: they can't bear to tell parents the truth. They think angry parents will blame schools.[7]

The problem is not parents, many of whom are ill equipped to help children stay on track academically. And the problem is not schools, which are often doing the best they can, given the small role our system allows them to play in children's lives. The problem is the skill-development system we impose on both of them—loaded with perfectly natural and perfectly fraught emotion and existential angst—that asks parents to solve almost the entire skill-building problem on their own, blames schools for the inevitable results, and robs children of skill growth worth hundreds of thousands of dollars in future wealth.

INFORMATION

Normally, when people struggle to solve problems on their own, they hire help. Can't fix a broken water pipe? Call a plumber. Can't fix a toothache? Call a dentist. Unfortunately, that's not so easy for parents struggling with skill development. Even if parents avoid overconfidence and recognize they need some help, they face a different problem.

The problem is that anxious feeling we all get when talking to a new plumber, dentist, auto mechanic, or lawyer—that feeling of being at someone's mercy. That vulnerable feeling is the essence of what economists call "asymmetric information."

Asymmetric information refers to situations where you don't know exactly what you're getting in a transaction. Many professional services in health care, education, law, and finance involve asymmetric information. Experts in all these fields can help us, but they can also rip us off, and that possibility reduces the value of their services. It also reduces the incentive to provide high-quality service because customers hesitate to shell out for quality they can't easily verify. This dynamic can lead to a self-reinforcing feedback loop known as "adverse selection" that degrades both service quality and consumer demand.

Asymmetric information and adverse selection can strangle entire lines of business that might otherwise provide enormous value. What if you could buy insurance against unforeseen career developments such as Chinese imports bankrupting your employer or new technologies rendering your professional skills obsolete? What if you could buy insurance against getting a divorce or dropping out of college or changing careers after realizing corporate law isn't as gratifying as you had hoped? All of these insurance products would be great, but none of them is freely available in open markets. One reason for their absence is asymmetric information: businesses know the first people to sign up will be those most at risk of needing the insurance—that is, the people who cost the most to insure.[8]

Asymmetric information and adverse selection may explain why parents, especially parents on tight budgets, are often wary of unfamiliar investments in their children. The problem is that all this understandable caution can also blind parents to real opportunities: opportunities such as college financial aid policies that make Stanford University cost less than Orange Coast Community College, tutoring that costs a lot but gets kids back on track at school, neighborhoods a few miles away with similar rents but better amenities, and protocols for treating chronic disease that seem overbearing but expand a child's horizons.

Here's the thing about this trust gap: it's larger for parents with less expertise in gathering and processing new information. And as we'll see, it's larger still for racial minorities who have been deceived and betrayed in every aspect of American life for generations.

Inadequate practice and feedback shove parents into a learning cage; then overconfidence and mistrust lock the door. One way to see the extent of this problem is to focus on how parents manage a special kind of skill-development technology. This technology costs parents almost nothing, has virtually no downsides, and protects children from major obstacles to skill growth.

What is this magical technology? Vaccines.

A WINDOW ONTO PARENTAL CONFUSION

Aside from anything COVID related, parental opposition to vaccines against infectious diseases, known today as the "antivax" movement, has been growing for years. In some places, vaccination rates have become dangerously low. The result has been new outbreaks of "old-time" diseases such as whooping cough, mumps, and measles that had previously almost disappeared.[9]

One of the main stated concerns of antivax parents is that vaccination may increase the rate of autism in children. This idea stems from a single study published in 1998 by a researcher named Andrew Wakefield in a prestigious medical journal, the *Lancet,* claiming to show evidence that 12 children who had received the measles-mumps-rubella vaccine had subsequently developed gastrointestinal problems and severe forms of autism. Wakefield arranged a press conference to announce the article's explosive findings, which brought him worldwide acclaim. He appeared in a flattering biopic movie, was interviewed on *60 Minutes,* and testified before Congress.

Over the following decade, however, a series of sensational investigations by journalist Brian Deer revealed that Wakefield's study was in fact an elaborate fraud. The 12 children in the study had been referred to Wakefield by lawyers pushing a lucrative class-action lawsuit against vaccine developers. These children, along with many others over the 1990s, had received a series of painful, invasive, unnecessary tests that came to be known as the "Wakefield protocol" in a fishing expedition for some kind of data that could insinuate vaccines caused harm in children. Wakefield had manipulated test results and case histories to support the argument. Deer also uncovered major conflicts of interest. The same lawyers who referred the 12 families to Wakefield for the study had paid him nearly a million dollars to produce evidence for their lawsuit. Before publishing the *Lancet* paper, Wakefield had filed a patent on an alternative vaccine that put him in a good position to profit once existing vaccines were rendered suspect. Unsurprisingly, given Wakefield's many deceptions, subsequent research failed to replicate his findings. Wakefield was ultimately found guilty of fraud and lost his medical license.[10]

Nonetheless, the fears sparked by Wakefield's discredited study live on among many parents. In a sense, this is puzzling. All parents have to do is listen to their pediatricians, who will be delighted to explain that mainstream vaccines pose no threat to children based on every large-scale, rigorous study that has ever been conducted.

The public-health researchers Matthew Motta, Timothy Callaghan, and Steven Sylvester surveyed 1,500 Americans to learn more about why so many parents remain confused about a topic affecting their children's basic health. They first asked an audacious question: Did respondents feel they themselves knew more or less about the causes of autism than professional physicians and scientists? More than *a third* of all respondents considered their knowledge in this domain equal or superior to that of experts who have spent a decade or more in training. Then the researchers gave respondents a short true/false quiz about autism, with statements including "Autism occurs in roughly equal numbers of boys and girls" (false, more prevalent in boys), and "Many scientists think that heredity and genes play a role in the cause of autism" (true). Finally, they asked respondents if they thought vaccines caused autism in children.[11]

The results uncovered a powerful Dunning-Kruger form of overconfidence. Respondents with the weakest autism knowledge and the strongest belief in a false vaccine–autism link also tended to believe they knew more about causes of autism than professional experts. Respondents with greater autism knowledge were more modest; they assumed they knew much less about the issue than experts.

But perhaps parents can maintain such misinformation only when the stakes are low. Today misinformed parents can skip most vaccines, and their children will remain protected by the high vaccination rates of other families in their community. In economic terms, antivax parents can free-ride on the safer behaviors of those around them, much like people who evade taxes can be sure their military security, roads, and parks will endure thanks to the compliance of other taxpayers.[12]

Unfortunately, misinformation is not limited to these lower-stakes decisions; it can thrive even in life-or-death situations. This is easy to see if we go back in time to a different vaccine, in fact the original vaccine, for smallpox. Throughout the 1800s, smallpox outbreaks terrorized American communities. During a Brooklyn outbreak in 1894, locals were so afraid they threatened to burn down the quarantine hospital that was caring for the victims. Known to Native Americans as "rotting face," smallpox killed a third of its victims and was highly contagious, but it could be neutralized by a cheap, effective, relatively safe vaccine that had existed since 1796. And yet even during these nightmarish outbreaks, with agony and death beating down their door, many parents ignored the advice of local experts and refused to vaccinate their children until public officials forced them into it.[13]

Clearly, many parents cannot easily ask experts such as pediatricians to guide them through hard decisions. Nineteenth-century opposition to the smallpox vaccine demonstrates that mistrust and overconfidence can short-circuit investments in transformative potions that cost virtually nothing and yield almost infinite benefits. Imagine how badly these forces can undermine investments in other kinds of skills, where up-front costs are significant and benefits are both finite and delayed.

BORROWING CONSTRAINTS

Complexity, barriers to learning, information problems: these are big obstacles to building skills in children. But we're not done. There is another force bearing down on parents.

This force sounds so compelling that it has captured the imagination of generations of economists, myself included. It sounds so obvious that many politicians and policy makers assume it is the single biggest problem facing parents. The leaders of the women's progressive reform movement in the early twentieth century, who founded and oversaw the landmark federal Children's Bureau, considered it the root problem of child underdevelopment.

The problem is *money*: parents' money. Namely, the lack of it.

We tend to fixate on K12 school budgets as a cover for how we collectively fund our children's development as a society. But as we have seen throughout this book, we neglect the much more important and more unequal realities faced by the people with the greatest burden of child skill building: parents.

Simply put, many parents do not have enough money to make big investments in children. Who can afford $80,000 or more for five years of good early childhood education, $100,000 or more for college, another $100,000 for consistent tutoring and extracurricular activities, and so many other big-ticket skill-building investments?

But if we step back for a moment, the problem becomes more interesting. It sounds odd, but, normally, lack of money is not such a big deal. This is what *loans* are for. Most people can't afford to buy a house, so they get a mortgage. Most people can't afford to start or expand a business, so they take out a business loan. Millions of people use these kinds of loans.

Investments in children's skills don't work this way, however, for a couple of reasons. Unlike homes, children's skills cannot act as collateral. If a homeowner defaults on a mortgage payment, the bank can seize the home and sell it to recover its losses. This reassurance, along with massive public financial support through Fannie Mae and Freddy Mac, allows banks to do something that might otherwise sound insane—lend large sums of money to regular people they barely know for decades at a time. But if parents default on a loan they took out to pay for their child's preschool, the bank cannot seize the child's new skills. Even if the literacy skills pay off and the child becomes richer as an adult, the bank has to bet that the child will voluntarily help her parents pay back the loan. This is a risky bet, to put it mildly.

Many business loans are safe for a different reason: they generate near-term profit that helps borrowers keep up with their payments. Think about how new restaurants, barber shops, and motels convert loans into customers and profits almost immediately. Children's skills do not generate new income quickly. Skills are less like conventional small businesses and more like tech startups in Silicon Valley that spend years building new technology and accumulating customers before ever turning a dime of profit. Startups often sell shares in their future profit rather than take out loans. But parents cannot sell shares in their children's future income because they don't own that income.

From a bank's perspective, therefore, "child-development loans" would combine the worst of all worlds. They would be long-term investments to build assets that do not yield near-term income and cannot be seized as collateral in event of default. And even worse, the new income from the investment ultimately accrues to the children, who have no legal obligation to share that income with their parents or use it to pay back the loan. The only chance to make such risky loans profitable would be to charge very high interest rates, but very high interest rates create an adverse-selection "death spiral" in which only the riskiest and least trustworthy people apply for the loans, further subverting lender profits.

If parents can't afford key investments in child skill development, they're stuck. Economists call this problem a *borrowing constraint*. It's hard to appreciate how strange borrowing constraints are because things have always been this way in child development, and we take it for granted. But consider how strange such constraints would be in other parts of the economy. Since 2015, oil companies have discovered about $275 billion worth of oil reserves off the coast of Guyana. They know the oil is there—all they need to do is extract it. But extracting the oil will cost about $192 billion. If they can do the extraction quickly enough, that's a rather sensational investment—more than $80 billion in profit. If oil companies were like parents, however, banks would say, "Too bad." No loans, no extraction, no oil.[14]

Many people studying inequality and child development have fixated on borrowing constraints as the fundamental problem. There are a few reasons for this. First, parental income is tangible, measurable, and malleable.

The solution to borrowing constraints is simple: just get the constrained parents more money.

Second, whenever parental income is measured, it correlates overwhelmingly with child skills. One reason the Children's Bureau considered poverty itself the main obstacle to child skill growth is that its groundbreaking research revealed such powerful correlations. Poor children died more often as babies. They also more often wound up out of school, in trouble with law enforcement, and sick with chronic disease. Julia Lathrop, first head of the Children's Bureau, stated in 1919, "The power to maintain a decent family living standard is the primary essential of child welfare."[15]

The third reason for the fixation on parental income is more subtle but might be the most important. In our twisted moral universe around parenting, focusing on money feels more *comfortable*. We admire parents such as Katie Nolan in *A Tree Grows in Brooklyn* as she rages against sheer poverty to invest in the education of her two older children. "Oh, if I could only get them into high school this fall! *Please God! I'll give twenty years off my life. I'll work night and day. But I can't of course. No one to stay with the baby.*"[16]

This can make the question of money in parenting seem very high stakes. In the back of our minds, we've learned to feel that parents who struggle with skill growth due to money are *valiant*, whereas parents who struggle with skill growth for other reasons are *just bad parents*. By now, I hope, we see that distinction is absurd. Complexity, limited learning and feedback, and understandable overconfidence and mistrust all conspire to prevent good parents from making sound investments in children—in some cases even investments with minimal costs and virtually infinite benefits.

So there's nothing shameful going on if it turns out parents *can't* be saved with some extra cash. But that still leaves the question: exactly how big a difference would the extra cash make?

TESTING A HYPOTHESIS

To really test the importance of borrowing constraints, we need to compare parents who are equally good at child skill development but have different access to money. This is difficult because one of the main ways that parents end up with more money is by excelling at work, and such parents will also tend to excel in many nonfinancial aspects of child skill development. As part of my work with the IRS Databank, I spent several years searching for a way to overcome this problem and pinpoint the role of money on its own.

Social scientists are supposed to be neutral toward their research, but that is rarely true. In my case, I was hoping to find that parental income played a large role in driving one important measure of skill development: college attendance. I wound up focusing on a natural experiment buried in the timing of parental *layoffs*. Economists already knew that layoffs caused sharp, long-term income losses.[17] So consider two kids, Penny and Lena. Penny's and Lena's fathers work in similar jobs with similar earnings. Suppose Penny's father loses his job when Penny is 15 years old. Poor Penny! This means that Penny now has to make college-attendance decisions in the shadow of her family's lower income. Lena's father also loses his job, but this happens when Lena is 25 years old—ten years later. Lucky Lena! By 25, Lena has already made her college investments. In that case, Poor Penny and Lucky Lena represent an almost ideal experiment for testing the importance of borrowing constraints, at least for older kids approaching college. If borrowing constraints are a major problem, we would expect kids like Poor Penny to attend college at much lower rates, or to attend much lower-quality colleges, than kids like Lucky Lena.[18]

The IRS Databank contained records on 7 million laid-off fathers. This allowed me to compare college outcomes for millions of children like Penny with college outcomes for millions of children like Lena. At the time of making college decisions, Penny's family was earning about $7,000 less per year than Lena's family. These income losses would continue in the future, meaning that Poor Penny's family had actually lost about $100,000 of future earnings relative to Lucky Lena's family. Overall, these 7 million layoffs shifted around $700 billion dollars of wealth. That's about 5 percent of total gross domestic product (GDP)—a very big experiment.

The simple correlations in my data looked just as stark as the correlations found by Children's Bureau researchers 100 years ago: rich children attended college at overwhelmingly higher rates than poor children. If parental income really caused these differences, I would expect layoffs to reduce college enrollment by several percentage points—a huge impact that would easily jump out given the powerful data. I put everything together, ran the numbers, and stared at the results in disbelief. Poor Penny and Lucky Lena's college behaviors looked almost indistinguishable. The effect was there, and thanks to the incredible data I could detect it—but it was tiny. Poor Penny was about *0.5 percentage points* less likely to attend college than Lucky Lena each year during ages 18 to 22. Because about 50 percent of kids in the United States attend college, that meant a 1 percent reduction in college attendance. This was only about *one-tenth* the impact you would expect if income itself really caused the rich–poor college-enrollment gap.

I found this result hard to believe. The extra $7,000 of annual income and $100,000 of future wealth had almost no impact on kids' educational outcomes. What about all the talk about "college affordability"? What about all the detailed, compelling stories of low-income children struggling to pay for college? One hundred thousand dollars is almost exactly the average out-of-pocket cost of an entire college degree; how could so much parental wealth make so little difference?[19]

I was so skeptical of my own findings that I spent the next year searching for mistakes in my code, problems in my data—anything that might resolve the puzzle. I've mentioned some of the thorny problems afflicting social science: bias toward publishing some results and dismissing others, cherry-picking results among multiple outcomes, and so on. But if you think all social scientists just manipulate statistics to validate their own biases, you're too cynical. I was hostile to my results, but I couldn't make them go away.

Eventually, I figured it out. The explanation was simple: parents don't spend additional income on helping kids attend college.

In surveys of parents with kids in college, parents who earn $1,000 more per year provide only about $20 to $50 more per year of college support. The same relationship holds for spending on early education: $1,000 of additional income results in only about $30 more spending on childcare. These patterns hold even for lower-income parents, who should be most vulnerable to borrowing constraints.[20]

This means that the layoffs I'd been studying probably reduced parental support for college by only a couple hundred dollars. In that light, the fact that college enrollment falls by even 1 percent is astonishing. Children themselves appear highly sensitive to college costs, but parents don't pour every available dollar into helping children overcome this problem, so parental income itself has minimal impacts.

My results made even more sense once I discovered the work of the sociologist Annette Lareau. Instead of distilling bone-dry numeric data into statistical insights in the manner of most economists, Lareau gets to know parents and observes their lives up close in their own homes and communities and even on trips to the dentist and the grocery store. After observing rich and poor families raising children for many years, she concluded: "Although it is very difficult to untangle economic and cultural factors, one possible thought experiment is to imagine the changes that could happen if a working-class or poor family won the lottery. The changes that could happen in the next few days or weeks could be reasonably tied to economic factors. It is unlikely, however, that working-class and poor families would be able to acquire knowledge about the inner workings of institutions such as schools or adopt middle-class practices in terms of the management of their children's lives outside the home."[21]

Lareau was predicting that income by itself probably did not account for the worse educational outcomes of children in lower-income families. She saw a much larger role for other factors, such as those discussed earlier: complexity, limited learning and feedback, overconfidence and mistrust. Instead of money being the primary force, it was parents' own cognitive, social, emotional, and professional skills that determined both their own income in the labor market *and* their ability to master child skill development. My work amounted to a Big Data confirmation of Lareau's Deep Data hypothesis. Given her intuition, my results didn't seem so shocking after all.

Soon after I conducted my study, another team of economists—George Bulman, Robert Fairlie, Sarena Goodman, and Adam Isen—used the same data and the same Poor Penny versus Lucky Lena approach, but with a big improvement: they did exactly what Lareau suggested and looked at parents who had literally won the lottery. Now Lena's parents won a $50,000 Powerball lottery prize when Lena was 16 (Lucky Lena!), while Penny's parents won a $50,000 Powerball lottery prize when Penny was 25, after she had already made her college decisions (Poor Penny!). Lottery wins offer a more ideal window onto borrowing constraints because they cannot possibly be anticipated, and they affect only family income, whereas layoffs combine income reductions with other factors such as ego deflation and more time at home. These researchers found exactly the same results. Lucky Lena's and Poor Penny's college outcomes looked almost identical, implying that parental income on its own made barely any difference.[22]

The small impacts of parental income become clearer if we compare them to impacts of a very different form of money: financial aid. Parents can spend labor income on anything they want, but financial aid has to be spent on college. Studies find $1,000 of additional financial aid raises enrollment by 2 to 5 percentage points. Recall that *$100,000* of additional parental wealth raises college enrollment by 0.5 percentage points. That means transferring a dollar to children directly in the form of financial aid for college increases attendance more than *100 times more effectively* than transferring that same dollar to parents. This makes sense once we realize 100 percent of financial aid goes toward college compared to only a tiny share of additional parental income.[23]

Apparently, the main determinant of investment in children is not so much parental income but other factors such as beliefs, knowledge, and skills that help parents overcome all the other hurdles involved in child skill development. The fact that all these other factors also help parents earn income is surprisingly incidental.[24]

Parental income does matter for very low-income families, especially when children are younger than five and have not yet gained access to public school. Programs such as the Earned Income Tax Credit, SNAP, and welfare expand parental income in different ways with different add-on elements such as employment, childcare, and nutrition, and these programs have been found to increase children's skill development in some cases. One possible explanation is that for very low-income families, basic expenditures on things such as food, housing, and peace of mind can improve the home skill-building environment without asking parents to make big new managerial leaps into complex aspects of schooling and health care.[25]

But even here the impacts of parental income appear small compared to alternative programs that invest directly in building skills. Consider, for example, the Special Supplemental Nutrition Program for Women, Infants, and Children (WIC). WIC provides mothers of young children with family nutrition support, health screenings, and help accessing other complex public benefits. WIC is not just income; it is a bundle of services designed to improve maternal health and child skill development.

Remarkably, WIC appears to reduce rates of low birth weight and improve rates of early academic achievement more than *five times* as much per dollar than cash transfers to parents.[26]

So parental income does improve skill growth in some cases. But even in these cases, money by itself is not particularly effective per dollar of public spending. Money won't cause most parents to become experts in architecture, carpentry, or law—and it won't cause them to become experts in child skill development, either.

So far, we've focused on structural forces that make it hard for parents to manage *their own* children's skill growth. The next force shows why that perspective is too narrow. When we fail to support parents, their own children's skill growth is just the first casualty.

SPILLOVERS

Researchers have asked parents what they consider to be the biggest problems facing their children at school. One factor consistently ranks at the top of the list. It's not school funding or large class sizes or school management or anything about teachers or administrators. Parents' number one concern is *other parents*. Specifically, it's the lack of support that some parents are able to provide to their children and the resulting behavioral problems that obstruct learning for everyone else.[27]

It turns out these parents are not making things up. When a child doesn't get the investments she needs to keep her skill growth on track, it affects her peers and classmates, almost like a contagious disease. These "spillovers," also known as "externalities," mean that skill-building obstacles cascade from families into schools, communities, and groups, exacerbating all the other problems already besetting parents.

Two economists, Steve Carrell and Mark Hoekstra, discovered a way to start measuring this problem. They mined publicly available courthouse records in Alachua County, Florida, for data on parents who had requested a *restraining order* on their partner due to domestic abuse from 1993 to 2003. These data pinpointed families undergoing domestic violence. Other research had suggested that kids in these families, rattled by fear and stress, were much more likely to act out in class at school.[28] Tragically, domestic violence turned out to be quite common in Alachua, directly affecting one in every twenty students.

Carrell and Hoekstra then spent a decade combining these data with progressively richer information about skill development for all kids in Alachua County—not just the children experiencing domestic violence but all their classmates as well. First, the researchers got test scores, then college outcomes, then labor-market earnings in early adulthood. These extraordinary data provided the first glimpse into the impacts of disruptive kids on their classmates.[29]

To see what Carrell and Hoekstra did, consider the third-grade class at Idylwild Elementary School in Alachua. In most years, there are about 115 third graders sorted into eight classes, with about 14 kids in each class.[30] In 1996, suppose 4 of 119 kids had experienced domestic violence at home. In 1997—same school, same grade—suppose 8 of 112 kids experienced domestic violence at home. Variation in small numbers like this often reflects pure random chance, like raindrops landing on leaves, and the authors provide compelling evidence to support this premise. For purely random reasons, then, third graders at Idylwind in 1997, as compared to 1996, would be twice as likely to share a classroom with kids exhibiting disruptive symptoms of anxiety, depression, and stress due to violence at home. By comparing outcomes of third graders in 1996 and 1997, the researchers can see how these kids affect their peers.

Unfortunately, the evidence supports the fears that parents express in surveys. Kids exposed to more disruptive peers score lower on tests, commit more disciplinary infractions, reach college at lower rates, and get lower-paying jobs. The impacts are big, and they add up across all the kids in the class. Adding one additional disruptive kid into a classroom for a single year reduces future earnings of other kids in the classroom by about $80,000. A dollar impact helps to illustrate that the impacts are large. Social and emotional impacts, in particular the impacts of externalizing behaviors such as bullying, may be even more important.

"We've called and talked to counselors in Alachua," says Carrell. "Every teacher and every counselor who we talk to about this totally 100 percent believe the results of the paper." In conversations with principals and counselors, Carrell heard a lot of talk about tipping points. It seems teachers can handle one or two troubled children, but classes containing three, four, or five of them quickly spin out of control. Subsequent research on schools in Switzerland has found exactly this pattern.[31]

I spoke with a school counselor who also expressed this intuition. The counselor works in a building with two elementary schools, one public and one private. "The private school is self-selected, higher-income, crisscross apple sauce and all that, the kids pay attention. The public-school side is mayhem. They always have kids from really tough situations in those classes, they're dealing with a lot. One kid was wreaking havoc on the class. So we took this kid who was a ringleader and convinced the principal to move him over to the private side. The first time he tried to act up, the well-behaved kids shut him down. Boom he falls in line, all of a sudden he's no longer a problem."

An $80,000 reduction in future earnings per 20-student classroom is a lot of disappearing wealth caused by one struggling little kid in one year, and it's just a fragment of the spillovers affecting children. Only a small share of parents experiencing domestic violence request restraining orders, and many kids act out at school for reasons other than background domestic violence.[32] Many children are abused by parents and siblings. Many parents struggle with anxiety and depression, poverty, substance abuse, unemployment, incarceration, and the added stress that comes from inflecting all these factors through discrimination.

Major court rulings in the 2000s have overturned decades of struggle toward greater integration and given us a window into these broader spillovers. Some of these rulings triggered sudden shifts toward greater school segregation in particular cities. Researchers studying these episodes in Charlotte, North Carolina, and Seattle, Washington, have documented a disconcerting pattern: adding one additional low-income child to a classroom reduces the future wealth of all children in that classroom together— rich and poor alike—by about $14,000. This is less than the impact of children with parental restraining orders in Carrell and Hoekstra's work, but there are ten times more children in poor or near-poor families than in families experiencing domestic abuse. The findings suggest that a student who spends her entire K12 career in classrooms with all-poor classmates will lose at least $180,000 in future earnings, on average, compared to what she would have earned had she attended schools with no poor classmates.[33]

Over and over, these studies turn up a particular form of spillover effect. Schools that serve more disadvantaged students struggle to hire and retain good teachers, and the scarcity of good teachers then in turn harms all students at the school. The problem is not that these schools can't pay equal salaries. As we've seen, funding gaps are no longer a major phenomenon in the K12 system. The problem is that teachers prefer to work with higher-achieving, higher-income students, largely because they associate these children with fewer academic and behavioral problems. In one study, the single job characteristic that teachers valued above all others was a principal who would help them manage disruptive students. Teachers in more-advantaged schools essentially have more assistant teachers to help them do their job. These assistant teachers are the students' own parents, who have the skills and resources to play this role effectively.[34]

Parents have three main options in response to spillovers.

One option is to embrace the more intangible benefits of economic diversity, even if, on average and other things equal, classrooms with more disadvantaged kids result in weaker test scores, college preparation, and future earnings. We might call this option the "Diversity" response.[35] A second option is for parents to seek shelter from adverse spillovers in the most exclusive, advantaged communities they can afford. We might call this the "Isolation" response. Finally, parents can advocate for policies that provide a more comprehensive skill-building ecosystem so that poor children no longer struggle so disproportionately in school. We might call this the "Elevation" response.

The Diversity response will not appeal to many parents, who are understandably reluctant to make such hard trade-offs when it comes to their children. These parents often turn instinctively to the Isolation response. But fleeing diversity comes at a high price. Homes in exclusive neighborhoods are expensive, as are private schools. Isolation turns society into an arms race, with parents jostling for their children to join the scarce pool of highly advantaged peers. For very rich families, isolation works fine. For middle-class families, it means constantly feeling on the brink of a precipice: *make more money, barely afford your life, or else watch your children fall behind.* For most families, the Elevation response would be a cheaper, more-effective, and less-stressful option. Elevation would also be more consistent with most people's sense of America's identity as a nation eschewing aristocracy and promoting a level playing field.

In America, we ask parents to carry almost the entire skill-development burden. In this endeavor, parents individually fight back flames of complexity, inadequate learning, information problems, and borrowing constraints. All of these forces weigh more heavily on lower-income and less-educated parents. When we concentrate these parents together in segregated communities, spillovers pour gasoline onto these fires, incinerating future wealth for millions of children.

And it is this predicament, more than any other, that perpetuates the cornerstone American pathology: racial inequality.

5 SKILL DEVELOPMENT AND RACIAL INEQUALITY

We saw in the introduction that opportunities to build the kinds of skills measured by the Armed Forces Qualifying Test early in life can explain about 70 percent of the income gap between children who grow up rich and poor. And we saw that these same skills can only account for about 50 percent of the Black–white income gap. You might see these numbers and assume that even if Black people gained the exact same skills as white people, discrimination in jobs, health care, criminal justice, and other systems might continue to drag Black incomes down far below white incomes.

In this chapter, I take a closer look at the determinants of Black–white income gaps in America and reach a different conclusion. I find that equalizing opportunities for skill growth in Black communities would eliminate much more than half of Black–white income inequality and would do so even if racial prejudice remained prevalent. The reason is that when an entire group gains access to greater skill development, as opposed to scattered individual members of the group, powerful and surprising multiplier effects kick in that serve to elevate the group's economic position. Closing racial income gaps, in turn, would likely close most of the racial wealth gap in one generation. Going further, an opposite strategy of reducing prejudice without equalizing Black skill growth would likely fail to close Black–white income or wealth gaps nearly as much as hoped.[1]

As we explore these issues, it's useful to keep in mind we're talking about averages, not individuals. For any pattern about group averages, there will often be many individuals who display the reverse pattern. If a pattern about group averages does not reflect your own experience or that of individuals you know personally, that is perfectly valid and important to keep in mind, but it need not indicate that the pattern about averages is false, and it likewise need not call your own experience into question. I also want to say up front that I think about race like most social scientists today: as a political, historical, and sociological category, *not* a biological category.

In this chapter, I focus on the ways our skill-development system affects racial groups differently. The key intuition is simple: *The more we rely on families rather than professionals to build skills in children, the tighter we link people's current prospects to the prospects of their ancestors.* Our egregious overreliance on parents to build skills thereby perpetuates inequality by race as well as by class. To see this, we start with a new look at America's founding sin: slavery.

AFRICAN AMERICANS AND SKILL PROHIBITION

African Americans have been striving to acquire economic skills since slave traders first brought them—stolen, tortured, starved, raped, and severed from their kin—to the shores of America.[2]

The abolitionist David Walker observed in 1829, "For coloured people to acquire learning in this country, makes tyrants quake and tremble on their sandy foundation." Terrified by slave rebellions such as the Stono Rebellion in 1739 and Nat Turner's Rebellion in 1831, Southern states erected harsh laws against teaching any enslaved person, and eventually any Black person whether enslaved or free, to read, write, or engage in "mental instruction" of any kind.[3]

Enforcement was strict, punishments medieval. An enslaved person caught with a book could receive hundreds of lashes, have fingers or hands sliced off, or be killed. The former slave James Lucas recalled how his former master "hung the best slave he had for trying to teach the others how to spell."[4]

But as the historian Heather Williams documents in her book *Self-Taught* (2007), these threats weren't enough. A valiant, subterranean market for education emerged early and persisted through the Civil War. Enslaved people held secret night schools "in secret places, sitting in the woods with spelling books." Black children carried books concealed in paper or dresses or hats to secret day schools in instructors' homes, coming and going one at a time. They charmed white children into "playing school." They traded money, food, nails and marbles, boxing and wrestling lessons for education from anyone desperate, naive, or sympathetic enough to provide it.[5]

Literacy allowed some to forge their own travel passes to freedom. Others discovered vindication in scripture, "God hath made of one blood all nations of men to dwell on all the face of the earth," and in secular passages, such as "liberty or death." Still others used literacy to assert their humanity. When one girl's master threatened to punish her for learning to write, she bent his whip into the shape of her own first initial.[6]

Slaves enlisting with the Union army during the Civil War filled the camps with makeshift classrooms. They read and studied while on guard, in hospitals, around campfires, in tents before work. Contemporaries recorded the widespread commitment of Black soldiers to gain literacy and noted that the "ability to read and write appeared to be an almost universal desire."[7]

Emancipation opened the floodgates. In 1870, after the Civil War had technically ended, only 20 percent of Blacks had achieved literacy compared to 92 percent of whites.[8] Booker T. Washington was nine years old when his Virginia family learned they were legally free. He later recalled the urgent demands for education by former slaves all over the South:

> This experience of a whole race beginning to go to school for the first time, presents one of the most interesting studies that has ever occurred in connection with the development of any race. Few people who were not right in the midst of the scenes can form any exact idea of the intense desire which the people of my race showed for an education. . . . Few were too young, and none too old, to make the attempt to learn. As fast as any kind of teachers could be secured, not only were day-schools filled, but night-schools as well. The great ambition of the older people was to try to learn to read the Bible before they died. With this end in view men and women who were fifty or seventy-five years old would often be found in the night-school. . . .

Day-school, night-school, Sunday-school, were always crowded, and often many had to be turned away for want of room.[9]

Southern whites took notice. One school official in Georgia thought, "The colored people manifest a great desire to have their children educated. Their schools are overflowing whenever opened." Another official in the state warned that "something is necessarily obliged to be done or the whites will not keep up with the darkey."[10]

And something was done. As the federal government phased out military occupation, the Confederacy rose again. Southern whites used raw terrorism and racist laws to shut down the Black vote. Then they set about embezzling money out of Black schools and plowing it into white schools. As one superintendent boasted, "The money allocated to the colored children is spent on the education of white children. We have twice as many colored children of school age as we have white, and we use their money. Colored children are mighty profitable to us."

By World War I, southern Black children attended schools that packed in nearly twice as many kids per class, taught a quarter fewer days per year, and paid teachers half as much.[11] "Separate but equal" was a pretext for paralyzing Black skill growth.

Even if Black students did manage to build skills in this hostile environment, their career choices remained slim. White-only professional schools and biased admissions policies closed off the most prestigious and lucrative professions to most Black students.[12]

But then things started to change. First, the National Association for the Advancement of Colored People (NAACP) launched a brilliant 50-year legal campaign to equalize educational opportunity from kindergarten through graduate and professional schools all across America. Many people thought trying to pressure the judiciary into upholding racial equality was a fool's errand, but they were wrong—the campaign worked. Even before *Brown v. Board of Education* (347 US 483) declared segregated schools unconstitutional in 1954, Black children no longer had to settle for egregiously larger classes, shorter school years, and lower-paid teachers.[13]

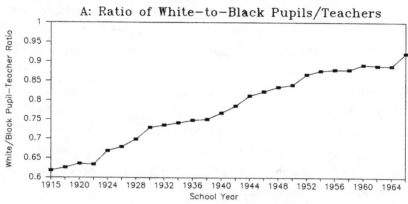

A: Ratio of White-to-Black Pupils/Teachers

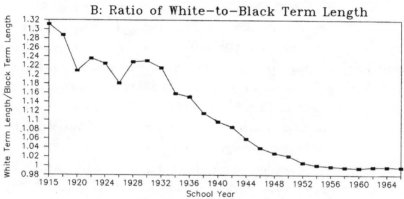

B: Ratio of White-to-Black Term Length

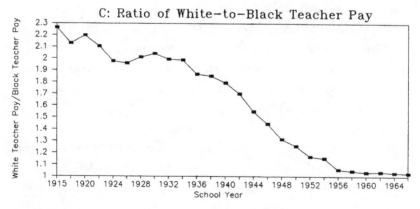

C: Ratio of White-to-Black Teacher Pay

Figure 5.1

Black–white school quality gaps, 1915–1965. *Source*: David Card and Alan B. Krueger, "School Quality and Black–White Relative Earnings: A Direct Assessment," *Quarterly Journal of Economics* 107, no. 1 (1992): 168.

Second, the nonviolent protest movement, led most prominently by Martin Luther King Jr., built up momentum toward the landmark Civil Rights Acts of 1964 and 1965. These laws kicked open the door to employment in all occupations.

This historic one-two punch appeared to lay a strong foundation for Black economic success. The playbook would be: gain skills in good integrated schools, then get jobs in good occupations now open to all races.

So how did things go? In 1970, Black men earned 50 percent less than white men. By 2014, they earned 65 percent less. The economic situation for African Americans got *worse*.[14]

What went wrong? Rising overall economic inequality is a major factor. Conditions grew worse for poor and working-class people of all races in America after the 1960s, and median wages have barely grown over this entire half-century period. Economists ascribe these trends to changes in technology that favored higher-skilled workers, stagnating minimum wages, falling unionization rates, and the failure of our education system to meet growing demand for college-educated workers. Centuries of discrimination left Black people disproportionately vulnerable to these trends.[15]

Another key factor has been skyrocketing incarceration rates, driven by harsh new policies such as the so-called war on drugs and mandatory-minimum sentences enacted in the wake of the civil rights movement. These policies increased nationwide incarceration rates after 1970 by a shocking *700 percent*, leaving about *one in ten* young Black men incarcerated at any given time in recent decades. By the 1990s, researchers estimated nearly *one-third* of Black men were cycling through incarceration at some point in their lives.[16]

Our nation has a long history of using criminal justice as a weapon to maintain white racial control, and new research over the past 20 years has documented the ongoing, staggering toll of this legacy. Racial bias begins with the choice of law enforcement priorities chosen by sheriffs. It continues with the initial detention and use of force by police. It then moves on to contraband searches and arrests, the size of fines, the severity of charges filed by prosecutors, the setting of bail, convictions by juries and judges, incarceration, sentence lengths, and use of capital punishment.

About three-fourths of the large Black–white employment gap for lower-income young men reflects the fact that so many more Black men are behind bars.[17]

Deteriorating conditions for lower-wage workers and mass incarceration hit even harder in the context of neighborhood segregation. Segregation had long been enforced by yet more racist practices such as restrictive covenants, redlining, exclusionary zoning, and straightforward terrorism. With minorities concentrated in distinct neighborhoods, they became more vulnerable to discrimination in public services such as education, transportation, and basic amenities, including clean air and water, garbage collection, and sewage. In some cases, upwardly mobile Black families have paid premiums for homes in higher-income, majority-white neighborhoods with mortgages secured at inflated prices, only to see their investments lose value as white families relocated to maintain segregation. Today, despite Supreme Court rulings that forbid explicit, legal forms of housing discrimination, real estate agents continue to "steer" Black clients disproportionately toward lower-quality neighborhoods.[18]

The combination of deteriorating incomes for lower-wage workers, mass incarceration applied with severe racial bias, and racial segregation in housing have left Black and white children growing up in radically different kinds of neighborhoods. Nearly two in three white children grow up in neighborhoods dominated by two-parent families with incomes above the poverty line. Less than *one in twenty* Black children grow up in such an environment.[19]

All these trends have pushed hard against Black economic progress in recent decades, curdling the optimism that prevailed in the 1960s as Martin Luther King Jr., A. Philip Randolph, Bayard Rustin, and other luminaries led the March on Washington, and President Lyndon Johnson assured Congress that "we shall overcome." But even without new obstacles, it is very possible that Black incomes would not have risen as dramatically as many civil rights advocates anticipated because the overall civil rights movement of the twentieth century was much more of a *beginning* than a resolution. Legal victories and new legislation really did narrow opportunity gaps in schools and occupations. But as we've seen,

American public schools provide only a sliver of the skill building that children need to pursue successful careers in adulthood because we still rely primarily on parents to build skills in children. *Brown v. Board of Education* and the civil rights movement barely touched the opportunities available to Black children during the 90 percent of childhood they spent outside of public school. Without anything even approaching equal access to skill development, Black children had little chance to capitalize on their new occupational opportunities.

You might be wondering why skill-building opportunities are so much weaker for Black children outside of public school. Well, we've seen how the legacy of segregation has left Black children to grow up in radically more precarious neighborhoods than white children, but this is only part of the story. The larger reason Black children face more difficulty in building skills outside of school is that many of the general obstacles to parental skill building in children weigh down Black parents with extra force.

Consider, for example, how asymmetric information bites harder for Black families. After getting burned so many times, it is easy to see why Black families may have developed greater skepticism toward new "opportunities." The broken "40 acres" promise of land redistribution after the Civil War; the great plunder of the Freedman's Savings and Trust Bank during Reconstruction; the medical betrayal in the Tuskegee Study of Untreated Syphilis; the massacre of "Black Wall Street" in Tulsa; the biased implementation of courts, unions, colleges, the minimum wage, Social Security, and GI Bills in education and housing—the betrayals have been kaleidoscopic and all-encompassing. Time after time, "opportunities" for Black people have turned out to be mirages or traps.[20]

Michelle Singletary, a Black personal finance journalist for the *Washington Post*, remembers this fear well. The grandmother who raised her refused to fill out the paperwork she needed to apply for federal financial aid to attend college. Singletary explains her grandmother "was afraid that disclosing her income and assets would somehow lead to her losing her home." This fear made perfect sense. Black people have seen their rightful homes seized by con artists, lawyers, and mobs throughout American history.[21]

So yes, sure, maybe all the very best colleges really are free for low-income kids. Maybe filling out the long invasive FAFSA really will bring thousands of dollars in federal financial aid for college with no strings attached. Maybe there really are nearby public schools and neighborhoods that can improve children's prospects at minimal additional cost. Maybe that free local Head Start preschool center really can improve low-income children's school readiness and later career outcomes. Maybe children's long-term health really can be improved by choosing a different diet or by implementing that complex asthma treatment the pediatrician recommended.

Maybe. Or maybe these opportunities are just more scams in a centuries-long string of betrayals. For all parents, but especially Black parents, it can be hard to tell. As the writer Damon Young puts it, "To question whether this bottomless skepticism is justified is like asking whether a cow has cause to be wary of butchers."[22]

And just like asymmetric information, all the other problems that parents face also bite harder for Black parents. Historical skill suppression means that Black parents have disproportionately been excluded from the kinds of training that help people identify and manage complex investments in child skill growth. The full tool kit of child skill building described in chapter 2—advocacy and negotiation, fluency in science and math and research, familiarity with educational and medical and financial institutions—consists of exactly the tools that so many Black people have been systematically denied for hundreds of years. Borrowing constraints—to the surprisingly small but still significant extent they matter—also bind more tightly for Black parents, who are disproportionately poor both in terms of income and in terms of the wealth that helps to cushion families against misfortune.[23]

This argument is easy to misinterpret. I am not suggesting that Black parents are worse than white parents. Most Black parents, like parents of all backgrounds, are in fact *experts* at caring for their children. If we talk about parenting in the right way, that means they are expert *parents*. As Ronald Ferguson, a Black economist and father of two, puts it,

We should not be surprised to find differences in how whites and blacks have coped and adapted over time to their positions in the nation's hierarchy of power and privilege. These differences reflect not only psychological self-defense mechanisms, but also social interaction patterns and disparities in access to opportunity. Such patterns help determine not only the economic wherewithal of families to provide for their children, but also the child-rearing methods that families grow accustomed to using and the ways that they understand and interact with mainstream institutions such as schools. There is no question that black parents love their children.[24]

Despite these reassurances, many people still worry that talking about the role of Black parents in child skill growth amounts to blaming Black parents for their children's economic setbacks. That concern makes sense. Often as a sort of backup strategy when other accusations of inferiority lose steam, Americans—specifically white Americans—have a long history of blaming minorities' "character" or "culture" for problems that are in fact rooted in discrimination. My argument here is *not* that we should blame Black parents for shouldering a monumental historical burden they never chose to carry. My argument is that the shadow cast by this burden is longer and larger than most Americans appreciate, that its consequences are insidious and pervasive today, and that Black families will need greater skill-building support to escape this shadow.

Are racial differences in parental skill development really large enough to account for any significant share of racial outcome gaps? To answer this, we need a way to quantify parental skill-building behavior. The most common measure of skill-building practices is known as the HOME assessment, or Home Observation Measurement of the Environment. It captures whether parents read to children regularly, discuss nature and science, explain numbers, letters, colors, shapes and sizes, and expose children to concerts, libraries, parks, and museums, along with many other practices considered beneficial for child skill growth.

HOME scores capture only a narrow range of parental skill-building behavior. They do not capture aspects of both caring and skill building where Black parents may have powerful advantages—for example, in teaching children how to navigate and reject racism or how to value an illustrious cultural heritage that has been widely ignored or misrepresented for most of American history. But in the subset of important parental practices that they measure, HOME scores indicate large Black–white differences.[25]

Based on rough calculations, the mapping of these differences into children's long-term outcomes suggest they could easily account for the *majority* of racial gaps in academic and economic success. This intuition lines up with other research concluding that broader measures of parental skill-building resources and practices can account for at least two-thirds of early Black–white gaps in academic achievement.[26] Measured impacts of discrimination in other systems—labor markets, law enforcement, housing—are large enough to account for the rest.[27]

In other words, there is not necessarily anything mysterious about the persistence of Black poverty, even after K12 school resources have been equalized and hard occupational exclusions have fallen away. In our parent-centric skill-building system Black children still have much weaker skill-building opportunities, just as they did under Jim Crow, because 90 percent of their skill-building time depends on the private resources of parents and communities encumbered by generations of structural discrimination.

This means the primary missing ingredient to realize the dream of racial equality is simple: much greater support for parents to build skills in children.

We saw this in high-quality early education programs that boosted early skill formation so dramatically for minority children. Greater support would mean easy, affordable access to these kinds of programs from infancy through the K12 years and continuing through to college and early career formation.

Skills appear to be the gateway to racial equality. But in a world still shot through by racist attitudes, how is that possible? Are skills really enough?

REALITY CHECK

Many people are rightly skeptical that closing skill gaps would close Black–white economic gaps. But there are three big reasons to be confident that equalizing skills would in fact be enough despite the persistence of racism in American life. One reason concerns individual skill growth. The other two reasons concern group-wide skill growth beyond what individuals can achieve in isolation.

The first reason for optimism is that Black people today who do have the opportunity to gain strong academic and professional skills wind up doing well economically in terms of both income and wealth.

Labor-market discrimination hits hard for less-educated Black workers. These Black workers earn lower wages than white workers with similar measured skills. They also receive fewer job offers, fewer promotions, and more dismissals for reasons tied to race, and the resulting experience deficit slows down their wage growth over time. These penalties concentrate in places where white people harbor more prejudice against Black people.[28]

But all this changes for the one in four Black workers with enough childhood support to graduate from college. If we compare individuals with similar cognitive test scores, Black college graduates earn *higher* wages than white college graduates. Studies that don't control for test score differences but examine earnings gaps within specific professions—lawyers, physicians, nurses, engineers, scientists—tend to find Black workers earn zero to 10 percent less than white workers. These gaps could reflect discrimination, unmeasured skill differences, or other factors such as geography. In any case, such gaps are small compared to the 50 percent overall Black–white earnings gap and reinforce the idea that closing skill gaps would go a long way toward closing income gaps. Once income and education gaps narrow, wealth gaps largely follow suit.[29]

A finding of small or even reverse wage gaps doesn't prove that Black college graduates escape the psychological toll of prejudice in their professional lives, but it does mean that Black workers are rewarded economically for building skills. The civil rights movement really did open up new opportunities. Perhaps this is why Black people report higher educational aspirations than white people and then follow through by obtaining more education than similarly skilled whites: they anticipate that skills will vault them out of more-prejudiced, lower-skilled labor markets and bring economic success.[30]

How is it possible that pervasive prejudice against Black workers does not necessarily yield large Black–white wage gaps for those able to obtain similar jobs? The reasons are choice and competition. In any local labor market, some workplaces operate with more prejudice than others. One study by the economists Kerwin Charles and Jonathan Guryan found that Black–white wage gaps depend entirely on the more moderate forms of prejudice that prevail among local whites whom Black people cannot easily avoid and don't depend at all on the most racist people in a local community. Prejudice still depresses Black wages significantly because in some places racism is so prevalent there aren't enough unbiased employers to hire all the Black workers. But in many other places, the white people who hire Black people are apparently quite reasonable compared to the fringe of local bigots.[31]

A famous example of this "choice and competition" dynamic occurred in pre–World War II Detroit, Michigan. In 1939, most Detroit automakers, such as General Motors and Chrysler, embraced openly racist hiring policies that excluded Black workers. Henry Ford saw the opportunity and seized it. The Ford Motor Company became known as a place where Black workers would be hired and paid wages equal to white people's wages in the same jobs. Black workers at Ford did not receive fully equal treatment, but they nonetheless gained enormously from their ability to choose among competing local employers.[32]

The same forces operate today for law firms, hospitals, schools, and all other organizations: a reputation for prejudice will push Black applicants to competing employers. This extra effort required of Black applicants to find unprejudiced employers is unfair and may help to explain the higher unemployment rates of Black workers as well as their lower wages. It is clearly much worse than a world free of prejudice, but choice and competition are still powerful reasons why racial wage gaps within similar jobs are often small or zero.

Even more surprisingly, this pattern is consistent with data going back much earlier in American history.[33] Paying Black workers less than similarly skilled white workers for the same work is not the way discrimination has typically played out. Instead, it has played out primarily by ensuring that Black people cannot get the skills they need to compete in the first place and by imposing blanket racial exclusions from entire occupations.[34] Now that blanket occupational exclusions have crumbled, the key missing link is equal access to skill development opportunities.

So that's the first reason to believe that deeper support for skill growth in Black communities will reduce racial income gaps: skills already do bring success for Black people with the opportunity to obtain them early in life.

The second reason to be optimistic that equalizing skills will bring economic equality is that group-wide skill shifts may undermine racist attitudes themselves. This is not about asking Black people to go out of their way to educate, convince, or cajole people out of their prejudice. It is about the automatic, ambient side effects of elevating a racial group's educational and occupational profile. If white people throughout their lives encounter more Black teachers and professors, managers and executives, engineers and entrepreneurs, nurses and physicians, the day-to-day contradiction between stereotype and reality will corrode prejudice for all Black workers, including those outside elite professions.

This is not just speculation. Racial attitudes are malleable, as are the ways people act on these attitudes. Today prejudice remains pervasive, but many Americans are willing to make friends, marry, and work across color lines in ways that would have been unthinkable for most of American history. Legal reforms, mass media, demographic shifts, and political leadership can alter prejudice, and evidence suggests a group's skill level can also matter. When high-skilled white and Black college students are randomly paired as roommates, for example, the white students' subsequent behavior toward other Black peers exhibits less prejudice. If a group's skill level affects how its individual members are perceived, then group-wide skill growth yields "double dividends" in the form of both stronger productivity and weaker discrimination.[35]

So the skills–prejudice link is the second reason. The third reason to focus on greater support for skill growth in Black communities is that it would short-circuit the downsides of de facto segregation in neighborhoods and schools. Direct efforts toward racial integration have unraveled in the face of continuing prejudice and deep market forces. One scholar has commented that "the problem of segregation is so entrenched in American culture and politics that solutions seem impossible." But a closer look suggests a focus on skills can break this cycle.[36]

The main reason segregation harms Black children is that we do not sufficiently support children's skill growth. If all children received high-quality early education, nutrition, health care, counseling, tutoring, and all the other critical skill-building investments that we currently foist onto overloaded parents, then vastly more children would start school on the right track. Classroom-disrupting behavioral and academic problems would no longer correlate with class and race starting at such young ages. Schools serving these students would no longer present so many challenges and would compete more effectively to hire and retain the best teachers.

In fact, it's obvious that certain kinds of voluntary segregation are benign for groups that already have ample skills. Think about world-class Historically Black Colleges and Universities such as Howard and Spelman or predominantly Asian American elite public schools such as Stuyvesant in New York City.[37] This kind of voluntary segregation may still have downsides—for example, it might obstruct mutual understanding or cultural cross-pollination—but it also has benefits. It allows minorities to avoid the distractions associated with prejudice and minority status, to build pride in their own rich cultural heritage, and to place more trust in authority figures who share their background. Consistent with this view, researchers have found that Black children learn more from Black teachers, and Black patients obtain better health care from Black physicians.[38]

Counterintuitively, we can see an example of this dynamic in Japanese internment camps. During World War II, America interned more than 110,000 Japanese Americans in isolated desert camps. These camps were hypersegregated: 100 percent Japanese American. Internment destroyed enormous wealth and traumatized a generation. However, the economist Jaime Arellano-Bover finds that this traumatic experience probably *improved* their career prospects on average. I want to be clear because economists can occasionally sound callous when talking about "data" divorced from the human lives that produce them: the internment of Japanese Americans was a national disgrace and a profound violation of human rights. But Arellano-Bover's finding nevertheless reveals an extreme case in which hypersegregation produced outcomes we can learn from, despite the abominable source.

One prisoner named Victor Ikeda entered camp as a vegetable broker. While in camp he learned how to sell insurance, and upon release he launched a successful insurance agency. Iwao Takamoto entered camp as a teenager, developed his drawing skills, and wound up launching a successful career in animation based on guidance from two fellow prisoners who had worked as art directors at Hollywood studios. Prisoners taught wildly popular adult-education programs in vocational subjects such as electricity, drafting, bookkeeping, radio, and machinery as well as English and the liberal arts. At the Minidoka camp in Idaho, "all of the instructors teaching technical courses possessed advanced degrees in their respective subjects." At the Topaz camp in Utah, where the famous artist and college instructor Chiura Obata led the Art Department, "seven out of twelve [music] instructors possessed advanced degrees in music, and all had prior teaching experience." Japanese Americans were already highly skilled, and the new skills and connections forged in the camps helped people move to better jobs in different occupations upon their release.[39]

Racial integration is surely a noble pursuit in many contexts. The legal scaffolds that have enforced segregation throughout American history— restrictive covenants, segregated schools, redlining, and all the rest—were always repugnant, and their demolition has been vital. But fixating on integration can also start to insinuate that Black people need association with white people to become whole. On the eve of mandatory school integration in Charlotte, North Carolina, in 1970, teachers from one proud all-Black ("segregated") public school wrote, "We have watched the efforts of integration, always meaning that blacks were to assimilate and, in fact, be absorbed by white institutions, white programs, white cultures. To this we say we are tired and resent your insult that you still presume our inferiority, that you still will presume that we are incapable of performing equally as well as whites."[40]

Writing about this tension during the civil rights movement, the historian Taylor Branch concludes: "Racial isolation and racial outreach can each be taken as foolish and cowardly or as wise and brave, depending on historical mood and circumstance."[41]

So—how essential is integration itself to equalizing opportunity? Do Black, Hispanic, Native American, and low-income kids all need to spend much more time around upper-class white kids to find success? Is there really something so magical about ski trips, Wes Anderson films, and avocado toast? Maybe not. Maybe all low-income and minority kids need to overcome negative spillovers is equal access to skill-development resources, not just in the stingy 10 percent of childhood covered by free K12 public education but more broadly. If a generation of minority children finally received much deeper and broader skill-building support, perhaps minority neighborhoods would no longer exhibit all the pathologies that prey on groups deprived of educational and professional success. Perhaps these communities would start to seem less like segregated slums reinforcing disadvantage and more like beacons of cultural pride. Think Harlem in its heyday, Little Saigon in Orange County, Little India in Queens, and the proud Chinatowns, Japantowns, and Koreatowns that dot America's urban landscape.

And that brings us to a fourth reason to be optimistic that skill development will bring economic equality: it's already happened for another group. Critically, this group never experienced slavery. But it did experience a century of deep, entrenched, institutional racism in America, and yet today the group is economically ascendant.

That group is Asian Americans, and their story is not the fable of cultural superiority we've been sold.

ASIAN AMERICANS

For several years I taught a college course called "Inequality of Opportunity in the United States" at Brown University. Every year I spent weeks describing the terrible impacts of discrimination against African Americans. And every year students would ask sheepishly about Asian Americans. Hadn't they experienced a lot of discrimination? Well, yes. Hadn't they started out poor, on average? Yes, that was my understanding. And aren't they just as rich as white people today, on average? Yes, pretty much.[42]

So what gives? I didn't know. And as I looked into it, I realized no one else knew, either. I read stories about the magical mind-expanding properties of rice farming, the superiority of Chinese mathematical symbols, the Chinese Imperial Civil Service Exam, the wisdom of a man named Confucius who died 2,500 years ago. All of this struck me as a bit elaborate, and I couldn't find any strong evidence that these factors had really prefigured Asian American economic success.[43]

Obviously, Asian Americans were never enslaved.[44] I knew any explanation had to start there. But there was still a puzzle. Asian Americans—a term I use throughout this chapter as shorthand for Chinese and Japanese Americans given their early predominance—first arrived in the United States in the nineteenth century without any conspicuously advanced skills.[45] They worked as manual laborers on railroads, mines, and farms. They were never enslaved, but they did experience 100 years of severe discrimination. Not the "You can't join our country club" kind of discrimination experienced by white immigrants such as Jews and Italians, but the "You are subhuman" kind of discrimination America has reserved for people of non-European descent.[46] Asian Americans experienced severe and pervasive discrimination, and yet by the 1970s they had somehow escaped poverty.

I quickly realized there was a simple reason why the origins of Asian American success had remained obscure: they are too small a group to study in most data sets. Progress on the issue would require a data set so large that it basically covered the entire US population, not only today but also historically. There is only one such data set: the US Census. In particular, the legendary (to data nerds) US Census of 1940 could potentially fill a major historical gap in our understanding of Asian American history.

This 1940 census covered all 132 million Americans alive at that time. Even better, it was the first census to collect information on earnings and educational attainment. This allows us to track economic progress better than in any prior census. The timing is also ideal because it just barely

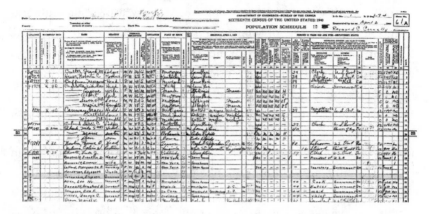

Figure 5.2

Example of raw data composing the US Census of 1940. *Source*: This page in the census covers the White House, whose residents were recorded just like all other American citizens. Downloaded from Ancestry.com, October 18, 2020, https://www.ancestry.com/imageviewer /collections/2442/images/M-T0627-00555-00436?treeid=&personid=&hintid=&queryId =809ea4947db8c22e39e314c95746f3d1&usePUB=true&_phsrc=Qgk21&_phstart =successSource&usePUBJs=true&pId=713024.

provides a unique window into minorities living in a world before World War II, when Jim Crow–style laws, practices, and attitudes still held full sway over American life.

There was only one problem: this data set was not really a data set. It was a mountain of documents, written with ink pens in cursive script. Turning these data into a proper data set that could be analyzed would require about 9 billion keystrokes. That would require hundreds of data-entry workers toiling away full-time for a year.

But then things changed. First, the underlying data became even more extravagantly useful in 2012, when the "72-year rule" kicked in. The 72-year rule stipulates that US Census records enter the public domain 72 years after their creation, the idea being that they would no longer be sensitive.[47] Suddenly, the full names and addresses of all 132 million Americans could legally be accessed by researchers or anyone else. Second, a company called Ancestry.com smelled profit. Ancestry is the world's largest for-profit company that helps people conduct genealogical research on their own family trees. From a business perspective, the 1940 census looked like a vast oil deposit waiting for extraction, so Ancestry teamed up with academics at the University of Minnesota to foot the bill to digitize the entire thing. Today, Ancestry is valued at more than six billion dollars, and census digitization is revolutionizing historical social science.

Armed with the 1940 census and a battery of other forgotten data sets, I was finally able to unravel some of the mystery of Asian American success.

The first finding was that Asian Americans had indeed achieved something extraordinary: their children were unusually upwardly mobile in every generation born at least back to the 1920s.

To see this pattern clearly—indeed, to think about Asian American history in general—we have to focus on California. California is the historical epicenter of Asian migration and of anti-Asian discrimination.

That means any comparison with Black economic mobility should focus on Black parents raising children in California. Fortunately, California was also an early home to many relatively skilled Black migrants who had abandoned the South in search of better lives. And this distinction turns out to be critical.

At the national level, Blacks always had much lower income than Asian Americans (still focusing on Chinese and Japanese Americans) due to a large concentration of very poor Blacks in the South. But in California things were different. Before World War II, Black families in California earned just slightly less than Asian American families. Thus, as of 1940 Black and Asian American children in California grew up in households with pretty similar financial resources. Yet after World War II only Asian Americans shot out of poverty and caught up to whites in a single generation.

So now at least we know the puzzle is real, not just an artifact of bad data. The question is, What happened? One common theory is that Asian American parents forced or cajoled their children to stay in school for longer than Black children. That turns out not to be very important. As of 1940, Asian Americans did exhibit higher education than other nonwhite minorities nationally, even after controlling for their income level. But that was just a matter of geography. All racial groups had unusually high educational attainment in California because California had a relatively high-quality and racially integrated education system. For any given level of family income, Asian American and Black parents in California raised children with similar educational attainment.

Another possibility is that Asians never really experienced harsh discrimination in California. This would mean they not only skipped slavery but also skipped Jim Crow. Is there any way to know *how much* discrimination Asian Americans faced in prewar California 80 years ago? This is a tough question, but many kinds of data point in the same direction: discrimination toward Asians was probably even harsher than discrimination toward other minorities in California.

One approach comes from an obscure body of research conducted by social psychologists in the 1920s and 1930s. At this time, researchers would ask (predominantly white) people to gauge their affinity toward different ethnic groups—and people would just answer because racism wasn't taboo. Some researchers asked respondents to compare their willingness to associate with one of two groups, such as Black people versus Chinese people or Chinese people versus Italian people or Japanese people versus Mexican people. They would then combine all these pairwise comparisons into a ranking of prejudice against different groups, much like we combine large samples of college football matches into performance rankings today. It was like the Prejudice Playoffs.

Other contemporaneous researchers asked respondents to assess how socially close they might be willing to get with members of various groups. Would the respondent be open to marrying an Italian or Black or Japanese person? Befriending one? Working with one? Living beside one? These data are kind of like the consumer-satisfaction surveys used in marketing. Like the Prejudice Playoffs, they also yield rankings of prejudice against groups.

All these data placed African Americans, Chinese Americans, and Japanese Americans toward the bottom of the prejudice hierarchy very consistently across the United States. In the two studies located in the American West, white respondents reported *greater* prejudice toward both Chinese and Japanese Americans than toward Blacks.

Of course, these data are still just survey reports—they do not reflect actual choices made by respondents. But they clearly do not support the idea that Asian Americans got off easy with respect to white prejudice relative to other groups *in prewar California.*

Other facts suggest pervasive white prejudice against both Asian Americans and Blacks in prewar California. Asian Americans experienced Jim Crow–style mob violence, including lynchings and more than 200 "round-ups" from 1849 to 1906, as well as open hostility from anti-Asian groups much like the Ku Klux Klan, including the Workingmen's Party of California and the Asiatic Exclusion League. This violence does not appear to have any counterpart for Blacks in prewar California history.[48]

There's also marriage. White people in California almost never married Asian or Black people. Much less than 5 percent of adult Asian Americans or Blacks of either gender living in California married whites in every census before 1970.

And then there's voting. Voters in California didn't hesitate to express their hostility toward Asian Americans. In 1920, 75 percent of California voters, both major political parties, and the governor all supported a direct ballot initiative to increase legal discrimination against Japanese farmers.

I also dug up some data on racial segregation across employers. The patterns were consistent with the tendency of markets to segregate workers in response to prejudice as minorities seek out unprejudiced employers. Most nonwhite workers in California were highly concentrated in a small number of firms, with many other employers—even large employers—hiring exactly zero or one to two nonwhite workers.

In fact, anti-Asian hostility has a much older and more virulent history than anti-Black hostility in the West, probably due to the greater local prevalence of Asians than Blacks.

If most citizens support discrimination, then democracy delivers discrimination. And that's what happened in California. From the mid-nineteenth century to well past World War II, all nonwhite groups in California faced discrimination in employment, union membership, marriage, court testimony, and residential segregation through restrictive covenants that closed off perhaps 75 percent of all homes to nonwhite owners.

And in California, many of these laws fell more heavily on the Asian American community than other nonwhite groups. Legally classified as "aliens ineligible for citizenship," Asian Americans born outside the United States were ineligible to vote, to seek political office, or to hold their own politicians accountable in normal ways, while also paying additional taxes and fees. Foreign-born Asian Americans in California also faced restrictions on land ownership and leasing in the form of the Alien Land Laws passed from 1913 to 1923. And during World War II, of course, the United States incarcerated nearly all West Coast Japanese Americans for multiple years. In addition to violating the Constitution and basic human rights, the chaotic internment process robbed the Japanese American community of a large share of its wealth.

Even in education, Asian Americans faced a harsher legal climate than Blacks in California. In a bizarre twist of racial jurisprudence, the California Supreme Court in 1890 prohibited segregation of Black children into separate schools but *permitted* segregation of Asian American and Native American children. And, indeed, while there are no records of legally segregated Black schools in California after this date, several legally segregated "Oriental schools" educated a small minority of California's Asian American students well into the 1940s.[49]

Asian Americans therefore faced all the normal contemporaneous obstacles confronting other nonwhite groups in California, plus additional legal disadvantages. If anything, this hostile environment should have made it *more* difficult for Asian American children to escape their parents' poverty, not less difficult. We thus need to look elsewhere to explain Chinese and Japanese Americans' upward mobility.

And this brings us to the most important area in which Asian Americans faced discrimination and the real secret to their success: *migration*.

FRUITS OF EXCLUSION

After the first waves of migration by Asian laborers to the West Coast, state leaders in California lobbied the federal government for new restrictions. The results were the federal Chinese Exclusion Act of 1882 and the Gentlemen's Agreement of 1907.

These restrictions barred migration of laborers and their spouses from China and Japan, respectively. From the passing of these restrictions all the way until the Immigration Act of 1965, only a small number of Asians migrated legally to the United States—and virtually all of them were merchants, professionals, or other skilled groups outside the broad category of "laborer."

Therefore, most Asian American children born in the United States after the 1920s—the children driving high upward mobility—would have been born to Asian American parents who entered the United States *after* restrictions set in.[50]

This means that for almost a century only a certain type of Chinese and Japanese nationals could start families in the United States. These people had something in common: they were highly skilled even before they migrated.

One way to see this is by examining educational attainment of Chinese and Japanese migrants to the United States in 1940 in comparison to educational attainment in their homelands. In 1940, Chinese migrants to the United States had completed almost seven years of schooling before they migrated. The average educational attainment in China at this time was a little more than *one* year. Thus, migrants had nearly six additional years of schooling—like the difference between a high school graduate and someone with a four-year college degree *and* a two-year master's degree. Likewise, Japanese migrants to the United States at this time had completed around nine years of schooling before migrating, compared to the average attainment of six years of schooling in Japan. By 1940 and probably well before then, Asian migrants to the United States were some of the most highly educated individuals in their home countries. It seems odd to search for the origins of these groups' success in ancient cultures of rice farming or Chinese number systems when such massive selection patterns jump out from the data.

Another clue to Asian immigrants' high skill levels comes from an astonishing new data set discovered recently in the US National Archives. Many Chinese Americans enlisted to serve in World War II and therefore took the detailed Army General Classification Test. These test scores were thought lost to history, but the economic historian Joseph Ferrie figured out that these scores had been accidentally entered into the "weight" field on more than 500,000 surviving World War II enlistment cards. In other words, for about three months in 1943 smarter people got recorded as heavier people.

These data allow a detailed comparison of test scores among Chinese, white, and Black enlistees in California in 1943, when Asian incomes still lagged far behind white incomes. Recruits taking this test had already passed physical and psychological assessments and were likely to wind up serving in the Army. If they scored higher on the test, they stood to receive more plum job assignments. Under these high stakes, most enlistees probably tried their best to perform well on the test.[51]

The results were striking. Much like today, Black, Hispanic, and Native American enlistees in 1943 scored much lower than white enlistees, even after adjusting for educational attainment. But for Chinese Americans there was no such gap—their scores were almost indistinguishable from whites. Japanese Americans are not present in these data because they had already been interned after the bombing of Pearl Harbor, but earlier research using test scores and grades also found high measured cognitive skills among Japanese school children in California.

Of course, immigration laws are just one ingredient shaping who enters the United States because immigrants, like all other groups, don't always obey laws.[52] But here, too, we find strong forces conspiring to raise the skill level of the Asian American population.

In 1906, the great San Francisco earthquake unleashed a fire that destroyed the immigration records of many Chinese immigrants. Many of these immigrants seized the "clean slate" opportunity to claim that they were in fact born in the United States, thereby gaining citizenship. By law, children born to US citizens abroad could also claim US citizenship, which created a black market in China for papers "proving" someone to be the son of a Chinese American with US citizenship as a way to secure access to American labor markets. Tens of thousands of Chinese migrants known as "paper sons" entered the United States using this trick. In 1956, the US government offered amnesty to Chinese Americans willing to confess to fraudulent immigration. More than 30,000 individuals confessed, about 15 percent of the Chinese American population at that time, and of course it's likely many paper sons did not confess.

In theory, paper sons could have been laborers and "sons" of laborers—they had found a loophole through the skill restrictions placed on new immigration. In practice, however, fake papers cost tens of thousands of dollars in today's currency, which would have excluded most lower-income families in a country as poor as China at that time.

Moreover, the US government soon caught wind of the scheme. Starting in 1910, it set up the Angel Island immigrant-processing station in order to interrogate Chinese migrants upon arrival and root out false family ties. Over the period 1910–1940, Angel Island agents rejected about 10 percent of immigration applicants, detained at least 6 percent of applicants in prisonlike conditions that could last more than a year, and ultimately deported 5 percent of arrivals. For immigrants, the costs of screwing up were high. Navigating these interrogations required potential migrants and their sponsors to study and memorize long texts containing detailed information about their fictional "family histories" prior to arrival. These histories could include family trees, characteristics of fake relatives, and features of homes, such as locations of staircases and colors of walls. Between the high price of fake papers and the difficult preparations required to navigate these interrogations, the "paper sons" loophole also likely selected higher-skilled migrants, much like the legal-exclusion restrictions.

When we take all these restrictions together—high financial and personal costs of entry, high educational and professional attainment, high motivation and persistence through bureaucratic hurdles—Asian American parents start to seem eerily reminiscent of another group of adults we have seen are particularly well suited to child skill development: *adopting* parents. The same issues that result in an advantageously "restricted range" in characteristics among adopting parents have also shaped the Asian American community.

What happened to the first waves of less-skilled laborers from China and Japan, such as the Chinese railroad workers? Did these lower-skilled

Chinese workers' children also experience upward mobility? Here's the short answer: *there were no children.*

At least, almost none.[53] More than *95 percent* of these early migrants were men. Most of these men returned to Asia, or they died alone in the United States. After immigration restrictions arose, these male laborers could not bring wives to join them in the United States, or if they left to start families in Asia, they could not return. By the early to mid-twentieth century, most US-born Asian American children were raised by higher-skilled immigrants who had arrived after the restrictions; they were not descendants of the laborers who had arrived in the nineteenth century.

In other words, the upward mobility of US-born Asian American children after World War II reflects the advantage of growing up with high-skilled parents, not a miraculous one-generation transition from downtrodden manual laborers to scientists and engineers. High-skilled Asian parents managed most of these children's skill-development process. Racially integrated, high-quality public schools in California managed the rest.

If Asian parents in the 1940s were high skilled and were imparting these high skills to their children, then why were their own incomes so low? In 1940, Asian American parents had incomes only slightly higher than Black parents in California at every level of educational attainment and more than 50 percent lower than white parents. These income gaps do not reflect English proficiency; even US-born Asian parents exhibited oddly low incomes.

Asian American adults in 1940 are in fact an anomaly: perhaps the only known example of a group with high educational attainment and high cognitive test scores but low income in American history. This low pay almost certainly reflects pure labor-market discrimination rather than lower skills. Asian Americans really could have been performing many higher-skilled, better-paid jobs given the skills they had brought with them from Asia, but no one would hire them: occupational walls stood firm. Asian Americans' unusually high self-employment rate at this time probably did not reflect some special entrepreneurial spirit. Rather, it reflected flight from jobs they felt were beneath their abilities. Apparently, discrimination before World War II in California was so harsh that even a relatively high-skilled minority could not get ahead.

And then things changed. They changed on the national stage but particularly in California. World War II was the turning point. Starting with President Roosevelt in 1941, the executive branch began prohibiting racial discrimination in federal agencies and in their vast network of private contractors. Soon after the war, California courts and legislatures overturned racial segregation in schools, laws against interracial marriage, and laws obstructing land ownership by Asian Americans. By 1959, California had passed a landmark law prohibiting racial discrimination by employers and unions, five years before the Civil Rights Act of 1964 enacted this policy nationwide.

By the 1960s, California was a new world. Employers, professional organizations, unions, and local governments faced crackdowns on racial discrimination, which had now become illegal. For Asian Americans, it was a bonanza. Many high-skilled Asian parents had toiled in low-wage jobs or operated small blue-collar businesses. Parents passed skills on to their children—as high-skilled parents of all groups always do in parent-centric skill-production systems—but now their children could actually apply their skills and their incomes shot through the roof.

As Asians found economic success, something interesting happened: they gained broader cultural acceptance that is still playing out today. We see this most clearly in rising white–Asian intermarriage rates. Apparently, toxic anti-Asian biases that prevailed in California for a century were anything but set in stone.

The life of Maxine Hong Kingston, the celebrated Asian American author of *The Woman Warrior* (1976), illustrates the pattern. In China, her parents had been educated professionals: her father a teacher and poet, her mother a trained midwife. Unable to find suitable employment after immigrating to prewar Stockton, California, they ran a laundry and gambling parlor. Despite their low income and working-class occupations, there was never any doubt Maxine would attend college. After graduating from high school in 1958, she won a scholarship to the University of California at

Berkeley, graduated with a degree in English, then worked as a teacher and author. She also wound up marrying a white man she met at Berkeley.[54]

In one sense, it was impressive that the daughter of working-class small-business owners could attend college and join the upper middle class. In another sense, Maxine Hong Kingston—like so many other Asian American children—was not really the daughter of working-class parents. She was the daughter of educated professionals disguised temporarily as working-class parents in the prewar California swamp of racial prejudice.

Asian Americans are unique among persecuted nonwhite groups in the United States. For African Americans, Native Americans, and many Hispanic Americans, skill destruction and suppression prevented many parents from orchestrating strong economic skill growth in their children. Legal reforms opened up the California labor market to minorities with strong skills to obtain high-paying jobs, but most minorities had not yet been able to accumulate these skills and therefore could not obtain these jobs any more than low-skilled whites could. Although antidiscrimination laws did boost earnings for Black workers, this increase was not nearly as profound or sustained as it was for Asians.[55]

In other words, Asian Americans skipped the hardest part of overcoming discrimination: they never had to lose and then regain skills. Discrimination undermined their income for a generation or two, making them blend in among other disadvantaged groups. Meanwhile, they were quietly passing on their high skills to their children. Then, when the civil rights movement broke down employment barriers, they shot into good jobs immediately, their imported skills finally gaining recognition and compensation.

"Confucian values" don't account for Chinese or Japanese American prosperity any more than "Ptahhotepian values" account for African American struggles. These Asian American children were set up for success in ways that no other nonwhite American minority could possibly have replicated. The upward mobility of US-born Asian American children reflects these special advantages, not some mysterious cultural antigravity. As Asian Americans got rich after World War II, China remained poor, and much of China remains poor today, alongside other Asian countries such as the

Philippines, Laos, Vietnam, Indonesia, Cambodia, and North Korea, while Japan's postwar economic boom has been stalled for decades. If Asians have a special cultural code for economic success, it sure hasn't been obvious in many of their native countries over the past few centuries.

A simpler story makes more sense. As a society, we leave skill building up to parents. Children benefiting from higher-skilled parents wind up accumulating more skills and doing better economically as adults. A large share of overall inequality, and most inequality between socioeconomic groups, reflects this differential management of investment in children's skills and all the potential productivity wasted along the way.

The real lesson from Asian American triumph is not that other groups can put on a new culture like some magical talisman and suddenly overcome the legacy of multigenerational skill suppression. It's that if we find a way to help these other groups manage the very challenging and expensive process of building skills in children, it probably will be enough to secure equality even if racist attitudes remain pervasive.

SKILL SUPPRESSION IN OTHER GROUPS

I have focused on African American and Asian American history to argue that structural obstacles to skill development are the primary cause of racial income inequality today. This view can also explain Native American and Hispanic American income gaps.

Like African Americans, Native Americans experienced widespread slavery in the United States. Many Hispanic Americans, descended from colonized Native American groups in Latin and South America, also experienced slavery both in the United States and in other countries before migrating to the United States in later generations.[56]

Both groups also experienced some aspects of Jim Crow–style institutions after slavery had technically been abolished. The federal government oversaw education and health care of Native Americans with minimal political accountability throughout the twentieth century. Periodic Senate investigations uncovered mismanagement, corruption, and disastrous levels of school quality. For decades, the government compelled many Native American children to attend segregated boarding schools that were devoted to cultural assimilation and were rife with abuse.[57]

Hispanic Americans also attended lower-quality schools in segregated neighborhoods throughout the Southwest.[58] The California Supreme Court case *Mendez v. Westminster* (64 F.Supp. 544 [S.D. Cal. 1946]) arose out of struggles for equal educational opportunity among Hispanic families in California and anticipated *Brown v. Board of Education* by seven years.

Today, researchers have found that earnings of Native and Hispanic Americans remain low but similar to wages of white workers with comparable skills. Once again, low incomes primarily reflect weaker skill accumulation during childhood rather than lower compensation for skills that have been successfully obtained.[59]

All of these groups have distinct, complex, monumentally rich histories, but one thing they all share in common is an experience of multigenerational skill suppression. As a consequence, children in these groups have received training and guidance from parents working with a weaker economic skill base and have grown up alongside similarly disadvantaged siblings and relatives. Meanwhile, educational institutions have exacerbated these disadvantages rather than compensating for them and continue to do so today through de facto segregation, if not any longer through legal segregation or K12 funding gaps.

So how do we help parents build more skills in children? That is the holy grail of racial equality in America today. Fortunately, the answers are sitting right in front of us.

6 GETTING MORE BY ASKING FOR LESS

BEATING THE MARKET

The fact that we don't help parents by publicly providing all the best investments in kids borders on collective insanity. What if you could open up a brokerage account and beat the stock market, no problem? That's basically the position we're all in, collectively, when it comes to investing in skill development for our own kids and for other people's kids through our public institutions.

We normally talk about "investments" in the context of stocks, bonds, real estate, and other business opportunities. Take stocks. If you had invested a dollar in the stocks of all US publicly traded companies such as Ford, Pfizer, and Amazon at any time over the past century, on average you would have earned an after-tax rate of return of about 7 percent per year. Put a dollar in today, get $1.07 next year. Over 20 years, $1 invested in US stocks has grown into $3.87 on average. That's the reward investors receive for waiting 20 years to spend the money they earned today and for accepting the risk that stocks can lose value, especially on a short time horizon. The total wealth created is greater because it includes new wealth paid to the government as taxes. That brings the overall or "social" rate of return closer to 10 percent annually. Warren Buffet, perhaps the most successful investor in modern history, has averaged a 20 percent annual rate of return. More risk-averse investors build wealth in safer assets such as Treasury bonds, which have typically yielded a 2–3 percent annual rate of return.[1]

Now, think about what happens if something better comes along. Say, it costs $1 million to start a multirotor drone factory that will earn $1.25

million in after-tax profit. That is a 25 percent return on investment (ROI), or nearly four times the return on stocks. At that rate of return, many investors will borrow funds to build their own drone factories. The resulting flood of new drones will decrease their price until drones are no longer so profitable. In this way, any investment with returns higher than 7 percent will tend to disappear rather quickly. In this world, the only reliable way to get higher returns is to accept greater risk—so you might earn 25 percent on your investment, but you also might lose all your money.

It's hard to pick stocks that perform better than a boring index of the entire market, which anyone can buy on demand from low-fee providers such as Vanguard. It's so hard, in fact, that economists still debate whether typical financial advisers who curate stocks for clients provide any value at all.[2] Just like it's hard to pick stocks, it's hard to come out ahead as a venture capitalist betting on new companies or as an entrepreneur trying to build new companies from scratch or as an existing company trying to create new products and services. There are not many easy wins in business for a simple reason: there's too much cutthroat competition.[3]

All this competition to snap up good investment opportunities is *great* for the rest of us, at least from a practical material perspective. When enough people want a product badly enough to pay for it, investors fund companies to make it. Over time, more investors jump on the bandwagon, driving prices down to the cost of production plus the return anyone can earn by investing in stocks. This means consumers wind up paying much less money for most products than what they'd be willing to pay if they had to, and that everyone willing to pay what it costs to make something winds up getting it.

Economists call this happy outcome "efficiency." Efficient systems feverishly realize potential value; inefficient systems squander it. What kind of system have we put in place to produce skills in children?

MISSED OPPORTUNITIES

For kids, there are no legions of experienced capitalists scouring the landscape to make every profitable investment as fast as possible. Potential investments in any individual child's skill growth hinge on the managerial acumen of just one or two parents.

This would be fine if most parents could easily master child skill growth. But as we've seen, that's not possible. Complexity, learning, over-confidence, mistrust, borrowing constraints, and spillovers cause many parents to miss out on great investments, thus costing their children hundreds of thousands of dollars in lifetime income.

Economists associate these conditions with extreme inefficiency. In this environment, though, we should expect ridiculously profitable investment opportunities to be common.

We can evaluate investments in children's skill development in terms of ROI, just like stocks and bonds.[4] The point here is not to view kids like financial assets. The point is to see how skill development stacks up against good alternative ways to save money and build wealth in younger generations. After all, any investment in a child's skill growth always could have been invested in financial assets on the child's behalf instead, earning interest over time as children grow up.[5]

Although it turns out that investments in skill growth often do beat investments in financial assets, not every investment in skill growth pays off. Only some do. The key thing about those skill-growth investments is simple: they don't ask *more* of parents, *more* of kids, *more* of teachers.

They ask *less*. And if they do ask more, they *give* more at the same time.

THE COLLEGE GAUNTLET

Let's think about one of the most obvious investments: college. The costs of college are tuition and the foregone income that students could have earned working and gaining experience if they weren't spending their time on college coursework. These costs typically add up to about $100,000 for a four-year degree. But over their lifetimes, college graduates earn nearly $600,000 more than high school graduates. They do so by developing economically useful skills in business, health, social science, natural science, and engineering, not by dabbling in wine tasting and basket weaving as many college skeptics seem to believe. If we just focus on this earnings benefit, the lifetime ROI in a college degree is about 15 percent.[6]

In other words, the return on a college degree is much higher than the typical return on stocks. But earnings are just a part of the value created by college. College graduates also enjoy more fulfilling, flexible, and secure jobs, better health, better relationships, and greater happiness—even compared to people who have similar incomes but didn't graduate from college. So the real ROI may well be more than 20 percent. It is almost impossible to get reasonably safe returns this high by investing in other financial instruments.

And once we include social returns to people other than the kids attending college, returns increase further. College graduates commit fewer crimes, claim fewer public benefits such as SNAP and Medicaid, and make their colleagues at work more productive.[7]

Despite these exorbitant returns, only one in three American children pull off a four-year college degree. To the trained eye, expanding college access looks like a very big missing investment and a very big opportunity.[8]

As we've seen, transitioning from high school to college is much easier for children when parents can manage the investment, but most parents are unfamiliar with the college ecosystem or too busy with other adult responsibilities to provide guidance. Programs bridging this gap offer prime candidates for high rates of return.

In one study, researchers tried two approaches: asking *less* of parents and asking *more* of parents. In the intervention asking less of parents, financial advisers helped them fill out the monstrous FAFSA. The FAFSA is 10 pages long and contains more than 100 questions that branch out into yet more forms and more questions. The researchers then explained how much federal financial aid the students were likely to receive and how this aid compared to costs at local colleges. For example, they might explain to a family that they would likely receive $5,400 per year of free money to help their child attend the local college, where tuition would be $11,000 per year, meaning out-of-pocket tuition would be $5,600.

Filling out the form with an adviser took eight minutes and cost $88 per participant. Those eight minutes of help both sped up and increased financial aid receipt, and ultimately raised college enrollment by about 0.2 years on average. These gains suggest about 2 percent higher earnings over the life cycle. Any low-cost intervention that raises college enrollment winds up delivering the same ROI as college itself, around 15–20 percent.[9]

The researchers also tried an approach that asked *more* of parents: they told parents how much financial aid they'd probably get if they filled out the FAFSA on their own. The results? No gains in college attendance.

Another team of researchers asked less of parents in a different way. They hired college students to act as mentors to high school students who were "on the fence" about college. These high school students had expressed interest in college and had the key academic requirements in place but were dragging their feet on applications.

The mentors provided the kind of support and information that many of the high school kids were not receiving from their parents. The mentorship program costs a few hundred dollars per recipient. It increased college attainment by nearly half a year. Half a year of college means about $50,000 of lifetime earnings. The rate of return on this program is also around 15–20 percent.[10]

Many other interventions that ask *less* of parents have nudged teenagers not only into college but also into higher-quality colleges. Examples include automatically guaranteeing financial aid to children before they even begin college applications, giving parents more organized and credible information about college costs, reducing the distance to college testing centers, automatically administering college entrance exams to all children, and defaulting students into sending college exam score reports to more colleges. Because all of these interventions facilitate more investments in college at virtually zero additional cost, they all yield very high rates of return.[11]

What about kids who don't want to obtain four-year college degrees or who struggle in academic environments, no matter how carefully their teachers and counselors nudge them along? Fortunately, young people also benefit enormously from good vocational training programs.

The federal government has sponsored a Registered Apprenticeship program for nearly a century. In 2019, a quarter-million new workers started apprenticeships in high-demand occupations such as construction, electrical repair, pipe fitting, carpentry, shipbuilding, welding, and information-technology support. Much like college, apprenticeships drive large income gains, high returns on public investment, and high job satisfaction among participants, but we invest almost nothing in these programs. The state of Indiana, with 6 million residents and the highest manufacturing employment share of any state in the United States, has recently employed *two* people to manage its entire state-wide apprenticeship program. As a result of underinvestment at a national level, the United States currently provides about one-tenth as many apprenticeships as other advanced nations.[12]

But are college and vocational training unique investment opportunities? Can it really be so easy to "beat the market" by investing in children's skill growth?

BABY COLLEGE

High-quality early education is expensive but yields big improvements in earnings, health, crime, and other outcomes later in life. Remarkably, the Abecedarian early education experiment raised children's future earnings by the same amount as college: about 12 percent per year of enrollment, or 60 percent overall. We may as well think about high-quality early education programs as a kind of baby college. Just as most rich kids go to college, most rich kids go to baby college. Their parents conduct baby college themselves (otherwise known as "stay-at-home parenting") or pay for high-quality formal programs or hire nannies to provide personalized care in ways that leverage parents' own personal and financial resources.[13]

The rate of return on high-quality early education programs can be very high, which might explain why rich parents are willing to shell out so much money and time to provide them to their own children. To give you a sense of how these rate-of-return calculations work, suppose a program costs $1,000 per child today and creates $10,000 of additional wealth in 20 years. This program would have an annual rate of return of 12.2 percent over that 20-year period, meaning the program is comparable to investing

$1,000 today in a financial asset that will pay 12.2 percent interest annually for 20 years.[14]

The overall annual rate of return on Perry Preschool—David Weikart's experimental preschool program for three- and four-year-olds in Ypsilanti, Michigan, in the 1960s—was 10 percent. The rate of return on Abecedarian—Craig Ramey's experimental preschool program in Chapel Hill, North Carolina in the 1970s, starting in infancy—was 13 percent. Abecedarian cost more, but the larger benefits more than made up for it. These figures include wealth created in the form of better health and lower crime in addition to higher earnings. However, they still omit impacts on total household wealth beyond individual earnings as well as many positive externalities on classroom peers and future colleagues.[15]

These numbers have astonishing implications. Five years of Abecedarian education cost around $80,000 per child in the original study. Another way to understand a 13 percent rate of return is that after 20 years that $80,000 investment had delivered more than $900,000 worth of goods and services for program participants and society more broadly.[16]

So investments in early education programs that increase the quality of children's learning environment can also "beat the market" from a broad social perspective. And yet, as with college, only a small minority of low-income families send their children to these kinds of programs because it is just too complex, time-consuming, and expensive for many of them to orchestrate these investments on their own.[17]

We can see this pattern starkly in the two largest national early education programs for low-income families in America. Both of these programs ask too much of parents, but one asks *way* too much.

The first and more sensible approach is Head Start. Head Start primarily serves preschool children ages three and four and to a lesser extent serves infants and toddlers through its Early Head Start offshoot. It provides relatively high-quality early education to about a million low-income children every year, typically in formal dedicated centers rather than private homes and with a strong dose of local control over program characteristics. The program was inspired in part by the preschool experiments by people such as Sam Kirk and David Weikart, who had drawn so much inspiration from the Iowa Child Welfare Research Station. Head Start emphasizes child skill development following a planned curriculum managed by trained professionals in healthy environments. For the most part, eligibility guidelines are simple and uniform: families qualify if their income falls below the federal poverty line. Once a child enters a Head Start program, she can remain enrolled until at least the end of the following year without having to reestablish eligibility.[18]

Head Start combines some good design elements of both the K12 and postsecondary systems. Like our K12 system, eligibility is pretty clear, and services have to meet basic quality standards. But like our postsecondary system, many kinds of public, nonprofit, and even a (very) few for-profit organizations can deliver the services rather than running all services through public entities such as school districts.[19]

Head Start is far from an ideal program. After half a century in operation, it still serves only about 40 percent of eligible children of preschool age and less than one in ten eligible infants and toddlers. Participation remains low for several reasons. First, legislation has never fully funded the program to guarantee a spot for every eligible child. Second, in contrast with Abecedarian's focus on convenience for parents, many Head Start programs do not provide enough care for parents to work a full-time job or save parents time and stress by offering transportation. Instead, Head Start pours resources into wraparound social services and complex governance structures mandated by the official Program Performance Standards. This means participating in Head Start can be a challenge for parents compared to using more convenient but (often) less educationally rich options such as family- and home-based arrangements.[20]

Depending on the perspective, Head Start can be thought of as underfunded or bloated. It spends about 40 percent less than a model program such as Perry Preschool, which offered very small classes with fully certified, college-educated teachers as well as intensive weekly home visits for all children. But Head Start spends 80 percent *more* per child than high-quality state preschool programs that don't offer such a rigid, expansive array of services. By spreading resources over so many different functions, some Head Start providers may wind up compromising the quality of their core skill-building services.[21]

Despite all these limitations, Head Start still drives significant improvements in child skill growth. The federal government funded a randomized controlled trial of Head Start called the Head Start Impact Study involving nearly 5,000 kids at hundreds of Head Start centers around the country. Results suggest a respectable 5 percent annual ROI if we focus only on individual earnings and a much higher ROI possibly exceeding 20 percent if we include impacts on health, crime, peers, colleagues, and other outcomes.[22]

So that's Head Start: a pretty simple way for low-income families to access reasonably high-quality early education without too much hassle or scrupulous research.

The other big federal program offering early education to low-income families in America is the Child Care Development Fund (CCDF). CCDF gives federal money to states to provide parents with childcare subsidies and currently serves more than a million children annually. If Head Start combines aspects of America's K12 and college systems, CCDF is reminiscent of K12 school voucher programs, but with unusually weak accountability and quality requirements. Compared to Head Start, CCDF has placed more emphasis on getting mothers into jobs than helping children build skills, and it tends to serve younger children. Despite these and other differences, comparing the two programs illuminates two very different approaches to child skill development. As it turns out, a freewheeling voucher program such as CCDF asks more of parents than Head Start. Much more.[23]

Every childcare center accepting CCDF subsidies manages its own snowflake application process involving its own arbitrary application fees and convoluted protocols. The application often requires multiple interviews, correspondence over phone and mail, invasive and complex paperwork, and at least one visit to a local agency in person during limited workday hours. These hassles are repeated every six months—more recently every year—as agencies reassess parents' eligibility based on minor changes in employment status, job-search behavior, hours worked, total earnings, and other factors. Parents who move or change work schedules face additional hurdles. Even after overcoming all these barriers, many parents wind up stuck on opaque waitlists with no further guidance. Anecdotally, many childcare providers decline to accept CCDF subsidies due to problems with families losing eligibility and defaulting on payment, which then results in fewer options and longer waitlists for participants. Whereas Head Start preschool serves around 40 percent of eligible children often for a year or more, CCDF serves only about one in 10 eligible children and often only for short, unstable periods as applicants' eligibility lapses. In fact, CCDF subsidies are so buried in red tape that many parents aren't even aware they exist.[24]

But red tape isn't the only way in which CCDF asks *much more* of parents than Head Start. Whereas Head Start mandates relatively high quality in all its providers, CCDF asks parents to assess childcare quality on their own.[25] Researchers have studied how low-income parents manage this burden, and the result is a rehash of all the usual skill-building problems. Parents don't have time to conduct thorough research and rarely consult available information about provider quality. Parents also exhibit overconfidence in the quality of their chosen provider and suffer from asymmetric information that prevents them from distinguishing better and worse providers in the first place.[26]

Faced with bewildering options, many parents wind up focusing disproportionately on the factors they can see clearly, such as cost, convenience, and cultural familiarity. The result is that educational quality takes a back seat. The best evidence on impacts of CCDF subsidies suggest they *reduce* children's skill growth. Similar findings have emerged for K12 school voucher programs that rely too heavily on parents to assess quality, and for publicly subsidized early education programs of inadequate quality in other countries.[27]

It's important to realize that asking *less* of parents need not mean excluding or ignoring them. Take, for example, the Child-Parent Centers. The Child-Parent Centers are a network of 20 public early education centers that have run half-day preschool programs in low-income neighborhoods around Chicago since 1967. Like many Head Start centers, they actively solicit parental involvement, but they go much further to accommodate the realities of parental life. Program administrators acknowledge that "busy life schedules prevent parents from following through in their commitment to participating at school events." Instead of excluding or scolding these parents, administrators search for ways to *serve* them. "If [parents] need a job, we can help them with resumes and applications. If they need a place to wash their baby's clothes, we invite them to use our washer and dryer." If parents live far from school, the centers provide "meet-and-greet teacher events in families' home-communities." Acknowledging that in-person meet-ups may not be feasible, administrators use text messages to "send parents reflection topics to work on at home with their children." This is what it means to *ask less* of parents while still leveraging their unique position to improve child development. And like Head Start, the Child-Parent Centers have demonstrated large positive impacts on children's academic and long-term outcomes.[28]

High-quality early education programs represent an astounding opportunity for nations to accelerate skill growth and build wealth. Making these kinds of programs easily, automatically available to children from birth would eliminate the massive skill gaps that separate children at the kindergarten door. Growing state and local public investments in preschool push in the right direction. These programs build on the best aspects of Head Start at lower cost and in some cases greater convenience for parents. But we've still barely scratched the surface of what is possible.

When we look for good investments both before and after kids enter K12 schools, we find extravagantly high-return opportunities foregone by millions of families. This is the essence of economic inefficiency. What about during the K12 years? Is there any limit to this inefficiency, or does it saturate every stage of childhood?

BECOMING A MAN

In 2001, a young counselor named Anthony Di Vittorio started mentoring a group of teenage boys at Clemente High School in Chicago. Di Vittorio is a massive, athletic figure with long, dark hair slicked back and gleaming with pomade. Di Vittorio grew up with four siblings and a single mother on welfare, surrounded by drugs and violence in a low-income Chicago neighborhood.

He credits his mother with instilling good values but sorely missed a father figure. "I met my first male mentor, a martial arts instructor who befriended and gave me life lessons and affirmation. I thought I was a man because I could bench 275 [pounds], smoke 3 joints and stay up all night. He taught me to push and focus and concentrate. I stopped smoking marijuana and grew up."[29]

Di Vittorio brought these experiences into his new high school mentoring sessions, but he didn't pretend to know what he was doing. The program evolved out of practice and repetition—the exact high-volume learning process that parents cannot achieve on their own. "I realized something unique and special was happening, but I didn't know what. I was bobbing and weaving. I was in one high school and a couple of grammar schools, working with white, Black, brown, and Ukrainian kids. I did hundreds and hundreds of groups, anywhere from 10 to 12 a week."

The program that emerged came to be known as "Becoming a Man" or BAM. BAM offered boys a new way to think about masculinity in terms of self-control, building on the ancient practice of initiating boys into manhood through formal rites of passage. In a modern twist, it leverages tools from cognitive behavioral therapy that teach kids to pause and reflect in tense situations, defusing rather than escalating conflicts. Some parents drill these kinds of skills into their children, but other parents may not have mastered these skills themselves and struggle to impart them at home.

In one BAM exercise, the facilitator gives a boy a tennis ball and asks another boy to find a way to get the ball. Most students dive into a wrestling match to grab the ball by force. After the interaction resolves, the facilitator asks if the student ever considered just asking for the ball. He then asks the other student what he would have done in response to the request. Typically, the student holding the ball replies that he would probably have handed it over without much fuss. Over and over, choreographed exercises like this help students to question their initial instincts and tap into broader options.

On its surface, BAM doesn't seem like a big deal. The program costs very little because it takes place in groups for one hour per week for less than a year. A cursory description can make it sound like the kind of self-help sideshow that naive, well-meaning college kids might dream up in their dorm rooms. I probably wouldn't have recommended investment in this program.

Well, I also thought the iPhone was a bad idea. Multiple large-scale experiments conducted by world-class, independent researchers find the BAM program makes a huge difference in children's lives. Arrests for violent crime drop by half during the program. High school graduation rates increase dramatically. We lack data on longer-term career outcomes among these children, but it doesn't matter: the savings from lower crime already suggest rates of return in the range of at least 500 percent, probably greater than *3,500 percent*. That figure is not a mistake—it's just as absurd as it sounds. The stock market yields a social rate of return of *10 percent*. BAM training for disadvantaged adolescent boys yields social rates of return that are *hundreds of times* larger. From society's perspective, funding programs like BAM would be like investing in Google back in 2001.[30]

It's useful to think about how BAM differs from the Parent Project, the court-mandated parent training program that I attended for twelve weeks. Both programs seek to help children slow down and make better decisions. The Parent Project tries to work through parents, whereas BAM hires counselors to work with children directly. In other words, the Parent Project asks *more* of parents, whereas BAM asks *less*. The Parent Project provides 30 hours of training to parents of all educational and professional backgrounds. BAM hires people with years of youth counseling experience as well as baccalaureate and even master's degrees. These people have already worked with hundreds of teenage children when they join BAM—compared to the one to three kids that most parents raise on their own. Then BAM provides counselors with *300 hours* of additional training—*ten times* the training provided to parents by the Parent Project.

However, few families whose children would benefit from programs such as BAM manage to pull off the investment on their own. Most schools don't offer such programs. Just as parents struggle to navigate complex college and early education landscapes, they also struggle to evaluate the extracurricular-program landscape. How do parents know that BAM is more effective than other similar-sounding programs? And how could they know this with enough confidence to seek out and pay for such services on their own?

The sociologist Margaret Nelson listened to a father explain his frustration around choosing extracurricular activities for his son, Sam: "I agonize over that a lot. . . . We try to make a decision as to whether these things are essential. . . . We're going to invest eleven hundred dollars next year in soccer . . . and it's not even the most competitive soccer echelon. . . . Summer camps and those kinds of things . . . you really don't know how beneficial they are and which ones are the good ones to do and given our financial situation, consideration of all those is always problematic."[31]

The lesson here is clear. Throughout all stages of childhood from birth through early career formation, if we make it easy for parents to access the best investments in their children's skill growth—ideally so easy it's automatic—then many families will participate, and our society will build wealth much more quickly, even compared to alternative forms of saving in financial assets such as stocks and bonds. In contrast, if we make it hard for parents to access these investments, then the investments will not happen.

When families miss out on key investments in skill growth, children face a dwindling set of options for career paths and personal identity. So what do children do when they approach adulthood facing only bad options? They choose one of them.

PERSONAL RESPONSIBILITY

Many Americans think we don't need to ask more or less of parents—we simply need to insist that children take more personal responsibility for their own lives. While I have focused on parents as managers of children's skill development, at some point in the purgatory of adolescence children start to become capable of making their own decisions, and it's right around that time when many kids start to make decisions that seem very bad.

Specifically, many teenagers get pregnant or commit crimes. Babies and crimes during adolescence are both associated with dropping out of school and starting adult life in poverty. Babies and crimes during adolescence are also much more common for children in lower-income families.

What should we make of these facts? Are these children making bad mistakes that ruin their otherwise bright futures? Or does inadequate prior skill growth leave these children with such bad options going forward that babies and crimes start to make a certain kind of sense?

Let's start with babies. Teen motherhood has declined dramatically since the 1950s in the United States due to a decline in teen pregnancy (not a rise in abortions).[32] Despite this decline, America still has the highest teen pregnancy rate of any developed country in the world. American girls don't have more sex than girls in other countries, but they use less contraception. And in states with the most teen sexual activity, contraception is *least* popular. That's how a state like Mississippi winds up with twice the teen birth rate of a country like Russia.

More sex and less contraception: it sounds almost like many of these teenage girls are *trying* to have babies. Why would they do that?

Are they counting on welfare to bail them out? Definitely not. Western European countries have much more generous welfare than the United States but much lower teen birth rates. We in the United States are uniquely stingy toward young, single mothers, yet we produce many more of them. And within the United States, the states with the *least*-generous welfare programs exhibit the *highest* teen birth rates. No one's having babies because they think their government will make it easy.

It also does not appear that teenagers simply need more information or stern warnings. Leading abstinence-training programs have been found, quite conclusively, to have zero impact on teen sexual behavior. Sex education programs focusing on contraception have shown somewhat greater promise but typically have small impacts at best. One of the most effective forms of sex education ever studied is MTV's hit reality show *16 and Pregnant* (2009–2014), which documents the grueling day-to-day life of teen mothers. Teenage girls who watch the show exhibit greater interest in contraception and also become significantly less likely to get pregnant.[33]

Policies restricting abortion vary a lot across states and over time, but these policies have only small effects on teen birth rates. When Medicaid expanded access to birth control in the 1990s among low-income women, it did reduce teen births slightly but not nearly enough to explain the massive variation across states and countries.

In fact, all the evidence points in the same direction: some teenage girls more or less decide to become mothers because they view motherhood as their best available "career" option. The problem is that they lack any better opportunities.

If teen pregnancy is really a reasonable option, we might expect it to have minimal impact on these girls' life prospects. To test this prediction, researchers have found many ways to compare girls with similar life circumstances but different age of motherhood. They have compared outcomes for girls in the same school and sisters in the same family. They have looked at outcomes for girls who get pregnant but then miscarry by sheer chance. They have looked at outcomes for girls who are more likely to avoid early pregnancy simply because they reach puberty at later ages. In all these studies, researchers find that for the girls most likely to become teen mothers, motherhood itself has minimal impact on their future education, careers, or marriage rates.

It appears motherhood is not derailing these women's skill development. Rather, it is a surprisingly reasonable response to their *already-derailed* skill development.

The sociologists Kathryn Edin and Maria Kefalas have interviewed hundreds of teen mothers over many years. They literally moved into a lower-income neighborhood, really got to know some of these young women, and dug into the kinds of considerations that gave rise to having babies. They wrote up their results in a fascinating book called *Promises I Can Keep* (2005). Here's what they found. These girls are not clueless. They understand that frequent, unprotected sex will lead to pregnancy. They also know they are not supposed to "want" babies they can't afford to raise confidently on their own. Some of these women abort their first pregnancy but then continue having unprotected sex and do not abort subsequent pregnancies. On some level, they know what they're getting into.

These women often told Edin and Kefalas how much they hated school, and no wonder. We have seen that low-income kids typically start out way behind in kindergarten after five years of minimal public support, then fall further behind as they miss out on more skill-building investments and hit more skill-corroding setbacks. By adolescence, school has become boring and frustrating because nothing makes sense and progress feels impossible. These girls also aren't "falling for bad guys" in the fun way described in edgy pop songs; they are simply taking the men they can get, and unfortunately that means men with a lot of problems stemming from mismanaged skill accumulation earlier in childhood—men very much like themselves.

Motherhood, even unmarried teenage motherhood, offers a sense of purpose that these girls have not been set up to find in any other sphere of life. Edin and Kefalas describe "the extreme loneliness, the struggles with parents and peers, the wild behavior, the depression and despair, the school failure, the drugs, and the general sense that life has spun completely out of control. Into this void comes a pregnancy and then a baby, bringing the purpose, the validation, the companionship, and the order that young women feel have been so sorely lacking. In some profound sense, these young women believe, a baby has the power to solve everything."[34]

Edin and Kefalas are describing girls who have been failed by our skill-development system, whose parents, despite the expertise many of them forged in caring about children as parents, were unable to equip them with tools required for educational persistence and economic success. These girls needed someone to help manage their skill-development process more fluently. By placing this burden primarily on parents, American society failed to provide that service.

Demanding greater personal responsibility from girls won't change their so-called bad behavior. For girls left behind by our skill-production system, teen motherhood *is* their expression of personal responsibility. If we want to see different behavior, we have to provide greater skill-building opportunities before kids reach adolescence.

All of these same patterns hold for crimes committed by young men. Men ages 15 to 25 commit most of the so-called index crimes recorded by police: murder, rape, robbery, aggravated assault, burglary, larceny, and motor vehicle theft.[35] Just as the United States stands out in terms of high teen-pregnancy rates, it stands out in terms of incarceration rates. And it's in a league of its own when it comes to *juvenile* incarceration.

The United States incarcerates children at five times the rate of any other country in the world, including China and Russia.[36] This is very expensive. It costs $88,000 per year to incarcerate a child, or nearly seven times as much as keeping that child in school.[37] And not only does it fail to help children, it strips away skill-development opportunities even further. Young people convicted of felonies lose access to many basic rights and benefits of citizenship, such as college scholarships, public housing, welfare, and voting.[38]

Why do so many young American men commit crimes despite all these harsh consequences? Are they throwing away bright futures? Or are they, like teen mothers, acting under constraints that have already throttled their future prospects?

The first important fact is that most crimes, perhaps more than 95 percent of them, go unpunished. It's simply too hard to catch most perpetrators in a society as (thankfully) free and open as the United States. So it's not hard to see how one-off or occasional crimes don't seem crazy to young men seeking additional income and who may be intuitively familiar with these odds.[39]

Second, arrests, incarceration, and longer sentences have surprisingly small negative impacts on these particular adult men's postrelease employment and earnings.[40] These studies rely on methods that control for hard-to-observe differences between individuals who get caught up in the criminal justice system and those who do not. One approach measures how people's earnings and employment change before and after experiencing an arrest or incarceration spell. Another approach compares people charged with identical crimes but randomly assigned to more and less severe judges. The individuals assigned to harsher judges wind up facing higher conviction rates and longer sentences due to random chance.

Unsurprisingly, incarceration does harm people. After their release, employment and earnings fall slightly from what they would have been otherwise. But the size of these impacts is surprisingly modest; they are smaller than impacts of common events such as layoffs and hospitalizations.[41] Harsher penalties also increase conviction rates for new crimes in the future, especially theft and drug-related crimes, consistent with adverse impacts on opportunities for lawful employment.

How is it possible that going to jail harms labor-market outcomes less than being laid off from a job? The reason is that people who go to jail tend to have such bad labor-market outcomes to begin with that there is little additional room for deterioration. Most of these men are not working in formal jobs, and those who do work earn poverty-level wages. Incarceration eats up men who already have very weak opportunities and spits them out with slightly weaker opportunities.

As we have seen, earnings largely reflect skills, and on average these men accumulate few productive skills before reaching adulthood. They are products of a long investment process that we foist almost entirely on parents. Just as some young women deprived of earlier skill investments turn to premature motherhood as a best bad option, some young men deprived of earlier skill investments turn to crime.

Impacts of incarceration are not always small. Most studies look at impacts on young men. Impacts of incarceration at earlier ages, during adolescence, are terrible: high school graduation rates collapse and future criminal behavior explodes.[42] Jail does not scare impetuous adolescents out of ruining their bright futures with a dose of "personal responsibility." It just darkens the long shadow of a skill gap acquired earlier in childhood.

Risky adolescent behavior is not a coincidence or a failure of "character" or a cultural malady. Our society has chosen to make parents responsible for managing 90 percent of children's skill-development process, thereby assuring vast inequality in skill growth. After 14 or 16 or 18 years in this system, some children are left with few skills and have no good options. The result of bad options is bad choices.

The path forward is not to demand more personal responsibility of children, any more than it is to ask more of parents. The path is to ask less of parents, and give more to parents, in some very big ways.

FAMILYCARE: THE DOOR TO THE ALTERNATE REALITY

What would it look like if we really invested in child skill growth by asking *less* not *more* of parents? It would look like professional experts managing more than the meager 10 percent of children's time currently managed by our public K12 system—much more. It would mean public funding for services that parents would no longer have to develop, identify, manage, and finance on their own.

It would look like a new policy package we might call "Familycare," the missing counterpart to Medicare.

Medicare solves elderly people's health problems. Familycare would solve young people's skill problems. Medicare costs $750 billion per year. Familycare would cost much less. Medicare benefits the elderly and all the rest of us who love them and hope to join their ranks in the future, but it doesn't do much for taxpayers. Familycare would benefit young people and all of us who love them, *and* it would yield massive benefits to taxpayers—as well as to anyone else who works, studies, marries, buys things, enjoys art, starts companies, or engages in any other activity dependent on the fully developed talents of other people in our society.

If we focus on the tax benefits alone and ignore all these other profound benefits, Familycare would increase future tax revenue by so much it would simply pay for itself. What does that mean? It means that for taxpayers starting their working life in the year that Familycare became law, the program would be expected to *lower* their lifetime tax burden—or, alternatively, to *increase* their receipt of valuable public services such as high-quality roads, schools, health care, and military security. How is that possible? As Familycare caused younger generations to reach adulthood with greater skills, they would earn more money and pay more in taxes. Governments would then choose between lower tax rates or better public services.

Familycare would essentially scale up the kinds of highly effective skill-development programs discussed throughout this book, which raises a concern. For a number of reasons, scaling up small experimental programs can sometimes dilute their quality. Small experimental programs may leverage an elite research team's unique talents, or freedom from real-world constraints such as red tape and lobbyists, or the unusual behavior of subjects recruited to act as guinea pigs in novel experiments. Fortunately, most of the key components of Familycare, from preschool to financial aid to apprenticeships, have already proven they can deliver major benefits at scale. In many cases where program impacts have not scaled as hoped, the main problem has been underfunding, which Familycare is specifically designed to address. Underfunding is not a mysterious, intractable problem; bridges and tunnels also "don't work at scale" if builders can't buy enough concrete and steel.[43]

I here describe the core features of one version of Familycare and provide more details in the appendix. The program is not a pipe dream. I helped write a version of Familycare into the policy platform of Pete Buttigieg's presidential campaign in 2020. The landmark American Families Plan, recently outlined by President Joe Biden, points in a similar direction even if it still asks too much of parents in some key ways.[44] More Americans are starting to recognize that serious public support for parents and children, much like public support for our military, advances our core shared interests as a nation.

Familycare would start with paid family leave, so parents and children don't have to get acquainted under a cloud of logistical and financial stress. New programs such as Creating Moves to Opportunity (discussed in chapter 2) would help more parents choose auspicious places to live and raise children and then capitalize on these opportunities by helping them apply for apartments, negotiate with landlords, sign contracts, and front security deposits in a pinch. As a matter of basic respect and good faith, Familycare would build on existing support for infant nutrition by assuring access to diapers and other infant essentials. Familycare would then provide universal access to full-day, full-year, high-quality early education programs built on successful models like Abecedarian and large-scale public-preschool programs. Quality, evaluation, and improvement over time would be essential; lower-quality programs have caused substantial adverse impacts on more-advantaged children in other contexts. These early investments would provide all kids with the healthy parent–child bonding and "baby college" experience that rich kids get as a kind of birthright. Acute stress would decline for millions of working parents.[45]

Familycare would continue with richer support for kids outside of existing K12 school hours and calendars. Additional resources would enable tutoring, extracurricular engagement in the arts and sciences, sports, politics, and business, and other interventions to address nutrition and health not only after school but also over weekends and longer breaks to suit the needs and interests of local families. The success of these initiatives would depend on their timing, content, design, and targeting. Done wrong, these kinds of programs have failed. Simply making classes or school years longer or adding a lightly supervised free study period to an already-tiring school day can harm participants and exacerbate existing inequalities. Done right, however, these programs have enriched children's lives. To assure high-quality programs, this aspect of Familycare would need to expand gradually and to include ongoing evaluation of different approaches. If successful models could be scaled up over time, they would further alleviate the overwhelming parental burden to manage children's homework, after-school time, and summer activities on their own. Empowering local public and nonprofit organizations to manage a larger share of children's skill development echoes a rich "community school" tradition stretching back more than 100 years.[46]

Familycare would streamline the college application and financing systems and provide richer forms of guidance during high school. Increased college financial assistance would cover not only tuition and study materials but also room, board, and transportation, so that college would represent a *comfortable* option for all kids, not just rich kids. Additional support programs would improve college persistence, graduation, and transition into the workforce. For children not interested in four-year college degrees, expanded funding for vocational programs such as apprenticeships would link college coursework more tightly to on-the-job training. All these programs would ask virtually nothing of parents; they would simply provide professional services directly to children. The new approach would make it *as easy as possible*—almost automatic—for children to harness effective training toward lifelong economic independence and productive service to their community and country.[47]

We would provide generous health care for all children's physical and mental health needs starting from birth. Medicaid, which serves low-income parents and children, pays only 72 percent of the reimbursement provided by Medicare, which serves the elderly. This stingy reimbursement rate prevents many health-care providers from accepting Medicaid and makes it harder for parents to keep their children healthy. It is also symbolically important that children's health care receive at least equal public support relative to health care of other groups.[48]

As children spend more time in publicly subsidized, high-quality learning environments starting from younger ages, new opportunities will arise to shift the burden of skill building from individual, overloaded parents to paid, experienced professionals operating effective programs at scale.

One very concrete example that many parents will relate to immediately is nutrition. Every day, millions of harried, working parents around the country independently cobble together meals and snacks for their children to bring with them to school. Under Familycare, this nonsense would no longer be required. Childcare centers, schools, and colleges would offer high-quality meals in bright, pleasant environments by means of public subsidies that guarantee affordable prices. By exposing children to nutritious foods routinely starting in early childhood, we can alter children's lifelong tastes and habits. Parents would no longer be the only defense against the onslaught of cheap, addictive food that leaves many children struggling with obesity before they are old enough to understand what "nutrition" or "obesity" even mean.

This is a snapshot of what a program such as Familycare might look like. At every step, Familycare would ask less of parents and more of publicly financed professionals. This is a vision for a country that takes skill development seriously rather than demanding that isolated, overloaded volunteers build the foundations of our economy in their spare time.

The public has been free-riding on the generosity of parents for too long. It is time to do right by parents and kids.

TOO EASY

Something seems wrong here. Finding great investments at every stage of childhood across such a wide range of children should not be so easy. It's as if we could easily find undervalued stocks, buy them, and make a fortune over and over again. Most experienced financial investors can't "beat the market" successfully. Why is it that so many child-development researchers seem to possess the investment acumen of Warren Buffett?

Indeed, something is wrong. Each child's skill-development process is still managed almost entirely by one or two loving parents from all walks of life. These parents labor under all the burdens we have seen including complexity, limited learning and feedback, overconfidence and mistrust, borrowing constraints, and spillovers. If every company trying to do something difficult had to hire one or two volunteer managers at random from the general population as its CEOs, isolate these individuals from reliable information or clear feedback, and forego all access to lending or outside investment—then yes, in that world sensational business opportunities would likewise routinely fall through the cracks.

In a way, the whole situation is puzzling. If it really is possible to increase productivity and wealth on a massive scale while reducing inequality, crime, and teen pregnancy, wouldn't America have made these investments long ago?

No, unfortunately—America and most other countries have some pathologies that block these investments. And, in fact, we'll see the situation is even more absurd than it sounds. Researchers have identified a lot of fabulous investments in child skill development. However, even a century after the women's progressive movement created the US Children's Bureau and Cora Hillis made way for the Iowa Child Welfare Research Station and half a century after Eunice Kennedy Shriver blazed a path for the National Institute of Child Health and Human Development, we have still barely even started trying to take advantage of these investments or build on them with any kind of urgency.

To understand why that is and—more importantly—to *change* it, we have to remember how a country like America makes decisions.

7 WHY WE DON'T INVEST IN SKILL DEVELOPMENT

UNFINISHED BUSINESS

Child skill development is the largest and most important industry in America. But just as in Cora Hillis's time 100 years ago, it still doesn't look anything like other industries.

Start with research and development (R&D). R&D helps industries increase efficiency over time. Think about military research on radar and computers, federally funded biomedical research on genomics and disease, Google's research on self-driving cars, or Merck's research on vaccines. Similar kinds of R&D on children yield new skill-building technologies ranging from folic acid supplements during pregnancy to the Carolina Infant Curriculum. R&D can also develop better ways to scale up effective programs without losing their punch.

In most industries, R&D combines a healthy mix of public and private funding, with governments covering the more fundamental, long-term, high-risk investments and private industry carving out a path from scientific discovery to marketable product. But the main institutions responsible for building skills in children—families, schools, school districts, and state departments of education—conduct little R&D, which leaves virtually all R&D on children to the federal government. Although many agencies conduct R&D on children, the single largest contributor is the Eunice Kennedy Shriver National Institute of Child Health and Human Development, the agency that funded Craig Ramey's Abecedarian preschool experiment and launched a thousandfold increase in research on child development relative to the Iowa Station's humble beginnings.[1]

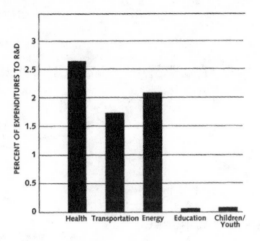

Figure 7.1

Share of expenditures devoted to R&D by sector, 1995. *Source*: Neal Lane and Harold Varmus, *Investing in Our Future: A National Research Initiative for America's Children for the 21st Century* (Darby, PA: DIANE, 1997), 22.

This investment was a big improvement, but viewed in the right context it's still tiny. Figure 7.1 shows the share of R&D in total spending in several other industries. R&D is around 2 percent of spending in health, transportation, and energy, which amounts to hundreds of billions of dollars. For example, the health-care industry has typically spent more than $100 billion per year on R&D since 2000. For child development, R&D spending is less than one tenth of 1 percent of total public spending—and basically zero as a share of public and private spending combined.[2]

In other words, the single largest and most important part of the US economy spends almost nothing on R&D to improve productivity over time. There is only one word to describe this behavior: *stupid*.

Once we appreciate the pittance we devote to understanding child skill development, some things that seemed puzzling begin to make more sense. Why were the Perry and Abecedarian experiments, among the most important social science projects ever conducted, so *small*—especially in comparison to routine clinical trials for adult drugs? Why have only a handful of large-scale social experiments tackled the monumental questions around how to craft more capable adult human beings, rather than hundreds of ambitious new studies every year? Why has the Parent Project only recently eked out its first kind-of-sort-of rigorous program evaluation after being court-mandated for nearly half a million families over 30 years? Why hasn't the federal government updated the landmark Head Start and Early Head Start Impact Studies or many other important experiments to see how these investments affect children's educational attainment, crime, teen pregnancy, employment, and other long-term outcomes, even though the participants are now well into adulthood and even though the IRS Databank and other administrative data sets have long rendered these follow-up studies relatively straightforward?

If the child-development industry spent a similar share of its total expenditure on R&D as other industries, its R&D spending would be around $100 billion per year. That's about *100 times* current levels. Cora Hillis's main point, that we take R&D in child development far less seriously than we take R&D in other critical sectors such as agriculture in her time and health or energy in ours, remains as true as ever. Why haven't we fixed this problem?

THE WORLD'S LARGEST DISENFRANCHISED MINORITY

Why doesn't our society invest more in understanding and improving child development? Because children can't vote. That's all there is to it.

It's not that children *should* vote; it's that children's inability to vote discourages politicians from serving their interests. Young people are the world's largest disenfranchised minority.

Parents can vote, but indirect representation is cold comfort. Women, racial minorities, poor people, "commoners"—every disenfranchised group in world history has been robbed, exploited, and ignored. It didn't matter that men claimed to represent women, white people claimed to represent nonwhite people, and wealthy landowners claimed to represent laborers. Only strong, direct representation has ever safeguarded a group's interests.[3]

As if that weren't hard enough on children's interests, America also makes it harder for their *parents* to participate in democracy. Younger and lower-income people—people such as young adults and parents—vote at around *half* the rates of older and richer people. So not only are children disenfranchised, but they remain underenfranchised in early adulthood, and their political custodians are also underenfranchised. For children, democracy is like trying to hold someone accountable by yelling at their uncle's former roommate's dentist.

The most obvious contrast for young people's lack of power is elderly people's surfeit of power. Elderly people vote at about twice the rate of young people raising children.[4] Elderly people lobby through the AARP, one of the most powerful organizations in the country. The AARP has 38 million members, each paying $16 per year.

Children do not have a monolithic lobbying juggernaut; they have a collection of smaller groups such as the Children's Defense Fund and Save the Children. In many years, lobbying expenditures on elderly people's interests exceed those on children's interests by more than 10 to 1.[5]

No voting and no lobbying mean no power, and policy makers respond accordingly. For every $1 of federal, state, and local public funds spent on a child, more than $2 are spent on a senior citizen. At the federal level, it's more than six to one in favor of the elderly. Private spending doesn't come close to compensating for this overall gap.[6]

Much of this greater spending on the elderly represents health care to address elderly people's costly health problems. But children likewise have costly skill problems—and as crass as it may be to say, those skill problems will be with us for a long time as their impacts compound and ripple through families, communities, and generations. The health problems of an 88-year-old? Not so much.

The elderly get a massive public program called Medicare. Children should be getting a comparable skill-development program such as Familycare, but it doesn't exist.

And, really, why is it that elderly people have such high medical expenditures? It's because medical technologies have advanced enormously over the past 50 years, creating many new ways for elderly people to spend money on their health. This is wonderful, and I'm grateful that my family and I can benefit from all this innovation. But while we've spent hundreds of billions of dollars developing these technologies for elderly adults, we've spent almost nothing on developing technologies for improving child skill development. That is the R&D gap coming to life. There should be a wide range of fancy, expensive treatments addressing children's various skill deficits; we just haven't bothered to develop them. Then we justify low spending on children by claiming they don't have anything expensive to buy.

Even the basic criteria we use to justify policies are different for elderly people. Researchers and policy makers sometimes suggest we should invest in young people if there is rigorous causal evidence that the returns on that investment are high or even that the policies "pay for themselves" in terms of higher tax revenue. That is an extremely high bar. Meanwhile, for investments in elderly people we simply ask if a new treatment has any benefit at all, no matter how small, no matter how expensive. Publicly financed Medicare frequently reimburses $10,000 per *month* for a new cancer treatment that might extend an elderly person's life by only a few months.[7] A single month of such costs are more than enough to provide a child struggling in school with an entire *year* of supplemental tutoring, something virtually all school districts consider prohibitively expensive.

Elderly people have spent their lives contributing to society, and they deserve great public services such as Medicare. But children have been born into our society—through no choice of their own—and they also deserve public assistance. It makes no sense to provide elderly folks with an almost-all-you-can-eat buffet to solve health problems big and small but provide children with leftover crumbs to build skills for a lifetime. If we focus on just health care alone, every dollar spent on care for children saves many times more lives and yields more years of healthy life than every dollar spent on the elderly.[8] It would be impossible to maintain current spending patterns if children held remotely equal seats at the table of democracy.

But children never will vote; it's a glitch in the very idea of democracy. So here is the one area where we certainly have to ask *more* of parents. It is up to parents—and to people who appreciate the sweeping benefits of this approach, whether they have kids or not—to advocate for children's political interests.

There is already a great deal of bipartisan agreement around some aspects of Familycare. Nearly 90 percent of Americans—including 75 percent of Republicans—support public investments to make high-quality early education universally affordable.[9] The main obstacle to political unity around child development more generally is a web of falsehoods that has served to pit parents against each other and blind them to the possibility of radical improvement. These falsehoods include, most prominently, the Myth of Nonaffordability, the Myth of Zero-Sum Parenting, and the Myth of Government Failure—and it's time we put them to rest.

THE MYTH OF NONAFFORDABILITY

Many parents buy into the dogma that taxpayers can't afford a larger role in child development. This is the Myth of Nonaffordability.

Right away, the entire concept of "affordability" is a red herring. Is military readiness affordable? Are roads and sewage systems affordable? Can you afford to fix the flat tire on your car? The hole in your roof?

Good investments cost money. Responsible adults make them anyway. Unlike claims that large tax cuts for rich families and corporations pay for themselves, the claim that Familycare would pay for itself is backed by all the credible evidence we have discussed on investments in children's skill development. Familycare is like fixing a flat tire or a leaky roof—it protects us from more painful and expensive problems down the road. The only thing more expensive than making these investments is *not* making these investments.

And, in fact, the costs involved are modest. I show in the appendix that Familycare would cost something like 2 percent of GDP. Let's put this number in perspective.

Today we spend 4 percent of GDP on Medicare. That means we could implement Familycare for half the money we currently spend on health care for the elderly. If we can't afford public investment in child skill development, then we definitely can't afford public health care for the elderly—but of course we can.

Alternatively, we currently spend about 3.2 percent of GDP on the military. If we want, we can think of Familycare like a new military, but instead of protecting us from foreign threats, Familycare protects us from a dire domestic threat—the destruction caused by foregone investments in children's skill growth.

Here's another angle. Over the past 50 years, the richest 1 percent of Americans have gotten a big raise. After taxes, they now keep about 7 more percentage points of GDP than they used to.[10] Many of these people are talented, work hard, and do great things that benefit all of us. Others get lucky or find ways to cheat the system at other people's expense. Whatever you think about the richest people in America, it's hard to argue they have become so much *more* talented or *more* hard-working than all other families over the past 50 years that they deserve this gigantic pay raise. So it certainly seems reasonable to use a third of this regressive windfall to fix our broken skill-development system.

In addition to being affordable, Familycare would create about 6 million new jobs in child care, teaching, counseling, administration, and other human services. These professions involve hard, creative, valuable work that cannot easily be replaced by artificial intelligence or offshored to foreign countries. The new jobs would be dispersed geographically throughout the United States in proportion to the distribution of children, especially low-income children, thus stimulating depressed local economies while empowering children to stay or leave for better opportunities as they wish.[11]

So affordability is a red herring. But here's another objection, one that many wouldn't so readily admit to or perhaps even realize they have: Why would any parent or nonparent want to invest in *other people's* kids?

THE MYTH OF ZERO-SUM PARENTING

Ned Johnson runs a tutoring and college-prep company based in Washington, DC. Several years ago he was working with a student, and the student's parents asked Ned a question: "How much could we pay you to ensure you work with our child only *and no other students in the class at this high school?*"[12]

These parents had gone in hard for the Myth of Zero-Sum Parenting, or the idea that help given to other parents' children hurts their children.

It's the second falsehood that prevents parents from uniting around their shared political interests.

Many affluent parents have learned to see the world through the prism of elite-university admissions. If *other* children gain more skills, it means more competition with *their* children for those precious few seats at elite universities that allegedly catapult kids into economic bliss.

The zero-sum fallacy is a wedge that distracts parents from their much larger *common* interests. Less than half of 1 percent of children wind up attending an Ivy League college. The primary impact of making better investments will *not* be to clog up your child's Harvard applicant pool. It will be to ensure more children stay healthy, graduate from high school, obtain useful postsecondary degrees at nonselective colleges, and build productive careers.

Even if your child gets to attend one of these superelite colleges, the economic advantages are likely quite modest, with a possible exception for minority and low-income children. Elite universities overwhelmingly enroll children predestined for economic success whether they attend Harvard or some other reputable four-year university. One of the great accomplishments of American society is its robust higher-education system. Any child who narrowly misses acceptance to an Ivy League university can still attend a different world-class university in any state in this country, where she can be educated in almost anything at the highest of levels. It's really quite extraordinary. In many ways, the most elite colleges basically engage in an arms race to attract and take credit for the skill-building achievements of children's parents and the sheer luck of children endowed with extraordinary aptitude—and then benefit from the virtuous social and professional circles that fund their endowment war chests.[13]

In fact, the vast majority of child development is *not* the zero-sum charade of elite-college admissions—it's the *supersum* reality of all of us using our skills to benefit each other in our inextricably shared lives. When more children get the investments they need outside school to relax and concentrate inside school, teachers spend less time putting out fires and more time helping children master academic content, while kids themselves spend less time disrupting each other and more time collaborating.

But supersum parenting is about much more than spillovers inside classrooms. As fellow citizens who benefit from tax revenue, we all—even those of us without children—collectively own about 30 percent of any additional income other people's children wind up earning. If Family-care investments help another parent raise a child whose annual income will be $30,000 higher than it would have been otherwise, that means $10,000 per year in additional tax revenue for public goods or tax cuts that help everyone else. And the converse is also true: if we fail to help other people's children build skills, our tax dollars pay for their repeat of grades, emergency health care, incarceration, and income supplements. We can either help parents prepare children to build our collective wealth or neglect parents and pay collectively for the consequences. There is no third option.

And tax revenue from higher income is just one part of supersum parenting. When we support investment in other people's children, they produce better goods and services, invent more technologies, start more businesses, create more works of art, and lead more social and political movements. More healthy, high-skilled children means more than a richer country in the narrow financial sense; it means a more dynamic, stronger, happier, and more culturally vibrant country for all of us.

But even if parents get past the affordability ruse and buy into their shared supersum interests, many Americans have a kind of learned help-lessness about government support. This is perhaps the largest myth that must be shattered for parents to defend the true interests of children.

THE MYTH OF GOVERNMENT FAILURE

It's funny. Many parents, including many who take immense pride in American history and freedom, have a strangely dour view of the very government that holds us together as a nation. These Americans have bought into the Myth of Government Failure: the belief that ambitious public programs tend to fail extravagantly at taxpayers' expense. But the Myth of Government Failure, like the Myths of Nonaffordability and Zero-Sum Parenting, is false.

This perception probably hits hardest for the federal government. America's federal government is not perfect, as anyone who has interacted with some of its more underfunded or dysfunctional agencies can attest. But it has a long, illustrious history of successful investments. Many of these investments have involved collaboration with the private and nonprofit sectors, especially universities. Federal programs fund research investments that are too audacious, risky, and long term for private businesses to undertake on their own.

Many of these projects have failed. And that's appropriate—that is the definition of *risk*. People who hate government hold up these failures and say, "We told you so," in a way they somehow forget to do when considering the vast majority of for-profit companies that also fail, including fraudulent, high-stakes implosions from Enron to Theranos. But when it comes to federal investments, this concern could not be more misleading because the overall effort has succeeded beyond anyone's wildest dreams.[14]

R&D investments coordinated, subsidized, and undertaken by federal agencies have created modern personal computers and smartphones, pharmaceuticals, biotechnology, nanotechnology, aviation, nuclear power and weaponry, the internet, agricultural technologies, green technologies, and many other fundamental technologies that have driven America's transformation into an economic and military superpower. Important federal agencies and programs driving this transformative R&D include the National Science Foundation, the National Institutes of Health (including the Eunice Kennedy Shriver NICHD), the Department of Defense, the Advanced Research Projects Agency, the Small Business Innovation Development Act, the Orphan Drug Act, the National Nanotechnology Initiative.

Private-sector innovation by companies such as Apple, Google, and Pfizer has typically followed the lead of US government investments. Businesses take taxpayer-funded, democratically created technologies, commercialize them for profit, and in the process burnish their own reputations for creative entrepreneurial genius.

Successful federal innovation showcases the power of our democratic government to make wise investments that benefit all Americans. But perhaps progressive public investments in social programs to help Americans overcome disadvantage or misfortune are different from scientific innovation. Haven't these progressive investments typically failed?

No, they have not failed. They, too, have been wildly successful. But no one can blame you for believing otherwise. The track record of these progressive investments has been refracted through decades of bad data, bad statistics, bad analysis, and propaganda. As Americans, we look upon our shared history of progressive government investment as if confronting a fun-house mirror image warped in all directions.

It is impossible to understand what we can achieve together in the future without understanding what we have already achieved together in the past. As I tell you this story, I promise not to overcompensate with exaggerated certainty. The reality is that evaluating success and failure of public investments is difficult, and there is still much we don't know.

Twice in American history we have initiated large-scale national investment campaigns to address poverty and inequality: the New Deal in the 1930s under President Franklin D. Roosevelt and the War on Poverty starting in the 1960s under President Lyndon B. Johnson. Child skill development played an important role in both of these campaigns.

The New Deal created Social Security Old Age Insurance, Assistance for the Elderly Poor, Unemployment Insurance, and Aid to Dependent Children (i.e., welfare, today rebranded in more insulting terms as Temporary Assistance for Needy Families), among other things. New Deal programs served their purpose: they reduced widespread poverty among the elderly, the unemployed, and children. That is why every affluent democratic nation in the world has adopted the same kinds of social insurance programs that America created during the New Deal—because voters all around the world demand them. And at least since the end of World War II, New Deal programs have not provoked sharp ambivalence in most Americans. Ronald Reagan himself voted for FDR four times, and as president he celebrated New Deal programs.[15]

Much like the New Deal, the War on Poverty focused on aiding families that had fallen on hard times, combining poverty relief for adults with some efforts to build more skills in children. The War on Poverty created Medicare, Medicaid, Head Start, Food Stamps, housing assistance, federal education grants, and many other programs that continue today. These programs were large. By 1970, inflation-adjusted federal spending on health, education, and welfare had tripled to 15 percent of the federal budget, or 2.7 percent of GDP.[16]

Today, however, most people take it for granted that the War on Poverty failed. In 1988, President Reagan quipped, "The federal government fought the war on poverty, and poverty won." Paul Ryan, former Republican Speaker of the House, wrote in 2016, "Even though the federal government has spent trillions of taxpayer dollars on [War on Poverty] programs over the past five decades, the official poverty rate in 2014 (14.8 percent) was no better than it was in 1966 (14.7 percent), when many of these programs started."[17]

Amazingly, this assertion that the War on Poverty "failed" is pure fiction. Let's see how this fiction emerged.

The Origins of a Myth: Part I

The main evidence cited by War on Poverty defeatists such as Reagan and Ryan is that poverty rates have not declined very much according to the "official poverty rate."

In fact, however, the "absolute poverty" rate in America—that is, the kind of poverty the official poverty rate is designed to capture based on a past standard of living—has plummeted. How is that possible? How can reasonable people disagree over something so basic as the share of Americans living in poverty? Here's why: the official poverty rate is such a flawed measure of poverty that only people who are dazzled by the word *official* take it seriously.

The official poverty rate suffers from three big, well-known problems: excessive inflation adjustment, excluded resources, and underreported resources. To understand these problems, we need to understand how the poverty rate is calculated.[18]

The official poverty rate measures the share of Americans earning an income below a fixed dollar threshold in a given year. This threshold was developed in 1964 by one federal civil servant named Mollie Orshansky.

The goal was to provide rough guidance to the White House's new Office of Economic Opportunity so it could focus its efforts on the most disadvantaged communities. In a pinch, Orshansky improvised: she took the Department of Agriculture's estimate of the bare-minimum food budget required to feed a family and multiplied this number by three. Since then, these thresholds have been updated annually for price inflation using the Consumer Price Index (CPI).

Given a threshold, we need to decide how to measure a family's income to see if it falls above or below the threshold. The official poverty rate captures the share of Americans who report pretax cash income from the prior year that falls below an inflation-adjusted poverty threshold fixed in 1964. By this measure, the poverty rate fell by about 20 percent from 1964 to 1966 and then remained steady for decades. This is the primary evidence that War on Poverty critics such as Reagan and Ryan cite when they declare surrender.

The first problem with the official poverty rate is the adjustment for *inflation*. The CPI overstates inflation. It implies that the value of a dollar has fallen by about 4 percent per year since the 1960s, on average. In reality, the value of the dollar has fallen annually by only 3 percent or less. To give you a flavor of the mistakes involved in the CPI, suppose bottles of baby formula suddenly include 10 percent more formula but cost 10 percent more money. The CPI assumes we can buy 10 percent less baby formula with our dollars, suggesting inflation, when in reality we haven't lost any purchasing power at all.[19]

Overstating inflation by 1 percentage point per year creates enormous distortions over time. In particular, it causes the threshold used to define poverty to go up much faster than it should in reality. In 1964, a family of four counted as poor if it earned less than $3,169 in a year. Today, due to adjustments for inflation using the CPI, that threshold is almost $25,000. Consensus estimates of actual inflation suggest that a poverty threshold preserving the same standard of living from 1964 would today be about $14,000 rather than $25,000. This lower threshold would classify a much smaller share of the population as poor, indicating a much greater decline in poverty.

The second problem with the official poverty rate is *excluded family resources*. By counting only pretax cash income, the official poverty rate excludes many kinds of income that are designed in part to alleviate poverty: tax credits such as the Earned Income Tax Credit and noncash assistance such as SNAP and housing subsidies. Excluding these income sources and arguing that poverty rates have not fallen is strange. It's like giving a sick person medicine that helps her recover and then arguing that she's still technically sick because you can't count the impact of the medicine.

The third problem with the official poverty rate is *underreported resources*. There is no perfect way to measure a family's income. The official poverty rate relies on people responding accurately and honestly to survey questions about their prior year's income. But it's hard to remember exactly how much money you made last year (I have only a rough idea), and it's hard to assess whether to be honest with a survey enumerator you've never met before. What if the survey enumerator is really a debt collector or program-eligibility officer trying to trick you into revealing your true income?

It turns out these reporting problems are real, and they have been getting worse over the past 20 years. That is, people have reported a decreasing share of their actual income to survey enumerators. Today, when we add up all the income from programs such as welfare and SNAP that respondents divulge in surveys, we can only account for 50–60 percent of known federal expenditures on these programs. Increasingly, respondents either forget or decline to report this income. If low-income people report less income over time, that will exaggerate the persistence of poverty.

When researchers adjust for all these problems, they find the poverty rate has fallen by *86 percent* since 1964. Recent claims that declining poverty has masked growth in "extreme poverty" also turn out to be artifacts of the same kinds of faulty data. Once we focus on more meaningful and accurate metrics than those used by War on Poverty defeatists such as Ronald Reagan and Paul Ryan, we see their surrender was premature.[20]

Does this mean we've eliminated poverty? No, it doesn't. America is the only developed country in the world that fixates on "absolute" poverty, or poverty based on a fixed standard of living from the past. Every other country focuses on "relative" poverty based on comparison to a current standard of living. The most common measures define a family as poor if its income falls below 50 percent of median national income. By this measure, the United States has a much higher poverty rate than most other advanced countries, especially for children.[21]

There are good reasons why other countries focus on relative poverty. Anyone with a shotgun, a refrigerator, and some protein bars would be living in luxury during the Middle Ages. Surely that doesn't make them rich today, as absolute poverty measures would have us believe.

But, then again, this entire debate over poverty rates is a bad way to assess the impact of War on Poverty programs. Even if War on Poverty programs succeeded, poverty rates could move in any direction due to unrelated demographic and technological trends. The better approach is to measure the impact of specific skill-building programs on the participants' outcomes as adults. And here we find that all the largest childhood investments composing the War on Poverty—Medicaid, Food Stamps, and Head Start—improve children's future income and health, yield high return on investment, and largely pay for themselves in the form of higher tax revenue from the participants.[22]

So the idea that the War on Poverty failed is pure fiction. Americans can and do create powerful programs to improve child skill development. There is every reason for optimism that a major new initiative such as Familycare would succeed if politicians wanted it to succeed and focused on making it work better over time rather than relitigating its legitimacy or sabotaging its implementation.

But if all this is true, then why do so many Important People still claim the War on Poverty failed? Why exactly has this myth persisted for so long?

The Origins of a Myth: Part II

Here's another way to frame the question: Why was the New Deal of the 1930s popular and today remembered with pride, whereas the War on Poverty of the 1960s was acrimonious and today remembered with disdain?

There are many reasons why these initiatives garnered such different receptions. The New Deal took place during the Great Depression. Many people at that time wondered if democratic capitalism had entered a permanent new phase of mass unemployment and feared that without some sense of hope the public would turn to communism or fascism. In this climate, even many conservatives sympathized with President Roosevelt's insistence that the federal government had to be viewed as taking action—every action, any action—to alleviate hardship.

In contrast, the War on Poverty took place at a time of economic prosperity. Fewer people saw a need for radical government intervention in 1964, compared to 1934. However, there is another difference between these two programs: how they interacted with white supremacy.

The New Deal took place at a time when white southern segregationists could block legislation at will. Southern senators chaired most key Senate committees and voted as a group on all legislation pertaining to civil rights and racial equality. This power assured that New Deal legislation had to respect the southern racial order.

New Deal policy makers responded to this power in two ways. First, they made sure programs couldn't be readily accessed by most Black workers. Second, they delegated program administration to state and local governments, which held no accountability to Black citizens due to their mass disenfranchisement after Reconstruction. The New Deal thereby carefully empowered southern governments to keep more funding in the pockets of white families.

For example, Social Security old-age insurance excluded agricultural and domestic workers in part to exclude the 75 percent of Black workers in these two occupational groups. States managed Aid to Families with Dependent Children and Assistance for the Elderly Poor, thus localizing program administration to permit racial discrimination. Unemployment Insurance combined both of these strategies.[23]

In contrast, the War on Poverty formed an important part of the National Democratic Party's overwhelming, explicit rejection of the southern racial order. This divorce between Democratic progressives and segregationists had many precursors, some of which began in the Roosevelt administration, even as it designed New Deal policies to exclude Black Americans. Examples include the embrace of Black leaders within the

Roosevelt administration, Roosevelt's Executive Order prohibiting racial discrimination in employment by federal contractors during World War II, and the inclusion of civil rights in Truman's Democratic Party platform in 1948. The Democratic Party had also become increasingly accountable to northern Blacks. While southern Blacks had been disenfranchised by terrorism and legal subterfuge, northern Blacks were very much able to vote.[24]

And then in 1963 John F. Kennedy ran for president, and all hell broke loose. In April 1963, Black leaders collaborating with Martin Luther King Jr. in Birmingham, Alabama, orchestrated a boycott of local stores to demand racial integration of employment and public accommodations (hotels, restaurants, etc.). White law enforcement responded, as usual, with violence. Americans watched on live television as police officers unleashed beatings, attack dogs, and water hoses on peaceful Black protesters, including children.

It was the middle of presidential campaign season. The public outcry over Birmingham jolted Kennedy. He finally declared support for national civil rights legislation.

The fallout was immediate. Southern whites poured out of the Democratic Party. In early 1963, before Kennedy endorsed civil rights legislation, 60 percent of southern whites supported his candidacy. From April to July, southern white support for him fell to 30 percent. Half of southern whites suddenly supported Goldwater. Outside the South, white support for Kennedy held firm.

The key thing about Goldwater? He opposed civil rights legislation. The other thing about Goldwater? He opposed every other kind of progressive government spending.

The economists Ilyana Kuziemko and Ebonya Washington have provided a clear view on the forces underlying this critical juncture. In the mid-2000s, the nonprofit Roper Center for Public Opinion Research released a trove of historical survey data from Gallup going back to the 1930s. As Kuziemko and Washington dug through the data, one survey question in particular caught their attention: "If your party nominated a well-qualified man for president, would you vote for him if he happened to be a Negro?" Between 1958 and 1972, Gallup asked the question nine separate times in exactly the same way. This gave the researchers a simple, consistent way to distinguish "racially conservative" whites from those with more tolerant views.[25]

Kuziemko and Washington found this one survey question overwhelmingly predicted which southern whites would shift party allegiance in the 1960s. Whites abandoning the Democratic Party didn't care what Goldwater thought about education or health care or Social Security. They didn't express unusual views toward women, Catholics, Jews, or immigrants. They were just racist. The Democratic Party had repudiated their worldview, so they left it.

Kennedy's announcement and the exodus of racist southern white voters it precipitated transformed the Democratic Party into the antisegregation party. In November 1963, Kennedy was assassinated, and Lyndon Johnson assumed the presidency. In March 1964, another peaceful protest led by Martin Luther King Jr. in Selma, Alabama, once again provoked police brutality captured live on television. Less than a week later, Johnson emphatically backed civil rights legislation while speaking at Howard University, a leading historically Black university. Johnson ended the speech with the words "we shall overcome," the gospel anthem of the Black civil rights movement.

Johnson followed words with action. The Civil Rights Act of 1964 prohibited racial discrimination in employment and public accommodations. Hotels, restaurants, markets—all would henceforth require racial integration as a matter of federal law. The Voting Rights Act of 1965 ensured Black citizens a right to vote. The Immigration Act of 1965 removed racial quotas on immigration, finally repudiating racist laws such as the Chinese and Japanese exclusion acts. The Civil Rights Act of 1968 prohibited racial discrimination in housing.

It was a new world. The fact that Lyndon Johnson ushered in this new world as president came as a double blow to southern white voters. Johnson had spent his career tacitly supporting white supremacy, chumming around with racist southern colleagues and mentors at every stage of his life. His fierce advocacy for civil rights legislation as president was a shocking, Shakespearean betrayal of his own lifelong relationships.[26]

The War on Poverty began in 1964 during the birth of this new political world. After 1963, white segregationists no longer acted as gatekeepers on Democratic progressive legislation because they were now Republicans. Lyndon Johnson therefore designed War on Poverty programs very differently than Franklin Roosevelt had designed New Deal programs three decades earlier. Instead of excluding Blacks and facilitating local white discretion, War on Poverty programs included Blacks, retained federal control, and prohibited racial discrimination by local administrators.[27]

The War on Poverty was labeled a failure by Republicans because to them it had failed from the start in a very simple way: it had rejected white supremacy. That is the primary origin of the Myth of Government Failure in America today.

Under the Hood

Want to see this political transformation up close? Meet Lee Atwater. Atwater was a Republican political strategist who grew up in South Carolina. His big break in politics came when he managed South Carolina senator Strom Thurmond's reelection campaign in 1978. Thurmond was a former member of the Ku Klux Klan and active defender of segregation.

In 1948, Thurmond ran for president as a "states' rights Democrat" in opposition to Harry Truman, who had embraced civil rights in the Democratic Party platform. As Thurmond accepted his "Dixiecrat" nomination, he made his views clear: "There's not enough troops in the Army to force the Southern people to break down segregation and admit the n----- race into our theaters, into our swimming pools, into our homes, and into our churches."[28]

Thurmond became the first high-profile southern Democrat to jump ship for the Republican Goldwater ticket in 1964. He would remain in office as a Republican senator until 2002. You might think association with a man like Thurmond and his naked racism would limit Atwater's career in the national Republican Party. Far from it. Atwater went on to become the preeminent national Republican campaign strategist of the 1980s and 1990s. He chaired Ronald Reagan and George H. W. Bush's presidential campaigns. He was close personal friends with future president George W.

Bush. And in 1988 he took over as chair of the national Republican Party. He wasn't shunned—he was celebrated.

In a famous interview in 1981, Atwater sketched out the genesis of Republican antigovernment ideology: "You start out in 1954 by saying, 'N-----, n-----, n-----.' By 1968 you can't say 'n-----'—that hurts you. Backfires. So you say stuff like forced busing, states' rights and all that stuff. You're getting so abstract now you're talking about cutting taxes, and all these things you're talking about are totally economic things and a byproduct of them is blacks get hurt worse than whites."[29]

The Republican Party before 1963 was mostly the party of business owners and rich people. They opposed higher taxes and greater government spending out of simple private self-interest, not because they believed a grandiose hypothesis that government programs never worked. Then, suddenly, in rushed a tsunami of white southern voters joining the party to defend white supremacy. How to unify these two disparate groups?

Here's how: the Myth of Government Failure. Working-class white southern voters have always had everything to gain from strong public investments in education, health care, and economic security. But if these programs could be assumed to fail or even backfire, then they could be repudiated with a straight face by white people cornered into alliance with plutocrats. Over subsequent decades the myth took on a life of its own. Today it is no longer only a smokescreen for racial prejudice, but a sincerely held belief of many Americans who are not aware of its origins or inaccuracy.

It's a sad story. But the story isn't over.

A PATH FORWARD

More than 100 years ago, American parents came together to launch the US Children's Bureau. Advocates hoped a single federal agency could represent the "whole child" against the onslaught of pressures to prioritize the needs of voting adults over nonvoting children. The strategy failed, and the Children's Bureau languished as parents failed to maintain a unified political front through two world wars and the Great Depression.

But it's not too late for parents to seize political power on behalf of children. I was motivated to write this book by my optimism that a different strategy can work. Parents together can pass something like Familycare, then protect and improve it over time. Familycare would modernize our skill-development system to ask less of parents and more of professionals. It would improve America for everyone and greatly attenuate the fissures of class and race that have circumscribed American lives for generations. This better, alternate reality is possible, but only if more parents understand how badly our current skill-development system damages their children's future prospects, and how grotesque it is to blame parents for failing at impossible tasks.

Fortunately, the political solution is right in front of us. Parents simply have to learn from the wisdom of their elders. AARP was not inevitable; it was the result of pioneering individuals working hard to wake up and organize a large group of people around their shared interests.[30] The obstacles undermining a similar movement for parents are not insurmountable. The Myths of Nonaffordability, Zero-Sum Parenting, and Government Failure can be debunked and counteracted.

There is one bipartisan organization that has tried to represent parents nationally for more than a century: the National Congress of Mothers. Founded in 1897, the Congress of Mothers helped launch and sustain the US Children's Bureau and swept Cora Hillis into her great quest to found the Iowa Research Station. Later, the Congress of Mothers morphed into the National Parent-Teacher Association—the good old PTA. With nearly 3.5 million members today, the National PTA is the largest member-supported, nonprofit organization advocating for children in the United States. In its own way, it emphasizes the key role of parents in child skill development, and its policy positions point toward many aspects of Familycare in areas such as early education, nutrition, and juvenile justice.

Unfortunately, today's PTA is not the organization that parents need. Its primary strategy is to ask *more* of parents—more volunteering, more leadership, more organizing, more training—and the results speak for themselves. Since the 1960s, as more mothers have pursued full-time careers, PTA membership as a share of the US population has fallen by *80 percent.*[31]

In addition to asking too much of parents, the PTA's emphasis on schools has narrowed its member-recruitment strategy and pushed its policy agenda toward modest, piecemeal improvements in the existing skill-development system that cannot possibly close skill gaps between children of different socioeconomic backgrounds. PTA member services have also become outdated. Parents don't need PTA groups to share and exchange information with teachers; they can use online social networks such as Edmodo or Class Dojo. They also don't need the PTA's premade programs for teaching fine arts, science and engineering, or social-emotional skills—all of which now face stiff competition from other outlets offering free, high-quality programs online.[32]

Parents need an organization that advocates for them in all aspects of child skill development, makes their lives as parents simpler and more manageable, and inspires fear in elected officials. Member recruitment should start in partnership with obstetricians and gynecologists serving pregnant women, then continue at childcare centers, libraries, places of employment, places of worship, and every corner of the internet. It should target online consumers buying pregnancy tests, diapers, and bassinets. The PTA could upgrade its value proposition for members through a time-tested strategy of *group discounts* for all the new goods and services parents need: bottles and formula, strollers and cribs, books and babysitters. Negotiating even a small additional member discount with Amazon, Walmart, or Target's baby-registry program would immediately cause membership to pay for itself. Instead of offering its own educational programs, the PTA could help parents and schools navigate the overwhelming variety of online resources and public services targeting child skill development. It could even offer members a complementary subscription to something like *Parents* magazine with stylish celebrity-parent profiles, expert perspectives on tough parenting issues, and sterling photography.

I'm not making up this strategy. I'm stealing it from the AARP. The PTA has fewer than 3.5 million members and $20 *million* of annual revenue. The AARP has nearly 40 million members and $2 *billion* of annual revenue. The AARP asks virtually nothing of the vast majority of its members. Anyone, elderly or not, can join by paying $16 per year, no questions asked. It's $12 with autorenew, and your spouse is free. People join AARP for the group discounts and to protect Social Security and Medicare.[33] *AARP: The Magazine* probably isn't a deal breaker, but it does sit on coffee tables radiating positive associations with AARP.

The PTA has inched toward the AARP's strategy, but it's moving *very* slowly. For $16 or less, the AARP offers more than 200 discounts to its members. For $25, the PTA offers six, and one of them is a discount on AARP membership. Recent issues of *AARP: The Magazine* have profiled Viola Davis, Bruce Springsteen, and Kevin Costner. Recent issues of PTA's magazine *Our Children* have featured articles such as "Handwashing Tips and Tricks" and "Tips to Make Better Connections," paired with stock photography and banner ads for Lysol.

Newer organizations have tried to fill this void. Examples include the Children's Defense Fund and Every Child Matters as well as more issue-specific organizations such as Zero to Three and Child Care Aware on early education and the Child Welfare League of America on child abuse and neglect. These organizations, however, have not pursued a strategy of mass membership by parents seeking to promote their own personal and political interests but instead rely on elite donor altruism. As a result, they look nothing like the AARP in terms of budget, membership, or heavyweight political clout. Elite donor altruism cannot get us out of the Parent Trap.

So what are busy parents to do? Join the National PTA and hope it somehow transforms into the advocacy juggernaut they deserve? Wait for some new organization to materialize? Right now, a Google search for "American Association of Parents" turns up the "American Association of Pet Parents," and AAP.com is the website for an industrial HVAC company.

Unfortunately, for now there is only one simple action most of us can take on this issue: *vote and help other people in your life to vote, too.* Voting can be a hassle, often a hassle manufactured by politicians and their wealthy donors to suppress the voice of busy, cash-strapped people like parents and young adults. So I end this book dedicated to making society ask less of parents by once again asking more of parents in this one key way. Despite the hassle, parents *must* vote and help other parents to vote. You—parents, young adults, and everyone else who cares about child development in America—are children's only political voice.

Use your vote to support public investments in child skill development that ask less of parents, and more of publicly financed professional support systems.

Advocate for policies that make it easier for parents to vote and access public programs in the first place.

Reject leaders who peddle the Mythologies of Nonaffordability, Zero-Sum Parenting, and Government Failure.

Insist that an alternate reality exists where class and race no longer short-circuit children's potential, and that we can access that reality together if we choose to do so.

Clarify that parents, no matter how much they undoubtedly love their children, can't bring about this alternate reality on their own due to profound structural obstacles such as complexity, inadequate learning, asymmetric information, borrowing constraints, and spillovers.

Explain that acknowledging parents can't build nearly enough skills on their own is no more threatening or judgmental than acknowledging parents can't fly their own helicopters.

Repudiate anyone claiming that kids will be just fine if only government gets out of the way, and help others recognize such people as charlatans tightening the screws of the Parent Trap.

If you do these things, you are doing more than your fair share to help future generations lead better lives.

I understand these actions may feel trite compared to the scope of the problems I have described. This is inevitable. It is always anticlimactic to be reminded that most of us, on our own, have little power to fix the world's biggest problems. At the end of the film *An Inconvenient Truth*, starring Al Gore, about the catastrophic risks of climate change, many viewers want to know how they can help and the answers provided by the movie are jarring letdowns.[34] "Buy energy-efficient light bulbs"; "Buy a hybrid car"; "Recycle." Come on, Al—we all know recycling our tuna fish cans won't make a dent in global climate change. If, like me, you're fired up to help parents and kids build skills more effectively, the individual actions I have recommended here may feel similarly trivial.

But that has never been the point of books arguing for change. The point is to make certain kinds of ideas more widely accepted and to hope they percolate into the agendas of mayors, governors, legislators, presidents, and other decision makers over time. *An Inconvenient Truth* probably succeeded in that regard; it made urgency around climate change more mainstream. It thereby increased the viability of policies that really can make a difference—policies such as carbon taxation, cap-and-trade, massive public investments in clean-energy innovation, and international treaties with credible enforcement mechanisms. The same can be said of all the best works in this tradition: *Silent Spring, Uncle Tom's Cabin, The Jungle, The History of Standard Oil.* By changing conversations among individuals, new collective choices become possible.

Things could be much better in America. Better for parents who are forced to carry far too large a share of the skill-development burden that represents our single largest and most important industry. Better for kids who could live more secure, fulfilling, and productive adult lives. Better for low-income, working-class, and minority children who could achieve economic parity with upper-middle-class white kids in a single generation rather than plodding along as underdogs for yet another century. And ultimately better for all Americans who will benefit from living in a stronger, safer, richer, more just, and more innovative nation that stands proudly at the forefront of global societies.

Without something like a bipartisan American Association of Parents that has tens of million members and billions in revenue, nothing like Familycare will take place. Even if the latest effort, the American Families Plan, were to pass Congress without major cuts, it would struggle to take root and improve adequately over time, just like Head Start and federal childcare subsidies have languished while Medicare and Social Security have blossomed. Parents and children can no longer afford to take a back seat to better-organized constituencies such as business, labor, and the elderly. Our kids deserve the ironclad advocacy that only well-informed, politically organized adults can provide.

There are 63 million parents living with children younger than 18 in America, and millions of other Americans of all backgrounds and political persuasions eager to advocate for children's best interests. We're a big team. We're a passionate team. If we can unite our shared interests around a better way to raise children in America, we will succeed.[35]

Appendix

In this appendix, I outline the costs of an ambitious version of Family-care that invests in children and supports parents. The goal here is not to pinpoint the one detailed, exactly right policy portfolio but to provide an example of what such a portfolio might look like and give a sense of costs for a program that acknowledges the magnitude of the problem to be solved. These programs would likely benefit from state variation within basic national quality requirements, local and decentralized service pro-vision, rigorous evaluation, competitive-bidding procurement procedures, and gradual phase-in.

- **Paid leave.** Introduce a national paid family-leave program offering 60 days of paid parental leave and 20 days of paid personal and family medical leave. This component focuses the new benefit on parental leave, which evidence has demonstrated has much larger benefits than costs, but also acknowledges a need for additional paid leave more gen-erally. Starting with a smaller amount of nonparental leave acknowl-edges the risk that workplace disruptions might reduce employment of low-wage workers.
  - Calculations: Adjust the cost estimates in Tanya Byker and Elena Patel, *A Proposal for a Federal Paid Parental and Medical Leave Program*, policy proposal (Washington, DC: Hamilton Project, 2021). By offering a shorter nonparental leave, annual costs fall to $32 billion/year, which could be financed by a 0.5 percentage

point increase in the Old Age and Survivors Disability Insurance payroll tax rate.

○ Cost: $32 billion/year.

- **Diapers.** Augment WIC to include assistance with diapers for low-income parents. This would likely be more convenient for parents than scaling up separate, fragmented diaper-support networks, as proposed, for example, by the Lee-DeLauro End Diaper Need Act of 2019.

  ○ Calculations: The National Diaper Bank Network estimates parents spend about $75/month on diapers, suggesting an annual cost of about $900/year. The average duration of a child's diaper usage is 2.25 years, according to Johns Hopkins Medicine, "Toilet Training," n.d., https://www.hopkinsmedicine.org/health/wellness-and-prevention/toilettraining. About 50 percent of babies participate in WIC, and about 4 million babies are born annually. This suggests that free diapers for all WIC participants would cost $900/year * 2.25 years * 4 million children * 0.5 WIC participation rate, or $4 billion/year. WIC could negotiate much lower prices on diapers using a competitive bidding process, as it already does for baby formula, and need not cover 100 percent of parents' diaper expenditures, likely reducing total costs closer to $2 billion/year or less. See Steven Carlson, Robert Greenstein, and Zoë Neuberger, *WIC's Competitive Bidding Process for Infant Formula Is Highly Cost-Effective* (Washington, DC: Center for Budget and Policy Priorities, 2017).

  ○ Cost: $2 billion/year.

- **Early education.** Introduce universal, high-quality, full-day, full-year childcare and preschool modeled on programs such as Abecedarian for all children from infancy through kindergarten, including at least 10 hours of operation per day and transportation assistance, as a fully funded entitlement rather than a block grant. This policy would assure that no family has to spend more than 7 percent of its income to obtain high-quality childcare.

  ○ Calculations: See the leading legislative proposals—for example, Mark Zandi and Sophia Koropeckyj, "Universal Child Care and Early Learning Act: Helping Families and the Economy," Moody's Analytics, February 2019; Elizabeth E. Davis and Aaron Sojourner, *Increasing Federal Investment in Children's Early Care and Education to Raise Quality, Access, and Affordability* (Washington, DC: Hamilton Project, 2021).

○ Cost: $100 billion/year.

- **Extracurricular activities.** Subsidies for high-quality after-school and summer extracurricular activities, assuring that all families can access these learning opportunities for less than 7 percent of their income.

  ○ Calculations: Author's estimates.

  ○ Cost: $100 billion/year.

- **Foster care.** Double the federal budget to support foster care and adoption with additional counseling, tutoring, coaching, financial aid, data management, and other services.

  ○ Calculations: Current federal spending is around $13 billion/year; see Kerry DeVooght and Hope Cooper, "Child Welfare Financing in the United States" (N.p.: State Policy Advocacy and Reform Center, 2012). Doubling that would cost $13 billion. Scale up 20 percent for inflation because the report gives figures for the year 2010.

  ○ Cost: $16 billion.

- **College guidance counseling.** Introduce personalized, intensive counselor support for high school seniors to implement postgraduation college and career plans. Reserve extra support for the quarter of seniors most in need of assistance.

  ○ Calculations: 25% of seniors * 4 million children/cohort * $300/child = $500 million. Cost from Scott Carrell and Bruce Sacerdote, "Why Do College-Going Interventions Work?," *American Economic Journal: Applied Economics* 9, no. 3 (2017): 124–151.

  ○ Cost: $300 million.

- **Family decision support.** Introduce "family decision support" to provide personalized, intensive counselor support for low-income families to make and implement key decisions regarding neighborhood, childcare, schools, physicians, and public-benefit claims, building on the Creating Moves to Opportunity (CMTO) program as described in Peter Bergman, Raj Chetty, Stefanie DeLuca, Nathaniel Hendren, Lawrence F. Katz, and Christopher Palmer, *Creating Moves to Opportunity: Experimental Evidence on Barriers to Neighborhood Choice*, NBER Working Paper no. 26164 (Cambridge, MA: National Bureau of Economic Research, 2019, rev. 2020).

- ◦ Calculations: The CMTO program includes $2,600 one-time direct costs at time of move and $2,800 per year in higher housing subsidies. The latter figure depends on the rent structure of Seattle, so I focus on direct costs here. Assume the lowest-income quartile of families are eligible, and eligible families take up the benefit once every three years, implying service to about 8 percent of families each year. Also assume lower costs for nonhousing interventions, and avoid double-counting costs from participation in other Familycare programs. Consultation is per family, not per child. Assume two kids per family. Assume all kids ages 0–18 eligible. So 4 million kids/cohort * 18 cohorts * 0.5 families/kid * 0.33 interventions/year * $2,000/intervention * 25% of families eligible = $6 billion/year.
- ◦ Cost: $6 billion/year.

- **Tutoring**.
  - ◦ Calculations: Cost of $2,500/student/year at scale, as given in Roseanna Ander, Jonathan Guryan, and Jens Ludwig, *Improving Academic Outcomes for Disadvantaged Students: Scaling Up Individualized Tutorials* (Washington, DC: Hamilton Project, 2016). Assume targeted at 10 percent of students most in need of assistance. Assume K12 only, so 13 cohorts. This is 4 million kids/cohort * 13 cohorts * 10% of students * $2,500/year = $13 billion/year.
  - ◦ Cost: $13 billion/year.

- **College support.** Increase funding for college support programs and financial aid, with greatly simplified or automatic aid-application procedures and aid commitments made well before students begin college applications.

○ Calculations: Current annual spending on Pell Grants is $30 billion on 7 million students (US Department of Education, "Distribution of Federal Pell Grant Program Funds by Institution," accessed May 26, 2021, https://www2.ed.gov/finaid /prof/resources/data/pell-institution.html). Doubling spending per student in the form of effective support services and aid, as needed, could increase the share of students enrolled in college by about 20 percentage points from baseline of around 30 percent (author's calculations based on *Indicators of Higher Education Equity in the United States: 2020 Historical Trend Report*, [Washington, DC: Pell Institute and PennAHEAD, 2020], http:// pellinstitute.org/downloads/publications-Indicators_of_Higher _Education_Equity_in_the_US_2020_Historical_Trend_Report .pdf, and Rachel Fulcher Dawson, Melissa S. Kearney, and James X. Sullivan, *Comprehensive Approaches to Increasing Student Completion in Higher Education: A Survey of the Landscape*, NBER Working Paper no. 28046 [Cambridge, MA: National Bureau of Economic Research, 2020]). This implies total enrollment in the Pell-eligible population should increase by a ratio of 20/30% = 67%. So spending would increase from $30 billion to (2 * $30 billion/year) + 67% * (2 * $30 billion/year) = $100 billion.

○ Cost: $70 billion/year.

• **Apprenticeships.** Expand apprenticeships and vocational training infrastructure.

○ Calculations: After Familycare, all children will achieve approximately the college graduation rates of higher-income children due to better academic preparation and postsecondary guidance, increasing the overall college graduation rate from 35 percent to 60 percent. This leaves 1.6 million kids/cohort without college degrees. Of these, suppose 1 million have the interest and the baseline skills to benefit from an apprenticeship. Assume costs to scale up participation around $5,000 per apprenticeship per year (Robert Lerman, *"Expanding Apprenticeship Opportunities in the*

United States [Washington, DC: Brookings Institution, 2014]), implying $5 billion for 1 million apprenticeships/year.

- ○ Cost: $5 billion/year.
- **R&D on children**. Gradually increase the budget of the NICHD, the Institute of Education Sciences (IES) within the US Department of Education, and other agencies engaged in similar work from $1.5 billion/year (NICHD 2019 budget of $1 billion/year and IES 2019 budget of $500 million/year) to $50 billion/year in order to conduct a level of R&D on child development more in line with R&D in other industries, at least 1 percent of total child-development expenditures (which is at least $5 trillion/year, see the introduction), with a focus on evaluating, scaling, improving, and augmenting public investments in child development programs and technologies, alongside basic science on child development.
  - ○ Cost: $50 billion/year.
- **Health care.** Improve Medicaid and the Children's Health Insurance Program (CHIP) for children.
  - ○ Calculations: Increase reimbursement rates for children to close the gap with Medicare rates. Current Medicaid expenditures on children as of 2018 were $117 billion/year; see Centers for Medicare & Medicaid Services, Division of Quality and Health Outcomes, "Medicaid and CHIP Beneficiaries at a Glance" (Baltimore, MD: Centers for Medicare & Medicaid Services, February 2020). Current reimbursement rates are 72 percent of Medicare; closing this gap means a 38 percent increase in Medicaid expenditures costing $44 billion/year. As part of this increase, modernize eligibility rules and processes and integrate these processes with other family support programs such as SNAP.
  - ○ Cost: $44 billion/year.

- **School meals.** Improve overall quality of the school dining experience.
  - ○ Calculations: Current spending on the school breakfast and lunch programs is $20 billion/year. To improve food quality and variety and to invest in better dining environments, we could start by doubling current funding from $20 billion/year to $40 billion/year.
  - ○ Cost: $20 billion/year.

The total nominal price tag on this version of Familycare is $458 billion/year. That is 2.1 percent of annual GDP in 2019 ($21.4 trillion). The real economic cost is much lower than the "fiscal" cost to the government because public financing would save many families from having to pay for similar services out of pocket.

TABLES AND FIGURES

Table A.1

Inequality by Class and Race

Outcome	Average	Standard Deviation	Rich–Poor Gap	Black–White Gap
SAT Reading	508	112	83	99
College Graduation	30%	46 PP	34 PP	12 PP
Household Income	$74,000	$65,000	$53,000	$36,000

Notes: "Rich" and "Poor" refer to fourth and first parental income quartiles, approximately. "PP" refers to percentage points.
Source for SAT data: The College Board, "2009 College-Bound Seniors Total Group Profile Report," 2009, https://secure-media.collegeboard.org/digitalServices/pdf/research/cbs-2009-national-TOTAL-GROUP.pdf.
Source for college graduation and income-gap data: Author's calculations based on National Longitudinal Survey of Youth (NLSY) 1979 data file, available at https://www.nlsinfo.org/content/cohorts/nlsy79/get-data. For NLSY 1979, sample weights used; oversamples of disadvantaged and military subsamples included; parental income calculated as average income across children's ages 14–18 during years when children were living with parents; children's income in adulthood calculated as average for ages 35–55. Rich–poor gaps are similar when restricting to white children.

Table A.2

Skill-Building Resource Gaps in Schools and Families, by Class and Race

Skill-Building Resource	Parents	School Gap	Family Gap
Per Pupil Spending	Rich vs. Poor	2%	1,576%
Teacher Skills (% with BA)	Rich vs. Poor	~ 0%	256%
Teacher Skills (Test Scores)	Rich vs. Poor	~ 10%	150%
Instructional Time	College Grad vs. HS Grad	~ 0%	23%
Class Size	College Grad vs. HS Grad	~ 0%	21%
Per Pupil Spending	White vs. Black	–17%	124%
Teacher Skills (% with BA)	White vs. Black	~ 0%	100%
Teacher Skills (Test Scores)	White vs. Black	~ 10%	160%

Notes: Positive gaps indicate an advantage in the specified quality measure for the more-advantaged group; negative gaps indicate an advantage for the less-advantaged group.

"Per Pupil Spending" for school gaps across districts with high versus low shares of low-income students and high shares of white students versus high shares of Black students in National Center for Education Statistics tables A-6_FY2012 and B-6_FY2012, respectively, based on National Center for Education Statistics, "School District Current Expenditures per Pupil with and without Adjustments for Federal Revenues by Poverty and Race/Ethnicity Characteristics," accessed September 14, 2021, https://nces.ed.gov/edfin/Fy11_12_tables.asp. Per pupil K12 school spending gaps within districts in Kenneth Shores and Simon Ejdemyr, "Pulling Back the Curtain: Intra-district School Spending Inequality and Its Correlates," working paper, May 25, 2017, https://sejdemyr.github.io/docs/ejdemyr_shores_schoolineq.pdf. Within districts, minority and poor students receive 1–2% more than other students, on average, so I focus on between-district gaps nationally. "Per Pupil Spending" for Family Gaps defined as "enrichment spending per child" in Neeraj Kaushal, Katherine Magnuson, and Jane Waldfogel, "How Is Family Income Related to Investments in Children's Learning?," in *Whither Opportunity? Rising Inequality, Schools, and Children's Life Chances*, ed. Greg J. Duncan and Richard J. Murnane (New York: Russell Sage Foundation, 2011), table 3, unpublished conference draft consulted. The rich–poor gap in enrichment spending reflects $7,207/year for rich parents and $430/year for poor parents; the Black–white gap reflects $3,423/year for white parents and $1,525/year for Black parents.

"Teacher Skills (% with BA)" is defined as the percentage of teachers with a BA for both School and Family Gaps. School Gap is approximately zero because BAs are required for virtually all K12 teachers. See "Table 209.20. Number, Highest Degree, and Years of Teaching Experience of Teachers in Public and Private Elementary and Secondary Schools, by Selected Teacher Characteristics: Selected Years, 1999–2000 through 2017–18," in Cristobal de Brey, Thomas D. Snyder, Anlan Zhang, and Sally A. Dillow, *Digest of Education Statistics, 2019*, NCES 2021-009 (Washington, DC: Institute of Education Sciences, National Center for Education Statistics, US Department of Education, February 2021), https://nces.ed.gov/pubs2021/2021009.pdf.

Family Gap between Black and white parents taken from "Table 104.70: Number and Percentage Distribution of Children under Age 18, by Parents' Highest Level of Educational Attainment, Child's Age Group and Race/Ethnicity, and Household Type: 2010 and 2018," https://nces.ed.gov/programs/digest/d19/tables/dt19_104.70.asp, in de Brey et al., *Digest of Education Statistics, 2019*.

"Teacher Skills (Test Scores)" for the Family Gap is defined as AFQT percentile of mothers in Petra E. Todd and Kenneth I. Wolpin, "The Production of Cognitive Achievement in Children: Home, School, and Racial Test Score Gaps," *Journal of Human Capital* 1, no. 1 (Winter 2007): 91–136. Analogous gap for rich and poor mothers based on author's calculations in NLSY79 in top and bottom parental income quartiles. "Teacher Skills (Test Scores)" for the School Gap calculated based on teacher performance on the WEST-Basic exam as reported in Dan Goldhaber, Lesley Lavery, and Roddy Theobald, "Uneven Playing Field? Assessing the Teacher Quality Gap between Advantaged and Disadvantaged Students," *Educational Researcher* 44, no. 5 (June 1, 2015): 293–307, combined with author's calculations to approximately convert these average scores gaps into percentile gaps based on properties of normal distributions and state-wide WEST-Basic score distributions reported in State of Washington Professional Educator Standards Board, "Washington

Prospective Teacher Assessment System: 2007–2008 Results," December 2008, https://app.leg.wa.gov /ReportsToTheLegislature/Home/GetPDF?fileName=Final07-08AssessmentReportPrintVersion_8d8f9d36 -9055-42a3-9b72-bdab8ceae096.pdf. These results are for Washington State, but Washington has similar demographics as the United States more broadly and exhibits similar teacher gaps found in North Carolina, as documented in Dan Goldhaber, Vanessa Quince, and Roddy Theobald, "Has It Always Been This Way? Tracing the Evolution of Teacher Quality Gaps in U.S. Public Schools," *American Educational Research Journal* 55, no. 1 (February 1, 2018): 171–201.

"Instructional Time" for School Gaps is defined as hours in school per year and inferred from term-length convergence in segregated Black and white schools in the South in David Card and Alan B. Krueger, "School Quality and Black–White Relative Earnings: A Direct Assessment," *Quarterly Journal of Economics* 107, no. 1 (1992): 151–200. "Instructional Time" for Family Gaps is defined as total childcare time for mothers and taken from Jonathan Guryan, Erik Hurst, and Melissa Kearney, "Parental Education and Parental Time with Children," *Journal of Economic Perspectives* 22, no. 3 (Summer 2008): 23–46.

"Class Size" for School Gaps is defined as the number of pupils per teacher and inferred from Card and Krueger, "School Quality and Black–White Relative Earnings." "Class Size" for Family Gaps is defined as the number of children per parent, based on the author's calculations combining figures by Wendy Wang, Kim Parker, and Paul Taylor as well as by Gretchen Livingston and D'Vera Cohn, where the class sizes for families defined in this way are 0.93 versus 1.19 children per parent. See Wendy Wang, Kim Parker, and Paul Taylor, *Breadwinner Moms* (Washington, DC: Pew Research Center, 2013), chap. 4, "Single Mothers," https://www .pewresearch.org/social-trends/2013/05/29/chapter-4-single-mothers/; Gretchen Livingston and D'Vera Cohn, *Record Share of New Mothers Are College Educated* (Washington, DC: Pew Research Center, 2013), http:// www.pewsocialtrends.org/2013/05/10/record-share-of-new-mothers-are-college-educated/.

a)

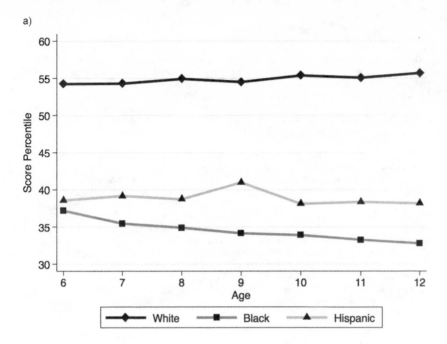

b)

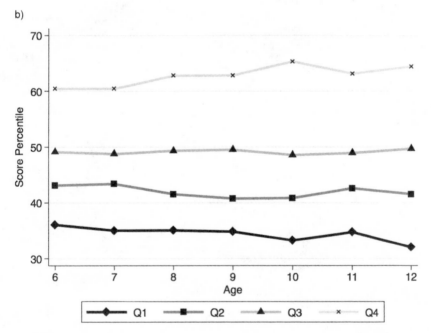

Figure A.1

Average percentile rank on PIAT-Math score by race and income (quartiles). *Notes*: Author's calculations using data from the children of the NLSY1979 survey, revising figures from James Heckman and Pedro Carneiro, "Human Capital Policy," in *Inequality in America: What Role for Human Capital Policies?*, ed. James J. Heckman and Alan B. Kruger (Cambridge, MA: MIT Press, 2003), figure 2.9, 130–131. Income quartiles calculated on average family income when children are ages 6 to 10. Test scores are average percentile ranks on PIAT-Math exam for each income group at each age.

Acknowledgments

Thank you to my agent, Eric Lupfer, who made what I have to assume are much, much larger contributions to this book than agents are supposed to provide. Thank you to my editor Emily Taber, who gave round after round of insightful feedback, and to the excellent reviewers she recruited. Thank you also to everyone else at the MIT Press whose work improved the final product, from copy edits to cover design, as well as to Jane Fransson for early editorial input and wisdom about the publishing world.

This book greatly benefited from detailed input by my own parents, Judith C. Green and Christopher Hilger, my wife, Bao Lam, and my BFF Vincent Ted Liao. Special thanks to Danny Yagan for being so insightful and so gracious in many ways over many years. I'm also grateful for valuable input from Annie Bernhard, Nathan Bernhard, Meredith Bock, Eric Gianella, Sandra Soghikian, and Chris Walters. Gabriele Borg provided valuable comments and excellent research assistance. Thank you also to Seth Stephens-Davidowitz for providing early guidance in crafting the proposal, introductions to the right people, and perspective on the book-writing process.

I want to thank Raj Chetty, John Friedman, and Emmanuel Saez for including me in their extraordinary early work on the IRS Databank, and for generous professional guidance and encouragement. I feel very lucky to have had the opportunity to work on their team. Thank you also to many wonderful former colleagues at Brown and NBER, and students in Economics 1375 at Brown, who have enriched my perspective on many topics in this book.

Many researchers and practitioners generously spoke with me about their own experiences and perspectives, answered questions, and offered expertise in ways that benefited the book immeasurably. In particular I want to thank Frances Campbell, Craig Ramey, and Joseph Sparling on the Abecedarian team; Ruby Hearn, Donna Spiker, Helena Kraemer, and Donna Bryant on the Infant Health and Development Program; Fran Benton and Wendy O'Shea from the Nurse-Family Partnership; and Roger Morgan and Ralph "Bud" Fry on the Parent Project, as well as the Parent Project administrators, teachers, and parents who tolerated my sometimes-awkward presence as a classroom observer. I gained valuable additional perspective from Anna Aizer, Nick Bloom, Jeanne Brooks-Gunn, Scott Carrell, Keith Edwards, Mark Hoekstra, Alan Kazdin, Ilyana Kuziemko, Trinnin Olsen, Bruce Sacerdote, Aaron Sojourner, and Michael Stoolmiller.

Bao, thank you for all the years of discussion, encouragement, and support that made this project possible. Felix, I hope someday you find this book interesting, or at least amusing. I love you both more than words can express.

Notes

INTRODUCTION

1. On federal lobbying expenditures, see OpenSecrets, "Top Spenders," accessed March 24, 2021, https://www.opensecrets.org/federal-lobbying/top-spenders?cycle=a.

2. For the figure 74 million children, see "Annual Estimates of the Resident Population for Selected Age Groups by Sex: April 1, 2010 to July 1, 2019," in US Census Bureau, "National Population by Characteristics: 2010–2019," last updated April 20, 2021, https://www.census.gov/data/tables/time-series/demo/popest/2010s-national-detail.html#par_textimage_1537638156.

    Various parenting activities in the United States can be valued at a total of more than $5 trillion per year, as determined by the market rates for equivalent work. I construct the market value of work for an average parent, pooling mothers and fathers, assuming two children per household.

    On average, each American parent spends about 50 hours per week on activities related to care, housework, and leisure activities that benefit children (e.g., cleaning, grocery shopping, playing) or being on call for assistance as needed. Overnight time counts as on-call time even for older children who aren't necessarily sleeping or at home, but in terms of salary equivalent hours I reduce the number of overnight hours (e.g., a 7:00 p.m. to 7:00 a.m. shift) from 80 per week to 20 because overnight childcare is often paid at half the rate, and two parents can often split on-call hours. Overtime pay sets in at more than 40 hours and is paid at a rate of time and a half, implying 55 hours per week. I multiply this number by the average full-time nanny salary of about $19 per hour (NannyLane, "How Much Do I Pay a Nanny?," accessed March 24, 2021, https://www.nannylane.com/guide/nanny/cost/cost#:~:text=The%20national%20average%20hourly%20rate,live%2Din%20nannies%20is%20%24670). Over 52 weeks, this yields a salary of $54,340. On parental time use, see Wendy Wang, *Parents' Time with Kids More Rewarding Than Paid Work—and More Exhausting* (Washington, DC: Pew Research Center, October 8, 2013). On the half-time pay rule for night shifts, see "How Much Should I Pay My Sitter for an Overnight?," accessed May 5, 2021, https://www.care.com/c/questions/3525/how-much-should-i-pay-my-sitter-for-an-overni/.

A typical surrogate pregnancy costs $100,000–150,000, according to Jessica Sillers, "How Much Can a Surrogate Earn?," *HavenLife Blog*, September 11, 2018, https://havenlife .com/blog/surrogate-mother-pay/. Wet nurses make $57,000 per year according to Comparably, "Wet Nurse Salary," accessed March 24, 2021, https://www.comparably.com /salaries/salaries-for-wet-nurse. On average, American mothers breastfeed for four months, according to Jennifer M. Weaver, Thomas J. Schofield, and Lauren M. Papp, "Breastfeeding Duration Predicts Greater Maternal Sensitivity over the next Decade," *Developmental Psychology* 54, no. 2 (2018): 220–227. Annualizing over 18 years of childhood adds $8,000 to the parental salary. Only mothers do this work, but on average for two children, so we count this once, averaging mothers and fathers.

Household spending per child apart from childcare (to avoid double counting) is $10,920 per year; we count this once when averaging across two parents. See Mark Lino, Kevin Kuczynski, Nestor Rodriguez, and TusaRebecca Schap, *Expenditures on Children by Families, 2015*, Miscellaneous Report no. 1528-2015 (Washington, DC: Center for Nutrition Policy and Promotion, US Department of Agriculture, January 2017, rev. March 2017), https://fns-prod.azureedge.net/sites/default/files/crc2015_March2017.pdf.

Summing up, that brings us to $73,260 per year per parent.

Taking parental work seriously would also involve putting a price tag on counseling services such as health advocacy, tutoring, college guidance, and job interview preparation, all of which expand beyond traditional nanny services.

To obtain aggregate parental output, sum up per child outlays for 74 million children (spending, pregnancy, breastfeeding), and sum up per parent time for 63 million parents living with children younger than 18, and assume single parents compensate for half the work of the absent parent and are paid overtime accordingly. This yields ($18,920 * 74 million) + ($54,340 * 63 million) + (.68 * $54,340 * 11 million) = $5.1 trillion. See table A3, "Parents with Coresident Children under 18, by Living Arrangement, Sex, and Selected Characteristics: 2020," in US Census Bureau, "America's Families and Living Arrangements: 2020," https://www.census.gov/data/tables/2020/demo/families/cps-2020.html.

The second-largest industry is health care, producing GDP around $3.8 trillion in 2019. See US Centers for Medicare and Medicaid Services, "National Health Expenditure Fact Sheet," last rev. December 16, 2020, https://www.cms.gov/Research-Statistics-Data -and-Systems/Statistics-Trends-and-Reports/NationalHealthExpendData/NHE-Fact -Sheet.html.

Conventional approaches to valuing household labor, of which direct and indirect childcare is a large component for parents, value it at 20–50 percent of GDP in the United States, consistent with my estimate here. These approaches do not acknowledge the unusual, intimate, and overtime nature of parental work and therefore understate its market value. See Nadim Ahmad and Seung-Hee Koh, *Incorporating Estimates of Household Production of Non-market Services into International Comparisons of Material Well-Being*, OECD Statistics Working Papers (Paris: Organization for Economic Cooperation and Development, 2011).

3. Ford Explorer price from https://www.ford.com/suvs/explorer/, accessed May 7, 2021.

4. Claudia Goldin and Lawrence F. Katz, *The Race between Education and Technology* (Cambridge, MA: Belknap Press of Harvard University Press, 2010); David J. Deming, "The Growing Importance of Social Skills in the Labor Market," *Quarterly Journal of Economics* 132, no. 4 (2017): 1593–1640.

5. George Stoddard, *The Meaning of Intelligence* (New York: Macmillan, 1942), 321.

6. Qin Jiang and James Kai-sing Kung, "Social Mobility in Late Imperial China: Reconsidering the 'Ladder of Success' Hypothesis," *Modern China,* May 2020; José-Antonio Espín-Sánchez, Salvador Gil-Guirado, W. Daniel Giraldo-Paez, and Chris Vickers, "Labor Income Inequality in Pre-industrial Mediterranean Spain: The City of Murcia in the 18th Century," *Explorations in Economic History* 73 (July 2019): 101274, table 2; N. Boberg-Fazlic, P. Sharp, and J. Weisdorf, "Survival of the Richest? Social Status, Fertility, and Social Mobility in England 1541–1824," *European Review of Economic History* 15, no. 3 (December 2011): 365–392, table 8; Joana-Maria Pujadas-Mora, Gabriel Brea-Martínez, Joan-Pau Jordà Sánchez, and Anna Cabré, "The Apple Never Falls Far from the Tree: Siblings and Intergenerational Transmission among Farmers and Artisans in the Barcelona Area in the Sixteenth and Seventeenth Centuries," *History of the Family* 23, no. 4 (October 2018): 533–567, table 4; Jason Long, "The Surprising Social Mobility of Victorian Britain," *European Review of Economic History* 17, no. 1 (February 1, 2013): 1–23; Maristella Botticini and Zvi Eckstein, *The Chosen Few: How Education Shaped Jewish History, 70–1492* (Princeton, NJ: Princeton University Press, 2012).

7. Loukas Karabarbounis and Brent Neiman, "The Global Decline of the Labor Share," *Quarterly Journal of Economics* 129, no. 1 (February 1, 2014): 61–103.

8. Luck includes such factors as graduating from high school or college during a boom or a recession, entering a field that does or does not encounter competition from robots or imports, and other factors that yield divergent incomes for people with otherwise similar characteristics. See Robert H. Frank, *Success and Luck: Good Fortune and the Myth of Meritocracy* (Princeton, NJ: Princeton University Press, 2017).

    Social connections are important but hard to distinguish from skills (including social skills). See Patrick Bayer, Stephen L. Ross, and Giorgio Topa, "Place of Work and Place of Residence: Informal Hiring Networks and Labor Market Outcomes," *Journal of Political Economy* 116, no. 6 (December 2008): 1150–1196.

    Preferences over different kinds of jobs include willingness to sacrifice time with loved ones to pursue career advancement, tolerance for financial and physical risk, and willingness to trade off pay against other objectives such as autonomy. See Isaac Sorkin, "Ranking Firms Using Revealed Preference," *Quarterly Journal of Economics* 133, no. 3 (August 2018): 1331–1393.

    On the role of institutions and policies in driving income inequality, see David Autor, Lawrence Katz, and Melissa Kearney, "Trends in U.S. Wage Inequality: Revising the Revisionists," *Review of Economics and Statistics* 90, no. 2 (May 2008): 300–323, and Nicole M. Fortin and Thomas Lemieux, "Institutional Changes and Rising Wage Inequality: Is There a Linkage?," *Journal of Economic Perspectives* 11, no. 2 (2009): 75–96.

9. The rich–poor income gap is found in the appendix table A.1 and was cross-checked against Raj Chetty, Nathaniel Hendren, Patrick Kline, and Emmanuel Saez, "Where Is the Land of Opportunity? The Geography of Intergenerational Mobility in the United States," *Quarterly Journal of Economics* 129, no. 4 (2014): 1553–1623, table 2, "Marginal Income Distributions by Centile," accessed on the Opportunity Insights website at https://opportunityinsights.org/data/?geographic_level=0&topic=0&paper_id=592#resource-listing, comparing the twenty-fifth and seventy-fifth percentiles of parental income when children are in their late twenties and early thirties. In these data, the gap is much larger, around $100,000, if we take the average income of all children below the twenty-fifth percentile compared to the average income of all children above the seventy-fifth percentile, suggesting that the National Longitudinal Survey of Youth (NLSY) data may be missing a large share of very high earners concentrated disproportionately among high-income parents. The approximate financial equivalence of a $50,000 annual income gap to a million-dollar trust fund at age 18 is based on author's calculations using a 5 percent discount rate over a career through age 65, with an annual $50,000 advantage.

   The Black–white income gap of $36,000 is also found in the appendix table A.1. This gap is cross-checked against median household income gaps reported in Raj Chetty, Nathaniel Hendren, Maggie R. Jones, and Sonya R. Porter, "Race and Economic Opportunity in the United States: An Intergenerational Perspective," *Quarterly Journal of Economics* 135, no. 2 (2020): 711–783. Given the problem of missing very high-income individuals in the NLSY data, it is likely that the true mean (not median) Black–white income gap is significantly larger.

10. Author's calculations in the NLSY79. Bureau of Labor Statistics, US Department of Labor, National Longitudinal Survey of Youth 1979 cohort, 1979–2016 (rounds 1–27) (Columbus, OH: Center for Human Resource Research [CHRR], The Ohio State University, 2019).

11. Author's calculations in NLSY79, consistent with findings for earnings documented in William R. Johnson and Derek Neal, "Basic Skills and the Black–White Earnings Gap," in *The Black–White Test Score Gap*, ed. Christopher Jencks and Meredith Phillips (Washington, DC: Brookings Institution Press, 1998), 480–497; George E. Schreer, Saundra Smith, and Kirsten Thomas, "'Shopping While Black': Examining Racial Discrimination in a Retail Setting," *Journal of Applied Social Psychology* 39, no. 6 (2009): 1432–1444; Cassi Pittman, "'Shopping While Black': Black Consumers' Management of Racial Stigma and Racial Profiling in Retail Settings," *Journal of Consumer Culture* 20, no. 1 (2017): 3–22; Kimberly Barsamian Kahn, Jean McMahon, Tara Goddard, and Arlie Adkins, *Racial Bias in Drivers' Yielding Behavior at Crosswalks: Understanding the Effect* (Portland, OR: National Institute for Transportation and Communities, 2017). On racial discrimination in other domains, see chapter 5 and its references.

   Some researchers have argued that test score gaps reflect racial bias in the tests rather than in skills. For example, William M. Rodgers III and William E. Spriggs claim to present evidence of racial bias in the AFQT ("What Does the AFQT Really Measure: Race, Wages, Schooling and the AFQT Score," *Review of Black Political Economy* 24, no. 4 [1996]:

13–43). James J. Heckman provides compelling reasons to reject their argument ("Detecting Discrimination," *Journal of Economic Perspectives* 12, no. 2 [1998]: 101–116). Christopher Jencks also presents evidence rejecting the idea that racial gaps in AFQT scores reflect a bias in the test toward concepts or situations more familiar to white test takers ("Racial Bias in Testing," in *The Black–White Test Score Gap*, ed. Jencks and Phillips, 55–85).

In contrast, Jencks also discusses studies that find racial gaps in job supervisor ratings are smaller than racial gaps in test scores, and interprets this as evidence that racial test score gaps may dramatically overstate economic skill gaps. However, supervisor rating gaps cannot be compared to test score gaps because the former ratings are determined relative to other employees selected for a job, and job distributions vary dramatically across races. For example, suppose workers in Group A have higher average skills than workers in Group B; most Group A workers get higher-skilled jobs; most Group B workers get lower-skilled jobs; and most workers receive satisfactory supervisor ratings for the jobs they were hired to do. In this example, group economic skill gaps are large, but supervisor rating gaps are small. Jencks, "Racial Bias in Testing."

12. Seth D. Zimmerman, "The Returns to College Admission for Academically Marginal Students," *Journal of Labor Economics* 32, no. 4 (October 2014): 711–754; Jonathan Smith, Joshua Goodman, and Michael Hurwitz, *The Economic Impact of Access to Public Four-Year Colleges*, NBER Working Paper no. 27177 (Cambridge, MA: National Bureau of Economic Research, 2020). See also the discussion of economic returns to college in chapter 6.

13. Raj Chetty, John N. Friedman, Emmanuel Saez, Nicholas Turner, and Danny Yagan, "Income Segregation and Intergenerational Mobility across Colleges in the United States," *Quarterly Journal of Economics* 135, no. 3 (2020): 1567–1633. These authors relied on data that permitted comparisons by parental income but not by race and do not control for many additional dimensions of skill (e.g., GPA, major, etc.).

14. Thomas D. Snyder, ed., *120 Years of American Education: A Statistical Portrait* (Washington, DC: National Center for Education Statistics, 1993). Public school is "free" in the sense that parents whose children use it do not pay additional taxes.

15. Joseph A. Buckhalt, "Insufficient Sleep and the Socioeconomic Status Achievement Gap," *Child Development Perspectives* 5, no. 1 (March 1, 2011): 59–65; Scott E. Carrell, Teny Maghakian, and James E. West, "A's from Zzzz's? The Causal Effect of School Start Time on the Academic Achievement of Adolescents," *American Economic Journal: Economic Policy* 3, no. 3 (August 2011): 62–81; Mona El-Sheikh, Erika J. Bagley, Margaret Keiley, Lori Elmore-Staton, Edith Chen, and Joseph A. Buckhalt, "Economic Adversity and Children's Sleep Problems: Multiple Indicators and Moderation of Effects," *Health Psychology* 32, no. 8 (August 2013): 849–859.

16. In 2018, public K12 schools spent $12,612 per year per child for 13 years of education, summing to about $164,000. This chapter calculated the annual value of parental spending and labor on children at $73,260 per year. Over 18 years, that is $1.32 million. Thus, public K12 spending is 12 percent of parental contributions in dollar terms. See US Census Bureau, "2018 Public Elementary–Secondary Education Finance Data," last rev.

April 14, 2020, https://www.census.gov/data/tables/2018/econ/school-finances/secondary
-education-finance.html.

17. In 1973, the Supreme Court upheld the constitutionality of these vast educational disparities in *San Antonio Independent School District v. Rodriguez* (411 US 1), https://supreme
.justia.com/cases/federal/us/411/1/.

18. Public spending does not close this private spending gap in extracurricular activities. See
Kaisa Snellman, Jennifer M. Silva, Carl B. Frederick, and Robert D. Putnam, "The Engagement Gap: Social Mobility and Extracurricular Participation among American Youth,"
ANNALS of the American Academy of Political and Social Science 657, no. 1 (2015): 194–
207; Annette Lareau, *Unequal Childhoods: Class, Race, and Family*, 2nd ed. (Berkeley: University of California Press, 2011). Low-income families do rely more heavily on unpaid help
from family members and friends; see Lynda Laughlin, *"Who's Minding the Kids?" Child
Care Arrangements: Spring 2013*, Household Economic Studies (Washington, DC: US
Department of Commerce Economics and Statistics Administration, US Census Bureau,
2013). However, the more limited unpaid help received by high-income families will tend
to have higher market value given strong correlations in potential earnings within social
networks. It is therefore not obvious this consideration narrows the gap.

19. Note that in this book I use the terms *Black* and *African American* interchangeably. See
Lydia Saad, "Gallup Vault: Black Americans' Preferred Racial Label," Gallup, July 13, 2020,
https://news.gallup.com/vault/315566/gallup-vault-black-americans-preferred-racial
-label.aspx.

20. See appendix table A.2.

21. Jonathan Kozol, *Savage Inequalities: Children in America's Schools* (New York: Broadway,
1991). For examples of articles that report extreme gaps, see Alana Semuels, "Good School,
Rich School; Bad School, Poor School," *Atlantic*, August 25, 2016; Emma Brown, "In 23
States, Richer School Districts Get More Local Funding Than Poorer Districts," *Washington
Post*, March 12, 2015.

22. Overall funding for children in low-poverty and high-poverty districts has been similar
since at least the 1990s. See Matthew M. Chingos, *How Progressive Is School Funding in the
United States?*, Evidence Speaks (Washington, DC: Brookings Institute, June 15, 2017);
National Center for Education Statistics, table 1-6, "Current Expenditures per Pupil . . . ,"
fiscal year 2012, and table B-6, "Current Expenditures per Pupil . . . ," fiscal year 2012,
https://nces.ed.gov/edfin/Fy11_12_tables.asp, which include federal funding and do not
overweight low-income students.

　　There are reasons to discount the value of federal funding relative to state and local
funding, but omitting it entirely is misleading in discussions of total realized funding
inequality. See Nora Gordon, *Increasing Targeting, Flexibility, and Transparency in Title I of
the Elementary and Secondary Education Act to Help Disadvantaged Students* (Washington,
DC: Hamilton Project and Brookings Institution, 2016).

23. Snyder, *120 Years of American Education*.

24. Emma Brown, "In 23 States, Richer School Districts Get More Local Funding Than Poorer Districts," *Washington Post*, March 12, 2015; see also Kenneth Shores and Simon Ejdemyr, "Do School Districts Spend Less Money on Poor and Minority Students?," *Brown Center Chalkboard* (blog), Brookings Institution, May 25, 2017, https://www.brookings.edu/blog /brown-center-chalkboard/2017/05/25/do-school-districts-spend-less-money-on -poor-and-minority-students/.

25. Urban Institute, "America's Gradebook: How Does Your State Stack Up?," accessed May 13, 2021, https://apps.urban.org/features/naep/. Utah has high household income. See US Census Bureau, "Historical Income Tables: Households," table H-8, "Median Household Income by State," last rev. September 8, 2020, https://www.census.gov/data/tables/time -series/demo/income-poverty/historical-income-households.html.

26. Shelby Webb, "School Districts in Houston, Statewide Feel Crushing Effects of Budget Troubles," *Houston Chronicle*, April 15, 2018; "2012 Excellence in Education Winners," H-E-B, accessed September 13, 2021, https://www.heb.com/staticpages/articletemplate.jsp ?name=2012-Excellence-in-Education-Winners. These low-spending districts are not unusually disadvantaged in terms of student socioeconomic characteristics. See "Cypress-Fairbanks Independent School District Demographics," Point2, accessed May 13, 2021, https://www.point2homes.com/US/Neighborhood/TX/Harris-County/Cypress-Fairbanks -Independent-School-District-Demographics.html, and "Cypress-Fairbanks IDS," *Texas Tribune*, accessed September 13, 2021, https://schools.texastribune.org/districts/cypress -fairbanks-isd/.

   For Capistrano Unified, see Ed-Data, "Capistrano Unified," accessed May 13, 2021, https://www.ed-data.org/district/Orange/Capistrano-Unified. In Capistrano, 25 percent of children in the district are eligible for free/reduced lunch, and 10 percent are English-language learners, percentages that are far below national averages. See Cristobal de Brey, Thomas D. Snyder, Anlan Zhang, and Sally A. Dillow, *Digest of Education Statistics, 2019*, NCES 2021-009 (Washington, DC: Institute of Education Sciences, National Center for Education Statistics, US Department of Education, February 2021), tables 204.10 and 204.20, https://nces.ed.gov/pubs2021/2021009.pdf.

27. William A. Fischel, "Did *Serrano* Cause Proposition 13?," *National Tax Journal* 42, no. 4 (December 1989): 465–473; William A. Fischel, "How *Serrano* Caused Proposition 13," *Journal of Law & Politics* 12 (1996): 607–636; Fabio Silva and Jon Sonstelie, "Did *Serrano* Cause a Decline in School Spending?," *National Tax Journal* 48, no. 2 (June 1995): 199–215.

28. I am focusing on public expenditures. Higher-income children do attend schools with greater private donations through parent–teacher associations. But private funding is only 1 percent of total school funding, too small to alter the conclusions drawn here. See Ashlyn Aiko Nelson and Beth Gazley, "The Rise of School-Supporting Nonprofits," *Education Finance and Policy* 9, no. 4 (October 2014): table 6.

29. C. Kirabo Jackson, Rucker C. Johnson, and Claudia Persico, "The Effects of School Spending on Educational and Economic Outcomes: Evidence from School Finance Reforms,"

Quarterly Journal of Economics 131, no. 1 (February 2016): 157–218; C. Kirabo Jackson, Cora Wigger, and Heyu Xiong, "Do School Spending Cuts Matter? Evidence from the Great Recession," *American Economic Journal: Economic Policy* 13, no. 2 (May 2021): 304–335.

30. Studies suggesting large teacher-quality gaps include Hamilton Lankford, Susanna Loeb, and James Wyckoff, "Teacher Sorting and the Plight of Urban Schools: A Descriptive Analysis," *Educational Evaluation and Policy Analysis* 24, no. 1 (March 1, 2002): 37–62; Dan Goldhaber, Vanessa Quince, and Roddy Theobald, "Has It Always Been This Way? Tracing the Evolution of Teacher Quality Gaps in U.S. Public Schools," *American Educational Research Journal* 55, no. 1 (February 1, 2018): 171–201; C. Kirabo Jackson, "Student Demographics, Teacher Sorting, and Teacher Quality: Evidence from the End of School Desegregation," *Journal of Labor Economics* 27, no. 2 (April 2009): 213–256.

    Studies suggesting smaller teacher-quality gaps include Eric Isenberg, Jeffrey Max, Philip Gleason, Matthew Johnson, Jonah Deutsch, and Michael Hansen, *Do Low-Income Students Have Equal Access to Effective Teachers? Evidence from 26 Districts* (Washington, DC: National Center for Education Evaluation and Regional Assistance, Institute of Education Sciences, US Department of Education, 2016); Raj Chetty, John N. Friedman, and Jonah E. Rockoff, "Measuring the Impacts of Teachers I: Evaluating Bias in Teacher Value-Added Estimates," *American Economic Review* 104, no. 9 (2014): 2593–2632.

    On teacher preferences to work with higher-achieving students, see Barbara Biasi, Chao Fu, and John Stromme, *Equilibrium in the Market for Public School Teachers: District Wage Strategies and Teacher Comparative Advantage*, NBER Working Paper no. 28530 (Cambridge, MA: National Bureau of Economic Research, 2021); Andrew C. Johnston, *Preferences, Selection, and the Structure of Teacher Compensation*, SSRN Scholarly Paper (Rochester, NY: Social Science Research Network, February 14, 2020).

31. See appendix figure A.1 on math. Language, reading, and social-emotional skills exhibit similar patterns. See Valerie E. Lee and David T. Burkham, *Inequality at the Starting Gate: Social Background Differences in Achievement as Children Begin School* (Washington, DC: Economic Policy Institute, 2002), https://www.epi.org/publication/books_starting_gate/; Emma García, *Inequalities at the Starting Gate: Cognitive and Noncognitive Skills Gaps between 2010–2011 Kindergarten Classmates* (Washington, DC: Economic Policy Institute, 2015), https://www.epi.org/publication/inequalities-at-the-starting-gate-cognitive-and-non cognitive-gaps-in-the-2010-2011-kindergarten-class/; Todd Elder and Yuqing Zhou, "The Black–White Gap in Noncognitive Skills among Elementary School Children," *American Economic Journal: Applied Economics* 13, no. 1 (2021): 105–132; Karl Alexander, Sarah Pitcock, Matthew Boulay, and Paul Reville, eds., *The Summer Slide: What We Know and Can Do about Summer Learning Loss* (New York: Teachers College Press, 2016); Anna Aizer, "Home Alone: Supervision after School and Child Behavior," *Journal of Public Economics* 88, no. 9 (August 1, 2004): 1835–1848; Marte Rønning, "Who Benefits from Homework Assignments?," *Economics of Education Review* 30, no. 1 (February 1, 2011): 55–64; Michael D. Kurtz, Karen Smith Conway, and Robert D. Mohr, "Weekend Feeding

('BackPack') Programs and Student Outcomes," *Economics of Education Review* 79 (December 1, 2020): 102040.

32. See, for example, Francesco Agostinelli, Matthias Doepke, Giuseppe Sorrenti, and Fabrizio Zilibotti, *When the Great Equalizer Shuts Down: Schools, Peers, and Parents in Pandemic Times*, NBER Working Paper no. 28264 (Cambridge, MA: National Bureau of Economic Research, 2020).

CHAPTER 1

1. Alice Boardman Smuts, *Science in the Service of Children, 1893–1935* (New Haven, CT: Yale University Press, 2008); Jeffrey P. Brosco, "The Early History of the Infant Mortality Rate in America: 'A Reflection upon the Past and a Prophecy of the Future,'" *Pediatrics* 103, no. 2 (February 1999): 478–485; Dorothy E. Bradbury, *Four Decades of Action for Children: A Short History of the Children's Bureau* (Washington, DC: US Department of Health, Education, and Welfare, 1956); Kriste Lindenmeyer, *A Right to Childhood: The U.S. Children's Bureau and Child Welfare, 1912–46* (Champaign: University of Illinois Press, 1997); Richard A. Meckel, *Save the Babies: American Public Health Reform and the Prevention of Infant Mortality, 1850–1929* (1990; reprint, Rochester, NY: University of Rochester Press, 2015).

2. Quoted in S. Josephine Baker, *Fighting for Life* (1939; reprint, New York: New York Review Books Classics, 2013), 188.

3. Quotes in Smuts, *Science in the Service of Children*, 102.

4. This section draws heavily on Smuts, *Science in the Service of Children*, and Hamilton Cravens, *Before Head Start: The Iowa Station & America's Children* (Chapel Hill: University of North Carolina Press, 1993). See also Ginalie Swaim, "Cora Bussey Hillis: Woman of Vision," *Iowa Heritage Illustrated*, Summer and Fall 2004, 116–127; H. L. Minton, "The Iowa Child Welfare Research Station and the 1940 Debate on Intelligence: Carrying on the Legacy of a Concerned Mother," *Journal of the History of the Behavioral Sciences* 20, no. 2 (1984): 160–176; and Cora Bussey Hillis, "How the Iowa Welfare Research Station Came into Being," 1919, Cora Bussey Hillis Papers, State Historical Society of Iowa, Iowa City, including all quotations from Hillis unless otherwise noted.

5. Smuts, *Science in the Service of Children*, 118. See also Shawn Kantor and Alexander Whalley, "Research Proximity and Productivity: Long-Term Evidence from Agriculture," *Journal of Political Economy* 127, no. 2 (April 2019): 819–854; Julian M. Alston, Matthew A. Andersen, Jennifer S. James, and Philip G. Pardey, "The Economic Returns to U.S. Public Agricultural Research," *American Journal of Agricultural Economics* 93, no. 5 (October 2011): 1257–1277.

6. Quote from University of Iowa Medical Museum, "ICRWS Nurses," in the exhibit *Bucking the System: Women in the Health Sciences at the University of Iowa, 1874–1950*, last modified June 5, 2006, http://web.archive.org/web/20121130190703/http://www.uihealthcare.com/depts/medmuseum/galleryexhibits/womeninhealth/icwrs/icwrsnurses.html.

7. Hillis began advocating for an Iowa state child research agency in 1901, two years before Lillian Ward first proposed the federal US Children's Bureau in correspondence with Florence Kelley in 1903. Ward also appealed to federal support for agriculture: "If the government can have a department to look after the nation's farm crops, why can't it have a bureau to look after the nation's child crop?" (quoted in Bradbury, *Four Decades of Action for Children*, 1). In *Science in the Service of Children*, Smuts documents the embrace of this analogy by Progressive reformers.

8. The cartoon is given as the frontispiece in Smuts, *Science in the Service of Children*.

9. Allison Atteberry and Andrew McEachin, "School's Out: The Role of Summers in Understanding Achievement Disparities," *American Educational Research Journal* 58, no. 2 (2021): 23–82; Allison Atteberry, Daphna Bassok, and Vivian C. Wong, "The Effects of Full-Day Prekindergarten: Experimental Evidence of Impacts on Children's School Readiness," *Educational Evaluation and Policy Analysis* 41, no. 4 (December 1, 2019): 537–562.

    Many studies have found larger benefits of early education programs for low-income kids compared to middle- and high-income kids. Some lower-quality programs even appear to adversely affect higher-income children. Exactly how far benefits extend up the income distribution into the middle and upper classes depends on the nature and quality of the program and the learning environment parents would provide otherwise. This is a critical area of ongoing research. On the Infant Health and Development program, see Greg J. Duncan and Aaron J. Sojourner, "Can Intensive Early Childhood Intervention Programs Eliminate Income-Based Cognitive and Achievement Gaps?," *Journal of Human Resources* 48, no. 4 (2013): 945–968. On Head Start, see Marianne P. Bitler, Hilary W. Hoynes, and Thurston Domina, *Experimental Evidence on Distributional Effects of Head Start*, NBER Working Paper no. 20434 (Cambridge, MA: National Bureau of Economic Research, 2014). On public preschool programs in the United States, see Elizabeth U. Cascio, "Does Universal Preschool Hit the Target? Program Access and Preschool Impacts," *Journal of Human Resources*, January 11, 2021, 0220; Mariana Zerpa, "Short and Medium Run Impacts of Preschool Education: Evidence from State Pre-K Programs," working paper, Department of Economics, University of Leuven, 2021.

    International evidence confirms these findings. On public early education programs in Germany, Norway, and Spain, see Thomas Cornelissen, Christian Dustmann, Anna Raut, and Uta Schönberg, "Who Benefits from Universal Child Care? Estimating Marginal Returns to Early Child Care Attendance?," *Journal of Political Economy* 126, no. 6 (August 2, 2018): 2356–2409; Tarjei Havnes and Magne Mogstad, "No Child Left Behind: Subsidized Child Care and Children's Long-Run Outcomes," *American Economic Journal: Economic Policy* 3, no. 2 (May 2011): 97–129; Tarjei Havnes and Magne Mogstad, "Is Universal Child Care Leveling the Playing Field?," *Journal of Public Economics* 127 (July 2015): 100–114; Christina Felfe, Natalia Nollenberger, and Núria Rodríguez-Planas, "Can't Buy Mommy's Love? Universal Childcare and Children's Long-Term Cognitive Development," *Journal of Population Economics* 28, no. 2 (April 1, 2015): 393–422. In Denmark, public early education targeting disadvantaged children had large, positive, long-run impacts: see Maya Rossin-Slater and Miriam Wüst, "What Is the Added Value of Preschool for

Poor Children? Long-Term and Intergenerational Impacts and Interactions with an Infant Health Intervention," *American Economic Journal: Applied Economics* 12, no. 3 (2020): 255–286.

While high-quality early education appears neutral or slightly beneficial for more-advantaged children, lower-quality early education systems in Quebec, Canada (rated pre-dominantly as "minimal quality" in third-party assessments), and in Bologna, Italy (with relatively high 6:1 student-teacher ratios), both caused significant harm to these groups. See Michael Baker, Jonathan Gruber, and Kevin Milligan, "Universal Child Care, Maternal Labor Supply, and Family Well-Being," *Journal of Political Economy* 116, no. 4 (2008): 709–745; Michael Baker, Jonathan Gruber, and Kevin Milligan, "The Long-Run Impacts of a Universal Child Care Program," *American Economic Journal: Economic Policy* 11, no. 3 (August 2019): 1–26; Margherita Fort, Andrea Ichino, and Giulio Zanella, "Cognitive and Noncognitive Costs of Day Care at Age 0–2 for Children in Advantaged Families," *Journal of Political Economy* 128, no. 1 (January 1, 2020): 158–205.

10. Smuts, *Science in the Service of Children*, 124.

11. The most ethically compromising aspect of the study was that some children could poten-tially have their out-placement to foster homes delayed by a few months until the preschool semester concluded. For the study, see Harold M. Skeels, Ruth Updegraff, Beth L. Well-man, and Harold M. Williams, "A Study of Environmental Stimulation: An Orphanage Preschool Project," ed. George D. Stoddard, *University of Iowa Studies* 15, no. 4 (1938): 207.

12. Skeels et. al, "A Study of Environmental Stimulation," 25.

13. Quote from George Stoddard, foreword to Skeels et. al, "A Study of Environmental Stimulation."

14. Dean L. May and Maris A. Vinovskis, "A Ray of Millennial Light: Early Education and Social Reform in the Infant School Movement in Massachusetts, 1826–1840," in *Family and Kin in Urban Communities, 1700–1930*, ed. Tamara K. Hareven (New York: New Viewpoints, 1977), 62–99; Carl F. Kaestle and Maris A. Vinovskis, "From Apron Strings to ABCs: Parents, Children, and Schooling in Nineteenth-Century Massachusetts," in "Turn-ing Points: Historical and Sociological Essays on the Family," supplement, *American Journal of Sociology* 84 (1978): S39–S80; Cristobal de Brey, Thomas D. Snyder, Anlan Zhang, and Sally A. Dillow, *Digest of Education Statistics, 2019*, NCES 2021-009 (Washington, DC: Institute of Education Sciences, National Center for Education Statistics, US Depart-ment of Education, February 2021), table 202.20: "Percentage of 3-, 4-, and 5-Year-Old Children Enrolled in Preprimary Programs, by Level of Program, Attendance Status, and Selected Child and Family Characteristics: 2018," https://nces.ed.gov/programs/digest /d19/tables/dt19_202.20.asp.

15. Kaestle and Vinovskis, "From Apron Strings to ABCs," S58.

16. Minton, "The Iowa Child Welfare Research Station," 163.

17. Minton, "The Iowa Child Welfare Research Station," 162.

18. One researcher who agreed with the Iowa findings nonetheless acknowledged that, given the state of prevailing evidence, "No doubter who believes in fixed intelligence need relinquish his cherished belief or feel intellectually dishonest." See J. McVicker Hunt, *Intelligence and Experience* (New York: Ronald Press Company, 1961), 33.

19. Robert Mcg. Thomas Jr., "Samuel A. Kirk, 92, Pioneer of Special Education Field," *New York Times*, July 28, 1996.

20. Samuel A. Kirk, *The Foundations of Special Education: Selected Papers and Speeches of Samuel A. Kirk*, ed. Gail A. Harris and Winifred D. Kirk (Reston, VA: Council for Exceptional Children, 1993).

21. Samuel A. Kirk, *Early Education of the Mentally Retarded: An Experimental Study*, 1st ed. (Urbana: University of Illinois Press, 1958). Kirk additionally cites work undertaken by Newell Kephart while a PhD student at the Iowa Station in 1939–1940.

22. David P. Weikart, *How High/Scope Grew: A Memoir* (Ypsilanti, MI: High/Scope Press, 2004).

23. "Charles Eugene Beatty," short bio, https://www.facebook.com/AACHMuseum/posts/the -first-charles-eugene-chief-beatty-of-ypsilantibecame-the-first-african-ameri/10154437 108578509/; Eugene Beatty, interviewed by A. P. Marshall, January 2, 1981, African American Oral History Archive, A. P. Marshall's Original Interviews, Ypsilanti (MI) District Library, http://history.ypsilibrary.org/oral-histories/eugene-beatty/?fbclid=IwAR0uW2EeV mdZmR2lgiPFH7bEE-bUfR6cB8r2pe78Gl87x47Qyu9ga617I-g. On helping to build trust among parents, see Louise Derman-Sparks and Evelyn K. Moore, "Our Proud Heritage: Two Teachers Look Back—the Ypsilanti Perry Preschool, Part I," *Young Children*, September 2016, https://www.naeyc.org/resources/pubs/yc/sep2016/ypsilanti-perry-part-1. On two and a half hours, see Edward Zigler and Sally J. Styfco, "Is the Perry Preschool Better than Head Start? Yes and No," *Early Childhood Research Quarterly* 9, no. 3 (January 1, 1994): 269–287.

24. Irving Lazar, Richard Darlington, Harry Murray, Jacqueline Royce, Anne Snipper, and Craig T. Ramey, "Lasting Effects of Early Education: A Report from the Consortium for Longitudinal Studies," *Monographs of the Society for Research in Child Development* 47, nos. 2–3 (1982): ix–xiv, 1–151.

25. Samuel A. Kirk, "Preschool and Early Education Programs for Handicapped Children," in *Foundations of Special Education*, 53.

26. Eileen McNamara, *Eunice: The Kennedy Who Changed the World* (New York: Simon & Schuster, 2018), 168.

27. Kate Clifford Larson, *Rosemary: The Hidden Kennedy Daughter* (Boston: Mariner Books/ Houghton Mifflin Harcourt, 2016).

28. McNamara, *Eunice*, 181.

29. The first five years of NICHD funding, 1964 to 1968, averaged around $50 million per year. In 2020 dollars, that is $400 million per year. In 1917, the Iowa Research Station

received $25,000. In 2020, that would be worth $500,000. So $400 million divided by $500,000 is 800 times more for national funding. On NICHD funding, see National Institutes of Health, "History of Congressional Appropriations, 1960–1969" (table), https://officeofbudget.od.nih.gov/pdfs/FY08/FY08%20COMPLETED/appic3806%20-%20transposed%20%2060%20-%2069.pdf.

30. John F. Kennedy, "Remarks Upon Signing Bill for the Construction of Mental Retardation Facilities and Community Mental Health Centers," October 31, 1963, Online by Gerhard Peters and John T. Woolley, The American Presidency Project, https://www.presidency.ucsb.edu/node/236620.

31. Janet F. Williams, Vincent C. Smith, and the Committee on Substance Abuse, "Fetal Alcohol Spectrum Disorders," *Pediatrics* 136, no. 5 (November 1, 2015): e1395–e1406; Centers for Disease Control, "CDC Grand Rounds: Newborn Screening and Improved Outcomes," *Morbidity and Mortality Weekly Report* 61, no. 21 (2012): 390–393; Centers for Disease Control, "Folic Acid & Neural Tube Defects: Data & Statistics," last rev. November 9, 2017, https://www.cdc.gov/ncbddd/birthdefectscount/data.html.

32. Due to funding constraints and stigma, the share of children receiving official special-education services is much smaller than the share of children with potentially severe learning obstacles. My statement here is based on the share of children scoring below "Basic" proficiency in the National Assessment of Educational Progress. See B. Hussar, J. Zhang, S. Hein, K. Wang, A. Roberts, J. Cui, M. Smith, F. Bullock Mann, A. Barmer, and R. Dilig, *The Condition of Education 2020*, NCES 2020144 (Washington, DC: National Center for Education Statistics, 2020).

33. See the documentary film *Dr. Frank: The Life and Times of Frank Porter Graham* (UNC Center for Public Television, 1994), https://vimeo.com/11191367, especially the statement by the historian Augustus Burns that Graham facilitated "the first studies done by any southern university that seriously challenged a number of southern practices and traditions."

34. Frances Campbell, phone interview by the author, April 1, 2020. All quotations from Campbell come from this interview unless otherwise noted.

35. University of Washington Capital Planning and Development Office, *Final Supplemental Environmental Impact Statement for the University of Washington Population Health Facility Project* (Seattle: University of Washington, 2017), 60–61, https://facilities.uw.edu/files/media/population-health-facility-final-seis-3-28-17.pdf. Nancy Robinson joined the University of Washington faculty a few years later: see Dave Shaw, "From Turmoil to Triumph," *Endeavors*, July 11, 2017, https://endeavors.unc.edu/from-turmoil-to-triumph/.

36. Craig Ramey, interviewed by the author, April 2 and 3, 2020. All subsequent quotations from Ramey come from this interview unless otherwise noted.

37. Frances A. Campbell and Craig T. Ramey, "Effects of Early Intervention on Intellectual and Academic Achievement: A Follow-Up Study of Children from Low-Income Families," *Child Development* 65, no. 2 (1994): 684–698.

38. Craig T. Ramey, Albert M. Collier, Joseph J. Sparling, Frank A. Loda, Frances A. Campbell, David L. Ingram, and Neal W. Finkelstein, *The Carolina Abecedarian Project: A Longitudinal and Multidisciplinary Approach to the Prevention of Developmental Retardation* (Chapel Hill, NC: Frank Porter Graham Child Development Center, 1974), 26.

39. Joseph Sparling reports that his primary theoretical motivation came from the works of Lev Vygotsky and Jean Piaget. See Joseph Sparling and Kimberly Meunier, "Abecedarian: An Early Childhood Education Approach That Has a Rich History and a Vibrant Present," *International Journal of Early Childhood* 51, no. 2 (August 1, 2019): 207–216.

40. Joseph Sparling, interviewed by the author, April 8, 2020. All subsequent quotations from Sparling come from this interview unless otherwise noted.

41. Jorge Luis García, James J. Heckman, Duncan Ermini Leaf, and María José Prados, "Quantifying the Life-Cycle Benefits of an Influential Early-Childhood Program," *Journal of Political Economy* 128, no. 7 (July 2020): 2502–2541, with an online appendix.

42. On the early and long-term impacts of the Perry and Abecedarian programs, see Eric I. Knudsen, James J. Heckman, Judy L. Cameron, and Jack P. Shonkoff, "Economic, Neurobiological, and Behavioral Perspectives on Building America's Future Workforce," *PNAS* 103, no. 27 (2006): 10155–10162. On the long-term impacts of Head Start, see, for example, Martha J. Bailey, Brenden D. Timpe, and Shuqiao Sun, *Prep School for Poor Kids: The Long-Run Impacts of Head Start on Human Capital and Economic Self-Sufficiency*, NBER Working Paper no. 28268 (Cambridge, MA: National Bureau of Economic Research, 2020); Pedro Carneiro and Rita Ginja, "Long-Term Impacts of Compensatory Preschool on Health and Behavior: Evidence from Head Start," *American Economic Journal: Economic Policy* 6, no. 4 (November 2014): 135–173. On fade-out in short-term outcomes and persistence in long-term outcomes, see Raj Chetty, John N. Friedman, Nathaniel Hilger, Emmanuel Saez, Diane Whitmore Schanzenbach, and Danny Yagan, "How Does Your Kindergarten Classroom Affect Your Earnings? Evidence from Project Star," *Quarterly Journal of Economics* 126, no. 4 (November 2011): 1593–1560.

43. Interestingly, the big average earnings impact combines a very large impact on males and a small impact on females, which suggests the average impact on total family income is likely larger because female participants completed much more education and likely wound up married to higher-income partners. The data on total household income and wealth were collected and remain in storage at the Frank Porter Graham Child Development Institute but have not been processed (Frances Campbell, interviewed by the author, October 14, 2020). The treated group is slightly more likely to be married and much less likely to be unmarried with two or more children (F. A. Campbell, E. P. Pungello, M. Burchinal, K. Kainz, Y. Pan, B. H. Wasik, O. A. Barbarin, J. J. Sparling, and C. T. Ramey, "Adult Outcomes as a Function of an Early Childhood Educational Program: An Abecedarian Project Follow-Up," *Developmental Psychology* 48, no. 4 [2012]: table 5). Due to greater support from higher-income spouses, more-advantaged women often wind up with lower individual income than their education and skills would predict (Derek Neal, "The Measured Black–White Wage Gap among Women Is Too Small," *Journal of Political Economy* 112,

no. S1 [February 2004]: S1–S28). Some economists might object that getting married to a higher-income spouse represents a zero-sum transfer rather than creation of new value, but that is not obviously true. The reason these women might be able to marry higher-income men is that their greater education and skill levels allow them to provide more value as partners and coparents.

See also Frances Campbell, Gabriella Conti, James J. Heckman, Seong Hyeok Moon, Rodrigo Pinto, Elizabeth Pungello, and Yi Pan, "Early Childhood Investments Substantially Boost Adult Health," *Science* 343, no. 6178 (March 28, 2014): 1478–1485; Jorge Luis García, James Heckman, Duncan Ermini Leaf, and María José Prados, *Quantifying the Life-Cycle Benefits of a Prototypical Early Childhood Program* (Cambridge, MA: National Bureau of Economic Research, June 2017); initial released version consulted. Black–white income gap based on appendix table A.1.

44. Carneiro and Ginja, "Long-Term Impacts of Compensatory Preschool."

45. Ruby Puryear Hearn, phone interviews by the author, June 12, 2020, and March 17, 2021. All subsequent quotations from Hearn come from these interviews unless otherwise noted.

46. The eight cities were Little Rock, AK; New York; Boston; Miami; Philadelphia; Dallas; Seattle; and New Haven, CT. The project originally cost about $40 million in 1984 dollars, or $100 million in 2021 dollars. Approximate project cost recalled by Ruby Hearn and Craig Ramey during interviews cited in notes 36 and 45 of this chapter.

47. Donna Bryant and Helena Kraemer, joint phone interview by the author, June 9, 2021.

48. Jeanne Brooks-Gunn, phone interview by the author, July 1, 2020.

49. I am not aware of any conclusive explanation for this isolated failure to replicate. Some researchers I spoke with ascribed it to unusually rich neonatal interventions already in place in Boston at that time. Others recalled a more advantaged mix of participants in Boston, but that theory conflicts with published data on income and education levels across the eight sites.

50. Greg J. Duncan and Aaron J. Sojourner, "Can Intensive Early Childhood Intervention Programs Eliminate Income-Based Cognitive and Achievement Gaps?," *Journal of Human Resources* 48, no. 4 (Fall 2013): 945–968.

Thanks to Perry, Abecedarian, IHDP, and the larger body of research cited in note 9 for this chapter, there is overwhelming evidence that high-quality early education programs can dramatically improve skill growth and long-term outcomes for low-income racial minorities. However, differential benefits by race have varied across programs. For studies finding larger benefits for minorities, see Katherine A. Magnuson and Jane Waldfogel, "Early Childhood Care and Education: Effects on Ethnic and Racial Gaps in School Readiness," *Future of Children* 15, no. 1 (2005): 169–196; Daphna Bassok, "Do Black and Hispanic Children Benefit More from Preschool? Understanding Differences in Preschool Effects across Racial Groups," *Child Development* 81, no. 6 (2010): 1828–1845. For studies not finding this pattern, see Bianca Montrosse-Moorhead, Shauna M. Dougherty, Tamika

P. LaSalle, Jennie M. Weiner, and Hannah M. Dostal, "The Overall and Differential Effects of a Targeted Prekindergarten Program: Evidence from Connecticut," *Early Childhood Research Quarterly* 48 (July 1, 2019): 134–145; Jason T. Hustedt, Kwanghee Jung, Allison H. Friedman-Krauss, W. Steven Barnett, and Gerilyn Slicker, "Impacts of the New Mexico PreK Initiative by Children's Race/Ethnicity," *Early Childhood Research Quarterly* 54 (January 1, 2021): 194–203.

51. Guthrie Gray-Lobe, Parag Pathak, and Christopher Walters, "The Long-Term Effects of Universal Preschool in Boston," NBER Working Paper no. 28756 (Cambridge, MA: National Bureau of Economic Research, May 2021); David L. Kirp, *The Sandbox Investment: The Preschool Movement and Kids-First Politics* (Cambridge, MA: Harvard University Press, 2009); Cascio, "Does Universal Preschool Hit the Target?"; Zerpa, "Short and Medium Run Impacts of Preschool Education"; Beth Meloy, Madelyn Gardner, Marjorie Wechsler, and David Kirp, "What Can We Learn from State-of-the-Art Early Childhood Education Programs?," in *Sustaining Early Childhood Learning Gains: Program, School, and Family Influences,* ed. Arthur J. Reynolds and Judy A. Temple (Cambridge: Cambridge University Press, 2019), chap. 5. Also see C. Weiland and H. Yoshikawa, "Impacts of a Prekindergarten Program on Children's Mathematics, Language, Literacy, Executive Function, and Emotional Skills," *Child Development* 84, no. 6 (2013): 2112–2130; Ellen S. Peisner-Feinberg, Jennifer M. Schaaf, Doré R. LaForett, Lisa M. Hildebrandt, and John Sideris, "Effects of Georgia's Pre-K Program on Children's School Readiness Skills: Findings from the 2012–2013 Evaluation Study," 2014, University of North Carolina Frank Porter Graham Child Development Institute.

CHAPTER 2

1. Although many researchers now consider the simple "genes versus environment" distinction outdated, adoption studies still offer the best way to gauge the overall importance of postbirth parental investments for child development. The genes–environment or nature–nurture distinction has fallen out of favor due to growing evidence of intricate interactions between these two kinds of forces. For example, environmental factors such as parental stress or trauma can alter genetic and cellular development (epigenetics), and genetic factors affecting a child's appearance and personality can strongly influence the child's environment. See, for example, Stephanie A. Tammen, Simonetta Friso, and Sang-Woon Choi, "Epigenetics: The Link between Nature and Nurture," *Molecular Aspects of Medicine* 34, no. 4 (July 1, 2013): 753–764. On genes influencing environments, see, for example, Prarthana Franklin and Anthony A. Volk, "A Review of Infants' and Children's Facial Cues' Influence on Adults' Perceptions and Behaviors," *Evolutionary Behavioral Sciences* 12, no. 4 (October 2018): 296–321. Some researchers have started using a distinction between "prebirth" and "postbirth" factors to capture the components that adoption research designs are more able to shed light on empirically. For my purposes here, I am interested in the potential for currently modifiable features of a child's environment to alter the child's future social and economic outcomes, whatever the mechanisms.

2. Harold M. Skeels and Marie Skodak, "Techniques for a High-Yield Followup Study in the Field," *Public Health Reports* 80, no. 3 (March 1965): 249–258.

3. Skeels and Skodak, "Techniques for a High-Yield Followup Study."

4. Bruce Sacerdote, phone interview by the author, January 24, 2018. All subsequent quotations from Sacerdote come from this interview unless otherwise noted.

5. Bruce Sacerdote, "How Large Are the Effects from Changes in Family Environment? A Study of Korean American Adoptees," *Quarterly Journal of Economics* 122, no. 1 (February 2007): 119–157. This imperfect 35 percent response rate leaves some room for caution, but sensitivity checks and outreach to additional families suggest it is not warping the results dramatically.

6. Sacerdote, "How Large Are the Effects," table 7, columns 2 and 4. I here use the term *moderate* to refer to one standard deviation. In this sample, this difference is similar to the child-development gap experienced by children raised by two higher-educated parents with fewer children and children raised by two less-educated parents with many children.

7. Christopher Avery and Sarah Turner, "Student Loans: Do College Students Borrow Too Much—or Not Enough?," *Journal of Economic Perspectives* 26, no. 1 (Winter 2012): 165–192; Anthony P. Carnevale, Stephen J. Rose, and Ban Cheah, *The College Payoff: Education, Occupations, Lifetime Earnings* (Washington, DC: Georgetown University Center on Education and the Workforce, 2013). Note that Carnevale, Rose, and Ban's estimates are consistent with Avery and Turner's once converted into present discounted value; see the technical appendix in *The College Payoff.*

    I focus on "wealth" in the sense of lifetime income, which is the primary determinant of most people's well-being. In more recent work extending Sacerdote's approach to Korean Norwegian adoptees, Andreas Fagerang and his colleagues show that adopting parents also have large impacts on children's adult financial wealth, stock-market participation, and portfolio risk. See Andreas Fagereng, Magne Mogstad, and Marte Rønning, "Why Do Wealthy Parents Have Wealthy Children?," *Journal of Political Economy* 129, no. 3 (November 2, 2020): 703–756.

8. Douglas Almond, Janet Currie, and Valentina Duque, "Childhood Circumstances and Adult Outcomes: Act II," *Journal of Economic Literature* 56, no. 4 (2018): 1360–1446.

9. Mike Stoolmiller, "Implications of the Restricted Range of Family Environments for Estimates of Heritability and Nonshared Environment in Behavior–Genetic Adoption Studies," *Psychological Bulletin* 125, no. 4 (1999): 392–409.

10. Sacerdote, "How Large Are the Effects," table 3, compared to college graduation rates in 1980 in the American Community Survey.

11. Jennifer Lanter, vice president at the Gladney Center for Adoption, phone interview by the author, January 4, 2019. The adoption fee at Gladney is currently about $50,000. See also Sarah K. S. Shannon, Christopher Uggen, Jason Schnittker, Melissa Thompson, Sara Wakefield, and Michael Massoglia, "The Growth, Scope, and Spatial Distribution of

People with Felony Records in the United States, 1948–2010," *Demography* 54 (2017): 1795–1818; Robin Munro, "Three Ways to Adopt a Child," *Holt International Magazine*, December 2, 2016, https://www.holtinternational.org/magazine/2016/12/02/three-ways-to-adopt-a-child/.

12. On the much lower rates of criminal activity among adopting parents versus biological parents, see discussion in Stoolmiller, "Implications of the Restricted Range of Family Environments," 397. On abuse rates in the United States, see Christopher Wildeman, Natalia Emanuel, John M. Leventhal, Emily Putnam-Hornstein, Jane Waldfogel, and Hedwig Lee, "The Prevalence of Confirmed Maltreatment among US Children, 2004 to 2011," *JAMA Pediatrics* 168, no. 8 (August 2014): 706–713. On abuse rates for adopted children in the Netherlands, see Marinus H. van IJzendoorn, Eveline M. Euser, Peter Prinzie, Femmie Juffer, and Marian J. Bakermans-Kranenburg, "Elevated Risk of Child Maltreatment in Families with Stepparents but Not with Adoptive Parents," *Child Maltreatment* 14, no. 4 (2009): 369–375.

13. Sacerdote's estimates, adjusted for restricted range, suggest that a one-standard-deviation ("moderate") advantage in parental skill building could increase children's college graduation rate by 40 to 60 percentage points and increase their incomes by 50 to 75 percent, which in Sacerdote's sample at mean child income around $50,000 would amount to $25,000 to $37,000. These numbers are large compared to college graduation and income gaps by class and race, as shown in appendix table A.1.

14. M. Schiff, M. Duyme, A. Dumaret, J. Stewart, S. Tomkiewicz, and J. Feingold, "Intellectual Status of Working-Class Children Adopted Early into Upper-Middle-Class Families," *Science* 200, no. 4349 (June 30, 1978): 1503–1504; Michel Schiff, Michel Duyme, Annick Dumaret, and Stanislaw Tomkiewicz, "How Much Could We Boost Scholastic Achievement and IQ Scores? A Direct Answer from a French Adoption Study," *Cognition* 12, no. 2 (September 1982): 165–196. Also see Christiane Capron and Michel Duyme, "Assessment of Effects of Socio-economic Status on IQ in a Full Cross-Fostering Study," *Nature* 340, no. 6234 (August 1989): 552–554; Mikael Lindahl and Erik Plug, "The Origins of Intergenerational Associations: Lessons from Swedish Adoption Data," *Quarterly Journal of Economics* 121, no. 3 (2006): 999–1028; Kenneth S. Kendler, Eric Turkheimer, Henrik Ohlsson, Jan Sundquist, and Kristina Sundquist, "Family Environment and the Malleability of Cognitive Ability: A Swedish National Home-Reared and Adopted-Away Cosibling Control Study," *Proceedings of the National Academy of Sciences of the United States of America* 112, no. 15 (April 14, 2015): 4612–4617.

15. These findings may surprise readers familiar with prominent research in the behavioral genetics literature by scholars such as Robert Plomin and T. J. Bouchard, who argue that parents matter much less than laypeople believe.

   Although identical-twin studies have captured the imagination of scholars and the public alike, in practice they suffer from a profound bias toward exaggerating the importance of genes and downplaying the importance of parental behavior and other aspects of children's developmental environment. This bias stems from an even more extreme version of the restricted-range problem if placement officers try to place identical twins in somewhat similar homes (for example, based on parental race or location) as well as from an interaction effect in which similar genes entail exposure to unusually similar treatment by parents, teachers, peers, and other key aspects of the learning environment. See Stoolmiller, "Implications of the Restricted Range," 404 and references therein, as well as Franklin and Volk, "A Review of Infants' and Children's Facial Cues." Modern hereditarians also ignore growing evidence demonstrating large impacts of environmental interventions that bear heavily on the role of parents and broader learning environments curated by parents in child skill development. I discuss this emerging research throughout the book.

For overviews, see Bruce Sacerdote, "Nature and Nurture Effects on Children's Outcomes: What Have We Learned from Studies of Twins and Adoptees?," *Handbook of Social Economics* 1 (2011): 1–30; Richard E. Nisbett, Joshua Aaronson, Clancy Blair, William Dickens, James Flynn, Diane F. Halpern, and Eric Turkheimer, "Intelligence: New Findings and Theoretical Developments," *American Psychologist* 67, no. 2 (February–March 2012): 130–159.

16. Classrooms in the United States are typically 900 square feet and cost $250 per square foot. See C. Kenneth Tanner, "Minimum Classroom Size and Number of Students per Classroom," unpublished manuscript, 2000, rev. 2009, https://www.scarsdaleschools.k12 .ny.us/cms/lib/NY01001205/Centricity/Domain/1105/2014-11-19%20Meeting%20of%20 Greenacres%20Building%20Committee%20Meeting%20Handout%203%20-%20 Classroom%20Size%20Standards.pdf; "School Costs: Did You Know . . . ?," Spaces 4 Learning, July 1, 2015, https://spaces4learning.com/articles/2015/07/01/school-costs.aspx #:~:text=The%20median%20cost%20of%20a,The%20cost%20is%20%242426.5 %20million.

On Army salaries, see Jim Woodruff, "How Much Does the Military Pay? Salary, Requirements, and Job Description," *Chron*, updated June 28, 2018, https://work.chron .com/much-active-duty-soldiers-make-22371.html#:~:text=All%20soldiers%20on%20 active%20duty,first%20four%20months%20of%20service.

On the cost of treating cancer, see Peter Moore, "The High Cost of Cancer Treatment," *AARP: The Magazine*, June 1, 2018, https://www.aarp.org/money/credit-loans-debt /info-2018/the-high-cost-of-cancer-treatment.html.

17. S. J. Pennycook, M. Varela, C. J. D. Hetherington, and A. I. Kirkland, "Materials Advances through Aberration-Corrected Electron Microscopy," *MRS Bulletin* 31 (2011): 36–43, doi:10.1557/mrs2006.4.

18. Tax records include the 1040 and other forms filed by taxpayers but also crucially include "information returns" filed by third parties, such as W2 wage-payment forms filed by employers, 1098T college-enrollment forms filed by colleges, 1099-INT interest payment forms filed by banks, and so forth. For details, see Chetty et al., "How Does Your Kindergarten Classroom Affect Your Earnings?"

19. Chetty et al., "How Does Your Kindergarten Classroom Affect Your Earnings?"

20. One sample question from the test used in STAR asks children to listen for the ending sound of the word *cup* and then circle one of three pictures that starts with that sound: a pencil or a duck or a ship. Although scores explain a small share of total variation in children's future outcomes, on average higher test scores in kindergarten are strongly associated with better future outcomes. See Chetty et al., "How Does Your Kindergarten Classroom Affect Your Earnings?"

21. Chetty, Friedman, and Rockoff, "Measuring the Impacts of Teachers I"; Raj Chetty, John N. Friedman, and Jonah E. Rockoff, "Measuring the Impacts of Teachers II: Teacher Value-Added and Student Outcomes in Adulthood," *American Economic Review* 104, no. 9 (September 2014): 2633–2679; Gray-Lobe, Pathak, and Walters, "The Long-Term Effects of Universal Preschool in Boston."

22. For more, see Susan Athey, Raj Chetty, Guido W. Imbens, and Hyunseung Kang, *The Surrogate Index: Combining Short-Term Proxies to Estimate Long-Term Treatment Effects More Rapidly and Precisely*, NBER Working Paper no. 26463 (Cambridge, MA: National Bureau of Economic Research, 2019). Of course, this mapping is an imperfect substitute for measuring long-run outcomes directly.

23. Will Brawley, *Restaurant Owners Uncorked: Twenty Owners Share Their Recipes for Success* (N.p.: CreateSpace Independent Publishing Platform, 2011), 118.

24. Brawley, *Restaurant Owners Uncorked*.

25. Melonyce McAfee, "The Decade of the Parenting Manual," *New York Times*, April 19, 2020; Amazon, "Best Sellers in Parenting," accessed June 8, 2020, https://www.amazon .com/Best-Sellers-Books-Parenting/zgbs/books/11401/ref=zg_bs_unv_b_3_11403_1.

26. Quoted in Annette Lareau and Kimberly A. Goyette, eds., *Choosing Homes, Choosing Schools* (New York: Russell Sage Foundation, 2014), Kindle Edition, location 6210.

27. Quoted in Lareau and Goyette, eds., *Choosing Homes, Choosing Schools*, locations 4031, 4076, and 4009, respectively.

28. Raj Chetty, Nathaniel Hendren, and Lawrence F. Katz, "The Effects of Exposure to Better Neighborhoods on Children: New Evidence from the Moving to Opportunity Experiment," *American Economic Review* 106, no. 4 (April 2016): 855–902; Peter Bergman, Raj Chetty, Stefanie DeLuca, Nathaniel Hendren, Lawrence F. Katz, and Christopher Palmer, *Creating Moves to Opportunity: Experimental Evidence on Barriers to Neighborhood Choice*, NBER Working Paper no. 26164 (Cambridge, MA: National Bureau of Economic Research, 2019, rev. 2020).

29. Quoted in Bergman et al., *Creating Moves to Opportunity*, 34 and 36, respectively.

30. Bergman et al., *Creating Moves to Opportunity*, 36. Many families have to choose their next home under conditions of extreme urgency and stress. Stefanie DeLuca, Holly Wood, and Peter Rosenblatt, "Why Poor Families Move (and Where They Go): Reactive Mobility and Residential Decisions," *City & Community* 18, no. 2 (June 2019): 556–593.

31. Quoted in Jessica McCrory Calarco, *Negotiating Opportunities: How the Middle Class Secures Advantages in School* (New York: Oxford University Press, 2018), 36. See also Learning Heroes, *Parents 2018: Going beyond Good Grades* (Arlington, VA: Learning Heroes, December 2018).

32. User, "What Do I Do When I Don't Understand My Child's Homework?," Care.com, May 23, 2015, https://www.care.com/c/questions/3032/what-do-i-do-when-i-dont-understand-my-childs-home/.

33. Quoted in Karl Taro Greenfeld, "My Daughter's Homework Is Killing Me," *Atlantic*, September 19, 2013.

34. Ipsos Mori, *Global Parents' Survey* (London: Varkey Foundation, 2018), https://www.varkeyfoundation.org/media/4340/vf-parents-survey-18-single-pages-for-flipbook.pdf.

35. Author's calculations based on Chetty, Friedman, and Rockoff, "Measuring the Impacts of Teachers II"; Philip J. Cook, Kenneth Dodge, George Farkas, Roland G. Fryer Jr., Jonathan Guryan, Jens Ludwig, Susan Mayer, Harold Pollack, and Laurence Steinberg, *Not Too Late: Improving Academic Outcomes for Disadvantaged Youth*, Working Paper no. WP-15-01 (Evanston, IL: Institute for Policy Research, Northwestern University, 2015).

   Many studies find large impacts of tutoring. See Andre Nickow, Philip Oreopoulos, and Vincent Quan, *The Impressive Effects of Tutoring on PreK–12 Learning: A Systematic Review and Meta-analysis of the Experimental Evidence*, NBER Working Paper no. 27476 (Cambridge, MA: National Bureau of Economic Research, 2020); Michela Carlana and Eliana La Ferrara, "Apart but Connected: Online Tutoring and Student Outcomes during the COVID-19 Pandemic," HKS Working Paper no. RWP21-001, *SSRN Electronic Journal*, February 1, 2021, https://ssrn.com/abstract=3777556 or http://dx.doi.org/10.2139/ssrn.3777556.

36. George Bulman, "The Effect of Access to College Assessments on Enrollment and Attainment," *American Economic Journal: Applied Economics* 7, no. 4 (2015): 1–36; Michael Hurwitz, Jonathan Smith, Sunny Niu, and Jessica Howell, "The Maine Question: How Is 4-Year College Enrollment Affected by Mandatory College Entrance Exams?," *Educational Evaluation and Policy Analysis* 37, no. 1 (2015): 138–159.

37. Joshua Goodman, Oded Gurantz, and Jonathan Smith, "Take Two! SAT Retaking and College Enrollment Gaps," *American Economic Journal: Economic Policy* 12, no. 2 (May 1, 2020): 115–158; Amanda Pallais, "Small Differences That Matter: Mistakes in Applying to College," *Journal of Labor Economics* 33, no. 2 (2015): 28.

38. The COVID-19 pandemic has accelerated a preexisting trend among colleges toward making college entrance exams optional. See FairTest, "1,400+ U.S. Four-Year Colleges and Universities Will Not Require ACT/SAT Scores for Fall 2022 Entry," April 27, 2021, https://www.fairtest.org/1400-us-fouryear-colleges-and-universities-will-no. For a taste of the complex strategic decisions introduced by the new test-optional policy, see Laura Berlinsky-Schine, "Should You Apply Test-Optional for the 2020–2021 Cycle?," *CollegeVine* (blog), September 3, 2020, https://blog.collegevine.com/test-optional-coronavirus-policies/.

39. Caroline Hoxby and Sarah Turner, *What High-Achieving Low-Income Students Know about College*, NBER Working Paper no. 20861 (Cambridge, MA: National Bureau of Economic Research, 2015); Stephanie Riegg Cellini and Nicholas Turner, "Gainfully Employed? Assessing the Employment and Earnings of For-Profit College Students Using Administrative Data," *Journal of Human Resources* 54, no. 2 (March 31, 2019): 342–370; Stephanie Riegg Cellini and Claudia Goldin, "Does Federal Student Aid Raise Tuition? New Evidence on For-Profit Colleges," *American Economic Journal: Economic Policy* 6, no. 4 (2014): 174–206; David J. Deming, Claudia Goldin, and Lawrence F. Katz, "The For-Profit Postsecondary School Sector: Nimble Critters or Agile Predators?," *Journal of Economic Perspectives* 26, no. 1 (2012): 139–164.

40. Eric P. Bettinger, Bridget Terry Long, Philip Oreopoulos, and Lisa Sanbonmatsu, "The Role of Application Assistance and Information in College Decisions: Results from the H&R Block FAFSA Experiment," *Quarterly Journal of Economics* 127, no. 3 (August 2012): 1205–1242.

41. Caroline Hoxby and Sarah Turner, *Expanding College Opportunities for High-Achieving, Low Income Students*, SIEPR Discussion Paper no. 12-014 (Stanford, CA: Stanford Institute for Economic Policy Research, 2012); Susan Dynarski, C. J. Libassi, Katherine Michelmore, and Stephanie Owen, "Closing the Gap: The Effect of Reducing Complexity and Uncertainty in College Pricing on the Choices of Low-Income Students," *American Economic Review* 111, no. 6 (June 1, 2021): 1721–1756.

42. Christine Mulhern finds better guidance counselors have large impacts on children's college outcomes. See Christine Mulhern, "Beyond Teachers: Estimating Individual Guidance Counselors' Effects on Educational Attainment," working paper, Harvard University, 2020, 76.

43. College-application essays show the same stark advantages for rich kids as SAT scores. See A. J. Alvero, Sonia Giebel, and Ben Gebre-Medhin, *Essay Content Is Strongly Related to Household Income and SAT Scores: Evidence from 60,000 Undergraduate Applications*, Working Paper no. 21-03 (Palo Alto, CA: Stanford Center for Education Policy Analysis, 2021).

44. See Zimmerman, "The Returns to College Admission for Academically Marginal Students"; Smith, Goodman, and Hurwitz, "The Economic Impact of Access to Public Four-Year Colleges." Also see the discussion of economic returns to college in chapter 6.

45. Quoted in Robin Marantz Henig, "Asthma Kills," *New York Times Magazine*, March 28, 1993. See also Kristen Stewart, "Nancy Sander, Founder of the AANMA, Retires after 28 Years," Allergy Advocacy Association, November 19, 2013, https://www.allergyadvocacyassociation.org/index.php/118-newsletters/november-2013-newsletters/111-nancy-sander-founder-of-the-aanma-retires-after-28-years; Allergy & Asthma Network, "About AANMA," accessed June 7, 2020, https://web.archive.org/web/20131022152315/http://www.aanma.org/about-aanma/; Asthma and Allergy Foundation of America, "Asthma Treatment," accessed June 7, 2020, https://www.aafa.org/asthma-treatment/.

46. Quoted in Henig, "Asthma Kills."

47. For example, see Jean Hanson, "Parental Self-Efficacy and Asthma Self-Management Skills," *Journal for Specialists in Pediatric Nursing* 3, no. 4 (October 1998): 146–154.

48. Anna Aizer and Laura Stroud, *Education, Knowledge, and the Evolution of Disparities in Health*, NBER Working Paper no. 15840 (Cambridge, MA: National Bureau of Economic Research, 2010); Irene Mahon, "Caregivers' Knowledge and Perceptions of Preventing Childhood Lead Poisoning," *Public Health Nursing* 14, no. 3 (June 1997): 169–182; Deborah M. Reed, "Parental Awareness and Lead Poisoning: A Suburban Analysis," master's thesis, Seton Hall University, 1999; Disha Kumar, Lee Sanders, Eliana M. Perrin, Nicole Lokker, Baron Patterson, Veronica Gunn, Joanne Finkle, Vivian Franco, Leena Choi, and Russell L. Rothman, "Parental Understanding of Infant Health Information: Health Literacy, Numeracy, and the Parental Health Literacy Activities Test (PHLAT)," *Academic Pediatrics* 10, no. 5 (September–October 2010): 309–316; Andrea K. Morrison, Matthew P. Myrvik, David C. Brousseau, Raymond G. Hoffmann, and Rachel M. Stanley, "The Relationship between Parent Health Literacy and Pediatric Emergency Department Utilization: A Systematic Review," *Academic Pediatrics* 13, no. 5 (September–October 2013): 421–429; Andrea K. Morrison, Marilyn M. Schapira, Marc H. Gorelick, Raymond G. Hoffmann, and David C. Brousseau, "Low Caregiver Health Literacy Is Associated with Higher Pediatric Emergency Department Use and Nonurgent Visits," *Academic Pediatrics* 14, no. 3 (May–June 2014): 309–314.

49. Anne Case, Darren Lubotsky, and Christina Paxson, "Economic Status and Health in Childhood: The Origins of the Gradient," *American Economic Review* 92, no. 5 (2002): 1308–1334; Daniel Prinz, Mike Chernew, David Cutler, and Austin Frakt, *Health and Economic Activity over the Lifecycle: Literature Review*, NBER Working Paper no. 24865 (Cambridge, MA: National Bureau of Economic Research, 2018); David M. Cutler and Adriana Lleras-Muney, "Understanding Differences in Health Behaviors by Education," *Journal of Health Economics* 29, no. 1 (January 2010): 1–28.

50. Carlos Dobkin, Amy Finkelstein, Raymond Kluender, and Matthew J. Notowidigdo, "The Economic Consequences of Hospital Admissions," *American Economic Review* 108, no. 2 (February 2018): 308–352; Petter Lundborg, Martin Nilsson, and Johan Vikström, "Heterogeneity in the Impact of Health Shocks on Labour Outcomes: Evidence from Swedish Workers," *Oxford Economic Papers* 67, no. 3 (July 2015): 715–739.

51. John Cawley, "An Economy of Scales: A Selective Review of Obesity's Economic Causes, Consequences, and Solutions," *Journal of Health Economics* 43 (September 2015): 244–268.

52. Gopal K. Singh, Mohammad Siahpush, and Michael D. Kogan, "Rising Social Inequalities in US Childhood Obesity, 2003–2007," *Annals of Epidemiology* 20, no. 1 (2010): 40–52.

53. Hunt Allcott, Rebecca Diamond, Jean-Pierre Dubé, Jessie Handbury, Ilya Rahkovsky, and Molly Schnell, "Food Deserts and the Causes of Nutritional Inequality," *Quarterly Journal of Economics* 134, no. 4 (November 1, 2019): 1793–1844.

54. Cawley, "An Economy of Scales"; Justine Hastings, Ryan Kessler, and Jesse M. Shapiro, "The Effect of SNAP on the Composition of Purchased Foods: Evidence and Implications," *American Economic Journal: Economic Policy* 13, no. 3 (2021): 277–315.

55. Melanie Pescud, Simone Pettigrew, and Nadine Henley, "Nutrition Beliefs of Disadvantaged Parents of Overweight Children," *Health Education Journal* 73, no. 2 (2014): 201–208; Melanie Pescud, Simone Pettigrew, Lisa Wood, and Nadine Henley, "Insights and Recommendations for Recruitment and Retention of Low Socio-economic Parents with Overweight Children," *International Journal of Social Research Methodology* 18, no. 6 (2015): 617–633; Melanie Pescud and Simone Pettigrew, "'I Know It's Wrong, but . . .': A Qualitative Investigation of Low-Income Parents' Feelings of Guilt about Their Child-Feeding Practices," *Maternal & Child Nutrition* 10, no. 3 (2014): 422–435; Alissa Smethers, Liane S. Roe, Christine E. Sanchez, Faris Zuraikat, Kathleen Keller, Samantha Kling, and Barbara Jean Rolls, "Portion Size Has Sustained Effects over 5 Days in Preschool Children: A Randomized Trial," *American Journal of Clinical Nutrition* 109, no. 5 (April 2019): 1361–1372; Alissa D. Smethers, Liane S. Roe, Christine E. Sanchez, Faris M. Zuraikat, Kathleen L. Keller, and Barbara J. Rolls, "Both Increases and Decreases in Energy Density Lead to Sustained Changes in Preschool Children's Energy Intake over 5 Days," *Physiology & Behavior* 204 (May 15, 2019): 210–218.

56. Nicholas Bloom, Benn Eifert, Aprajit Mahajan, David Mckenzie, and John Roberts, "Does Management Matter? Evidence from India," *Quarterly Journal of Economics* 128 (February 2013): 1–51.

57. Bloom et al., "Does Management Matter?," 37.

58. Nicholas Bloom, interviewed by the author, February 22, 2019.

59. Nicholas Bloom and John Van Reenen, "Measuring and Explaining Management Practices across Firms and Countries," *Quarterly Journal of Economics* 122, no. 4 (November 2007): 1351–1408; Nicholas Bloom and John Van Reenen, "Why Do Management Practices Differ across Firms and Countries?," *Journal of Economic Perspectives* 24, no. 1 (Winter 2010): 203–224.

60. Zero to Three, *Tuning In: Parents of Young Children Speak Up about What They Think, Know and Need*, Tuning In: National Parent Survey Report (Washington, DC: Zero to Three, 2016); Ellen Galinsky, *Ask the Children: What America's Children Really Think about Working Parents* (New York: Morrow, 1999), 134–135.

CHAPTER 3

1. Smuts, *Science in the Service of Children*, 150. In 1929, the various Rockefeller Foundation entities consolidated, and Frank served as director of the child-development program at the Rockefeller Foundation. On the consolidation of the Laura Spelman Rockefeller Foundation, see Rockefeller Archive Center, "Laura Spelman Rockefeller Memorial," Rockefeller Foundation: A Digital History, accessed September 13, 2021, https://rockfound.rockarch.org/laura-spelman-rockefeller-memorial.

2. Cravens, *Before Head Start*, 154.

3. Weikart, *How High/Scope Grew*, 102–103; see also Craig T. Ramey, Donna M. Bryant, Joseph J. Sparling, and Barbara H. Wasik, "Project CARE: A Comparison of Two Early Intervention Strategies to Prevent Retarded Development," *Topics in Early Childhood Special Education* 5, no. 2 (July 1985): 12–25.

4. Ariel Kalil and Rebecca Ryan, "Parenting Practices and Socioeconomic Gaps in Childhood Outcomes," *Future of Children* 30, no. 1 (Spring 2020): 26.

   For the full report evaluating home-visit programs financed under the Affordable Care Act through children's first 15 months, see Charles Michalopoulos, Kristen Faucetta, Carolyn J. Hill, Zimena A. Portilla, Lori Burrell, Helen Lee, Anne Duggan, and Virginia Knox, *Impacts on Family Outcomes of Evidence-Based Early Childhood Home Visiting: Results from the Mother and Infant Home Visiting Program Evaluation (MIHOPE)* (Washington, DC: Office of Planning, Research, and Evaluation, Administration for Children and Families, US Department of Health and Human Services, 2019).

   The comparison of impacts of Abecedarian to impacts of home-visiting programs is based on my calculations using published results of 0.02 standard deviation (sd) on "reading receptivity" as a measure of cognitive skill and 0.05sd on behavioral skills. I compare these impacts to impacts around 0.75sd on IQ as a measure of cognitive skills given in Campbell and Ramey, "Effects of Early Intervention on Intellectual and Academic Achievement," taking the average of 12-month and 18-month impacts. These impacts are similar in work on Project CARE and IHDP. I obtain a 0.66sd impact of Abecedarian on behavioral skills, averaging impacts on "goal-directed behavior" and "social confidence" at 12 months and 18 months given in Craig T. Ramey and Frances A. Campbell, "Compensatory Education for Disadvantaged Children," *School Review* 87, no. 2 (1979): 171–189.

   Some nonexperimental evidence has also suggested that home visits, when supplementing more formal center-based care, can improve outcomes in children. See Christopher R. Walters, "Inputs in the Production of Early Childhood Human Capital: Evidence from Head Start," *American Economic Journal: Applied Economics* 7, no. 4 (2015): 76–102; John M. Love, Ellen Eliason Kisker, Christine Ross, Helen Raikes, Jill Constantine, Kimberly Boller, Jeanne Brooks-Gunn, et al., "The Effectiveness of Early Head Start for 3-Year-Old Children and Their Parents: Lessons for Policy and Programs," *Developmental Psychology* 41, no. 6 (2005): 885–901.

   However, experimental evidence from Project CARE did not find any additional benefits of home visits over center-based care; see Ramey et al., "Project CARE: A Comparison." Researchers have also found no measurable benefits of Head Start relative to other kinds of formal center-based care that probably do not provide home visits or other wraparound services in most (though not all) cases; see Patrick Kline and Christopher R. Walters, "Evaluating Public Programs with Close Substitutes: The Case of Head Start," *Quarterly Journal of Economics* 131, no. 4 (November 2016): 1795–1848; Avi Feller, Todd Grindal, Luke Miratrix, and Lindsay C. Page, "Compared to What? Variation in the Impacts of Early Childhood Education by Alternative Care Type," *Annals of Applied Statistics* 10, no.

3 (2016): 1245–1285. These findings suggest that additional experimental evidence on the value of costly wraparound services would be useful.

5. This history of David Olds draws heavily on Andy Goodman, *The Story of David Olds and the Nurse Home Visiting Program*, Grants Results Special Report (Princeton, NJ: Robert Wood Johnson Foundation, 2006), https://www.rwjf.org/en/library/research/2006/07/the-story-of-david-olds-and-the-nurse-home-visiting-program.html.

6. Meckel, *Save the Babies*; Baker, *Fighting for Life*.

7. On the NFP training requirements, see Nurse-Family Partnership, *Nurse-Family Partnership Education Overview* (Denver: Nurse-Family Partnership, 2019), https://www.nursefamilypartnership.org/wp-content/uploads/2019/04/NFP-Education-Overview_2019_EXTERNAL.pdf.

    A college degree requires four to five years of study or 1,800 hours of instructional time. See "What Are Credit Hours in College?," College Raptor, updated June 18, 2020, https://www.collegeraptor.com/find-colleges/articles/questions-answers/what-are-credit-hours-in-college/.

    Becoming an advanced commercial helicopter pilot typically requires about two years of study and practice, or about 900 hours. See Jaidyn Crookston, "How Long Does It Take to Get a Helicopter Pilot's License?," *T-Bird Nation Blog*, March 2, 2020, https://www.suu.edu/blog/2020/03/aviation-how-long-to-get-helicopter-pilot-license.html.

8. On Elmira, see John Eckenrode, Mary Campa, Dennis W. Luckey, Charles R. Henderson Jr., Robert Cole, Harriet Kitzman, Elizabeth Anson, et al., "Long-Term Effects of Prenatal and Infancy Nurse Home Visitation on the Life Course of Youths: 19-Year Follow-Up of a Randomized Trial," *Archives of Pediatrics and Adolescent Medicine* 164, no. 1 (January 2010): 9–15. On Memphis, see Harriet Kitzman, David L. Olds, Michael D. Knudtson, Robert Cole, Elizabeth Anson, Joyce A. Smith, Diana Fishbein, et al., "Prenatal and Infancy Nurse Home Visiting and 18-Year Outcomes of a Randomized Trial," *Pediatrics* 144, no. 6 (December 2019). On Denver, see David L. Olds, JoAnn Robinson, Lisa Pettitt, Dennis W. Luckey, John Holmberg, Rosanna K. Ng, Kathy Isacks, et al., "Effects of Home Visits by Paraprofessionals and by Nurses on Children: Follow-up of a Randomized Trial at Ages 6 and 9 Years," *JAMA Pediatrics* 168, no. 2 (February 1, 2014): 114.

    For years, despite Olds's extraordinary commitment to research, NFP still faced pushback. Olds himself, rather than independent researchers, had played an outsize role in evaluating his own program, which led to concerns he may have tilted the scales consciously or unconsciously toward "proving" his own success. One red flag had been that the various studies found impacts of NFP on different mother and child outcomes for different subgroups but no impacts on a wide range of other outcomes for other subgroups. These kinds of scattershot findings can occur when researchers check for impacts on a large number of outcomes—test scores, health, birth weight, crime, and so on—and then cherry-pick the lucky positive findings that can easily happen by chance. In 2017, a major independent analysis of the Memphis trial data by James Heckman and colleagues put many of these fears to rest. Heckman, a Nobel Prize–winning economist and statistician who has also reanalyzed Perry Preschool and Abecedarian data, confirmed significant positive impacts of NFP on children and parents even after adjusting for the number of outcomes under consideration. See James J. Heckman, Margaret L. Holland, Kevin K. Makino, Rodrigo Pinto, and Maria Rosales-Rueda, *An Analysis of the Memphis Nurse-Family Partnership Program*, NBER Working Paper no. 23610 (Cambridge, MA: National Bureau of Economic Research, 2017).

9. Wendy O'Shea, interviewed by the author, June 12 and July 10, 2019. All quotations from O'Shea come from these interviews unless otherwise noted.

10. Nurse-Family Partnership, *Annual Report 2019* (Denver: Nurse-Family Partnership, 2019), 5, https://www.nursefamilypartnership.org/wp-content/uploads/2020/07/annual-report -2019.pdf.

11. Author's calculations. About 20 percent of American children live in poverty. See Kids Count Data Center, Annie E. Casey Foundation, https://datacenter.kidscount.org/data #USA/1/0/char/0, especially the table "Children in Poverty (100 Percent Poverty) in the United States," https://datacenter.kidscount.org/data/tables/43-children-in-poverty-100 -percent-poverty?loc=1&loct=1#detailed/1/any/false/1729,37,871,870,573,869,36,868,8 67,133/any/321,322. Poverty rates are higher for families with infants or young children. See Children's Defense Fund, *The State of America's Children 2020*, https://www.childrens defense.org/wp-content/uploads/2020/02/The-State-Of-Americas-Children-2020.pdf. This suggests at least 1 million children are born into poverty each year. On average in recent years, American women have two children, suggesting approximately half of these women are first-time mothers. Thus, 500,000 children are eligible for NFP per year, implying that NFP serves about 12 percent of its target population.

12. Alan E. Kazdin, *Parent Management Training: Treatment for Oppositional, Aggressive, and Antisocial Behavior in Children and Adolescents* (New York: Oxford University Press, 2005), 8.

13. The history of psychological treatments for behavioral disorders that I describe here leans heavily on Leonard P. Ullman and Leonard Krasner, *Case Studies in Behavior Modification* (New York: Holt, Rinehart and Winston, 1965).

14. H. J. Eysenck, "The Effects of Psychotherapy: An Evaluation," *Journal of Consulting and Clinical Psychology* 16, no. 5 (October 1952): 319–324; E. E. Levitt, "The Results of Psychotherapy with Children: An Evaluation," *Journal of Consulting and Clinical Psychology* 21, no. 3 (June 1957): 189–196.

15. H. J. Eysenck, "Learning Theory and Behaviour Therapy," *British Journal of Psychiatry* 105, no. 438 (January 1959): 61–75.

16. See Ullman and Krasner, *Case Studies in Behavior Modification*; and Warren W. Tryon, "Whatever Happened to Symptom Substitution?," *Clinical Psychology Review* 28, no. 6 (July 2008): 963–968; Alan Peterson, Joseph McGuire, Sabine Wilhelm, John Piacentini, Douglas Woods, John Walkup, John Hatch, et al., "An Empirical Examination of Symptom

Substitution Associated with Behavior Therapy for Tourette's Disorder," *Behavior Therapy* 47, no. 1 (January 2016): 29–41.

17. These researchers were products of their times, and some of them held noxious views on race, gender, and other political issues. I cite them here exclusively for their contributions to behavioral modification techniques, not for their general opinions.

18. Carl D. Williams, "The Elimination of Tantrum Behavior by Extinction Procedures," *Journal of Abnormal and Social Psychology* 59, no. 2 (1959): 269.

19. For an overview, see Kazdin, *Parent Management Training*.

20. Marion Forgatch and Gerald Patterson, "Parent Management Training—Oregon Model: An Intervention for Antisocial Behavior in Children and Adolescents," in *Evidence-Based Psychotherapies for Children and Adolescents*, 3rd ed., ed. John R. Weisz and Alan E. Kazdin (New York: Guilford Press, 2014), 159–178, 167.

21. Quoted in Olga Khazan, "No Spanking, No Time-Out, No Problems," *Atlantic*, March 28, 2016.

22. Isaiah Andrews and Maximilian Kasy, "Identification of and Correction for Publication Bias," *American Economic Review* 109, no. 8 (August 2019): 2766–2794.

23. Many of the studies of Incredible Years, Parent–Child Interaction Therapy, and the Oregon Model cited in various editions of Weisz and Kazdin's collected volume *Evidence-Based Psychotherapies for Children and Adolescents* reach surprisingly mixed or even discouraging conclusions, especially studies conducted by independent researchers. Philip Wilson and his colleagues cast doubt on the evidence base for Triple P: see Philip Michael John Wilson, Robert Rush, Susan Hussey, Christine Puckering, Fiona Sim, Clare S. Allely, Paul Narh Doku, et al., "How Evidence-Based Is an 'Evidence-Based Parenting Program'? A PRISMA Systematic Review and Meta-analysis of Triple P," *BMC Medicine* 10, no. 1 (November 2012): 130.

Mairead Furlong, Sinead McGilloway, Tracey Bywater, Judy Hutchings, Susan M. Smith, and Michael Donnelly, "Behavioural and Cognitive-Behavioural Group-Based Parenting Programmes for Early-Onset Conduct Problems in Children Aged 3 to 12 Years," Cochrane Database of Systematic Reviews, February 15, 2012, https://doi.org/10.1002/14651858.CD008225.pub2; Daniel Michelson, Clare Davenport, Janine Dretzke, Jane Barlow, and Crispin Day, "Do Evidence-Based Interventions Work When Tested in the 'Real World'? A Systematic Review and Meta-analysis of Parent Management Training for the Treatment of Child Disruptive Behavior," *Clinical Child and Family Psychology Review* 16, no. 1 (March 2013): 18–34; Nicholas Long, Mark C. Edwards, and Jayne Bellando, "Parent Training Interventions," in *Handbook of Childhood Psychopathology and Developmental Disabilities Treatment*, ed. Johnny L. Matson, Autism and Child Psychopathology series (N.p.: Springer Nature, 2017), 63–86.

24. Kalil and Ryan, "Parenting Practices and Socioeconomic Gaps in Childhood Outcomes," 43.

25. Diana Hernández, Alice Topping, Carole L. Hutchinson, Anne Martin, Jeanne Brooks-Gunn, and Amélie Petitclerc, "Client Attrition in the Nurse-Family Partnership: Revisiting Metrics of Impact in a Home Visitation Program in the United States," *Health and Social Care* 27, no. 4 (July 2019): e483–e493; Ruth A. O'Brien, Patricia Moritz, Dennis W. Luckey, Maureen W. McClatchey, Erin M. Ingoldsby, and David L. Olds, "Mixed Methods Analysis of Participant Attrition in the Nurse-Family Partnership," *Prevention Science* 13 (2012): 219–228. Mother quoted in Margaret L. Holland, Julie J. Christensen, Laura P. Shone, Margaret H. Kearney, and Harriet J. Kitzman, "Women's Reasons for Attrition from a Nurse Home Visiting Program," *Journal of Obstetric, Gynecologic, & Neonatal Nursing* 43, no. 1 (January–February 2014): 64.

26. For my calculations based on Incredible Years, see Invest in Kids, *Annual Report, 2017–18* (Denver, CO: Invest in Kids, 2018), https://www.iik.org/media/1678/2018iikannualre port.pdf. See also Carolyn Webster-Stratton, *Bringing the Incredible Years Programs to Scale* (N.p.: Incredible Years, n.d.), 20, http://www.incredibleyears.com/wp-content/uploads /Bringing-IY-Programs-to-Scale.pdf.

27. In *Parent Management Training*, Kazdin reviews the evidence finding that lower socioeconomic status predicts higher dropout rates from these programs. Quote from Michelson, et al., "Do Evidence-Based Interventions Work?," 23.

28. Unless otherwise noted, all quotes by Roger Morgan and Bud Fry in this section are based on the following sources: Roger Morgan, interviewed by the author, March 24, 2018, and Ralph "Bud" Fry, interviewed by the author, July 23, 2020.

29. To protect the confidentiality of the parents in the class, I omit the location of the Parent Project session I attended as well as all real names and individually identifying details about both teachers and participants. The class took place over 12 weeks in 2018 on a public school campus in a racially and economically diverse metropolitan area. I was open about my status as an observer without any children of my own (at that time), but I did participate in group exercises at the recommendation of Roger Morgan as a way to experience what the course might feel like for parents. I explained when asked that I did not have any children and was participating in the class as part of a research project.

30. Animals and children share a long-interwoven history in American law. When Henry Bergh, founder of the Society for the Prevention of Cruelty to Animals, helped petition the courts to rescue a child from her abusive foster parents in 1874, a reporter observed that "the first chapter of children's rights was being written under warrant of that made for the dog" (quoted in Eric A. Shelman and Stephen Lazoritz, *The Mary Ellen Wilson Child Abuse Case and the Beginning of Children's Rights in 19th Century America* [Jefferson, NC: McFarland, 2005], 9).

31. For an example of how "reversion to the mean" can generate a powerful yet false perception of program efficacy, see Amy Finkelstein, Annetta Zhou, Sarah Taubman, and Joseph Doyle, "Health Care Hotspotting—a Randomized, Controlled Trial," *New England Journal of Medicine* 382, no. 2 (January 9, 2020): 152–162.

32. A preliminary draft of the Parent Project study was graciously provided by the principal investigator, Keith Edwards, a recently retired professor of psychology at Biola University. The study also sought to measure impacts several months after the program's completion at week 24, but due to substantial attrition from a small baseline sample these impacts are estimated too imprecisely to be informative. On leveraging random assignment of cases to judges, see for example Anna Aizer and Joseph J. Doyle, "Juvenile Incarceration, Human Capital, and Future Crime: Evidence from Randomly Assigned Judges," *Quarterly Journal of Economics* 130, no. 2 (May 1, 2015): 759–803.

33. "Parenting in America," Pew Social Trends, December 17, 2015, https://www.pewsocial trends.org/2015/12/17/parenting-in-america/.

CHAPTER 4

1.   Andrea Prado Tuma, Laura S. Hamilton, and Tiffany Berglund, *How Do Teachers Perceive Feedback and Evaluation Systems? Findings from the American Teacher Panel* (Santa Monica, CA: RAND, 2018).

2.   John P. Papay and Matthew A. Kraft, "Productivity Returns to Experience in the Teacher Labor Market: Methodological Challenges and New Evidence on Long-Term Career Improvement," *Journal of Public Economics* 130 (October 2015): 105–119.

3.   Learning Heroes, *Parents 2016: Hearts & Minds of Parents in an Uncertain World* (Arlington, VA: Learning Heroes, 2016); Learning Heroes, *Parents 2017: Unleashing Their Power and Potential* (Arlington, VA: Learning Heroes, 2017); Learning Heroes, *Parents 2018: Going Beyond Good Grades*; Peter Bergman, "Parent–Child Information Frictions and Human Capital Investment: Evidence from a Field Experiment," *Journal of Political Economy* 129, no. 1 (January 1, 2021): 286–322; Sheila Bonilla, Sarah Kehl, Kenny Y. C. Kwong, Tricia Morphew, Rital Kachru, and Craig A. Jones, "School Absenteeism in Children with Asthma in a Los Angeles Inner City School," *Journal of Pediatrics* 147, no. 6 (December 1, 2005): 802–806.

4.   Learning Heroes, *Parents 2016*, *Parents 2017*, and *Parents 2018*; Josh Kinsler and Ronni Pavan, "Local Distortions in Parental Beliefs over Child Skill," *Journal of Political Economy* 129, no. 1 (August 20, 2020): 81–100.

5.   Quoted in Sharon Hays, *The Cultural Contradictions of Motherhood* (New Haven, CT: Yale University Press, 1998), 75.

6.   Justin Kruger and David Dunning, "Unskilled and Unaware of It: How Difficulties in Recognizing One's Own Incompetence Lead to Inflated Self-Assessments," *Journal of Personality and Social Psychology* 77, no. 6 (January 2000): 1121–1134; David Dunning, "Chapter Five—the Dunning-Kruger Effect: On Being Ignorant of One's Own Ignorance," *Advances in Experimental Social Psychology* 44 (2011): 247–296. For evidence that Dunning-Kruger effects are probably not statistical artifacts in many cases, see Matthew Motta, Timothy Callaghan, and Steven Sylvester, "Knowing Less but Presuming More: Dunning-Kruger Effects and the Endorsement of Anti-vaccine Policy Attitudes," *Social Science & Medicine*

211 (2018): 274–281; Bergman, "Parent–Child Information Frictions"; Kinsler and Pavan, "Local Distortions in Parental Beliefs."

7.   Learning Heroes, *Parents 2018*.

8.   The other major reason why these markets don't exist is "moral hazard," referring to the problem that people may behave differently (e.g., more recklessly or leisurely) once they have insurance. George A. Akerlof, "The Market for 'Lemons': Quality Uncertainty and the Market Mechanism," *Quarterly Journal of Economics* 84, no. 3 (August 1970): 488–500; Michael Rothschild and Joseph Stiglitz, "Equilibrium in Competitive Insurance Markets: An Essay on the Economics of Imperfect Information," *Quarterly Journal of Economics* 90, no. 4 (November 1976): 629–649; Raj Chetty and Amy Finkelstein, "Social Insurance: Connecting Theory to Data," in *Handbook of Public Economics*, vol. 5, ed. Alan J. Auerbach, Raj Chetty, Martin Feldstein, and Emmanuel Saez (Amsterdam: Elsevier, 2013), 111–193; Nathaniel Hendren, "Knowledge of Future Job Loss and Implications for Unemployment Insurance," *American Economic Review* 107, no. 7 (July 1, 2017): 1778–1823.

9.   Emily Oster, "Does Disease Cause Vaccination? Disease Outbreaks and Vaccination Response," *Journal of Health Economics* 57 (January 1, 2018): 90–101; Jorge L. Ortiz, "Anti-vaxxers Open Door for Measles, Mumps, Other Old-Time Diseases Back from Near Extinction," *USA Today*, March 28, 2019.

10. Seth Mnookin, *The Panic Virus: A True Story of Medicine, Science, and Fear* (New York: Simon & Schuster, 2011); Brian Deer, *The Doctor Who Fooled the World: Science, Deception, and the War on Vaccines* (Baltimore: Johns Hopkins University Press, 2020).

11. Motta, Callaghan, and Sylvester, "Knowing Less but Presuming More."

12. For example, see James G. Hodge Jr. and Lawrence O. Gostin, "School Vaccination Requirements: Historical, Social, and Legal Perspectives," *Kentucky Law Journal* 90 (2001): 831–890; Oster, "Does Disease Cause Vaccination?"

13. Nineteenth-century opposition to the smallpox vaccine was different from the modern "antivax" movement in that smallpox was a much graver, more pervasive, and more immediate threat. This was not a matter of free riding strategically on the safety afforded by other families' vaccinations; it was fear and confusion. On vaccines and school mandates, see John Duffy, "School Vaccination: The Precursor to School Medical Inspection," in "George Rosen Memorial Issue," special issue of *Journal of the History of Medicine and Allied Sciences* 33, no. 3 (July 1978): 344–355; W. A. Orenstein and A. R. Hinman, "The Immunization System in the United States—the Role of School Immunization Laws," *Vaccine* 17, suppl. 3 (October 29, 1999): S19–S24. On risk factors of the smallpox vaccine, see Edward A. Belongia and Allison L. Naleway, "Smallpox Vaccine: The Good, the Bad, and the Ugly," *Clinical Medicine and Research* 1, no. 2 (April 2003): 87–92.

14. Among economists, the idea that borrowing constraints can reduce investment in child skill development is most associated with Gary Stanley Becker, *Human Capital: A Theoretical and Empirical Analysis with Special Reference to Education* (Chicago: University of Chicago

Press, 1964). On Guyana's offshore oil deposits, see David Blackmon, "World's Largest Recent Offshore Oil Discovery Progresses amid Political Tensions, Disputes," *Forbes*, July 29, 2019, https://www.forbes.com/sites/davidblackmon/2019/07/29/worlds-largest-recent -offshore-oil-discovery-progresses-amid-political-tensions-disputes/#5213341f672f. For illustration, I assume a price of $50 per barrel.

15. Quoted in Smuts, *Science in the Service of Children*, 97.

16. Betty Smith, *A Tree Grows in Brooklyn*, 75th anniversary ed. (New York: Harper Perennial Modern Classics, 2018), 355, emphasis in original.

17. The seminal paper is Louis S. Jacobson, Robert J. Lalonde, and Daniel G. Sullivan, "Earnings Losses of Displaced Workers," *American Economic Review* 83, no. 4 (1993): 685–709.

18. Nathaniel G. Hilger, "Parental Job Loss and Children's Long-Term Outcomes: Evidence from 7 Million Fathers' Layoffs," *American Economic Journal: Applied Economics* 8, no. 3 (2016): 247–283. I began this research focusing on mothers, found similarly puzzling small impacts, then shifted to fathers to obtain larger impacts on family income.

19. On the cost of a degree, see Adam Looney and Michael Greenstone, "Where Is the Best Place to Invest $102,000—in Stocks, Bonds, or a College Degree?," *Brookings* (blog), June 25, 2011, https://www.brookings.edu/research/where-is-the-best-place-to-invest-102000-in -stocks-bonds-or-a-college-degree/. Note this cost does not include the opportunity cost of foregone earnings.

20. Spending by parents with children in college: Hilger, "Parental Job Loss and Children's Long-Term Outcomes." Spending by parents with children in early education: author's calculations in Urban Institute, and Child Trends, "National Survey of America's Families (NSAF), 2002," Inter-university Consortium for Political and Social Research [distributor], October 3, 2007, https://doi.org/10.3886/ICPSR04582.v1. Note that it does not matter for the point here if parental income affects access to other public or private benefits; what matters is that parents on average spend a very small share of new resources they control on direct investments in child skill development. There may be an attenuation bias from restricting to families with children who attend college or child care, but other biases push in the opposite direction, and these biases are unlikely to be off by an order of magnitude.

21. Annette Lareau, *Unequal Childhoods: Class, Race, and Family Life*, 2nd ed. with an update a decade later (Berkeley: University of California Press, 2011), 411.

22. George Bulman, Robert Fairlie, Sarena Goodman, and Adam Isen, "Parental Resources and College Attendance: Evidence from Lottery Wins," *American Economic Review* 111, no. 4 (April 2021): 1201–1240.

23. Susan Dynarski and Judith Scott-Clayton, "Financial Aid Policy: Lessons from Research," *Future of Children* 23, no. 1 (2013): 67–91.

24. In sharp contrast with results in Hilger, "Parental Job Loss and Children's Long-Term Outcomes," and those in Bulman et al., "Parental Resources and College Attendance," Randall Akee and his colleagues find extremely large impacts of parental income on educational

outcomes for adolescent children. However, the conditions observed in that study also allowed children (not their parents) to start collecting their own payouts, and those payouts were structured to incentivize high school graduation both in direct ways and through changes in the local labor market. The study is therefore best thought of as estimating impacts of higher parental income along with large, salient new financial and professional rewards for completing high school. See Randall K. Q. Akee, William E. Copeland, Gordon Keeler, Adrian Angold, and E. Jane Costello, "Parents' Incomes and Children's Outcomes: A Quasi-experiment Using Transfer Payments from Casino Profits," *American Economic Journal: Applied Economics* 2, no. 1 (2010): 86–115.

25. SNAP (originally Food Stamps) has been found to benefit children's long-term outcomes, but only if parents receive the benefits when children are younger than age five. Although economists have traditionally viewed SNAP as an income-transfer program, recent work suggests it should be viewed more as a nutrition-support program due to a large, surprising "label" effect that tilts household budgets toward food. See Martha Bailey, Hilary Hoynes, Maya Rossin-Slater, and Reed Walker, *Is the Social Safety Net a Long-Term Investment? Large-Scale Evidence from the Food Stamps Program*, NBER Working Paper no. 26942 (Cambridge, MA: National Bureau of Economic Research, 2020); Justine Hastings and Jesse M. Shapiro, "How Are SNAP Benefits Spent? Evidence from a Retail Panel," *American Economic Review* 108, no. 12 (December 2018): 3493–3540; Hastings, Kessler, and Shapiro, "The Effect of SNAP on the Composition of Purchased Foods"; Allcott et al., "Food Deserts and the Causes of Nutritional Inequality."

Earned Income Tax Credit (EITC) benefits have been found to improve elementary-school children's academic achievement for the least-advantaged families. EITC benefits could also be subject to a labeling effect that tilts household spending toward children, in comparison to income transfers, given that the EITC benefit eligibility and amount depend heavily on having dependent children. See Gordon B. Dahl and Lance Lochner, "The Impact of Family Income on Child Achievement: Evidence from the Earned Income Tax Credit," *American Economic Review* 102, no. 5 (August 2012): 1927–1956; Hilary Hoynes, Doug Miller, and David Simon, "Income, the Earned Income Tax Credit, and Infant Health," *American Economic Journal: Economic Policy* 7, no. 1 (February 2015): 172–211.

Welfare experiments combine various elements of income support, center-based childcare, and parental employment. These studies tend to find benefits of parental income only for children younger than age five, before they enter public school. And in some cases, impacts of welfare programs appear to arise primarily from access to center-based childcare rather than from parental income itself. See Pamela A. Morris, Lisa A. Gennetian, and Greg J. Duncan, "Effects of Welfare and Employment Policies on Young Children: New Findings on Policy Experiments Conducted in the Early 1990s," *Social Policy Report* 19, no. 2 (June 2005): 1–20; Pamela A. Morris, Greg J. Duncan, and Elizabeth Clark-Kauffman, "Child Well-Being in an Era of Welfare Reform: The Sensitivity of Transition in Development to Policy Change," *Developmental Psychology* 41, no. 6 (2005): 919–932; Greg J. Duncan, Pamela A. Morris, and Chris Rodrigues, "Does Money Really Matter? Estimating Impacts of Family Income on Young Children's Achievement with Data from Random-Assignment Experiments," *Developmental Psychology* 47, no. 5 (September 2011): 1263–1279.

26. Author's calculations. The impacts of EITC are typically reported per $1,000 in transfers. The impacts of WIC are typically reported as impacts of overall participation, not per $1,000. Yonatan Ben-Shalom and his colleagues report one year of WIC participation entails $648 of transfers in 2007 dollars. Both WIC and EITC typically entail three to four years of participation. Putting estimates into the same inflation-adjusted dollar terms suggests that $1,000 of public spending raises average academic achievement at early ages by about 0.33sd for WIC versus 0.06sd for EITC and welfare experiments, and reduces rates of low birth weight by more than 10 percent for WIC versus 1.5–3.0 percent for EITC.

On the costs of WIC, see Yonatan Ben-Shalom, Robert A. Moffitt, and John Karl Scholz, *An Assessment of the Effectiveness of Anti-poverty Programs in the United States,* NBER Working Paper no. 17042 (Cambridge, MA: National Bureau of Economic Research, May 2011).

On low birth weight, see Brent Kreider, John V. Pepper, and Manan Roy, "Does the Women, Infants, and Children Program Improve Infant Health Outcomes?," *Economic Inquiry* 58, no. 4 (2020): 1731–1756; Maya Rossin-Slater, "WIC in Your Neighborhood: New Evidence on the Impacts of Geographic Access to Clinics," *Journal of Public Economics* 102 (June 2013): 51–69; Hilary Hoynes, Doug Miller, and David Simon, "Income, the Earned Income Tax Credit, and Infant Health," *American Economic Journal: Economic Policy* 7, no. 1 (February 2015): 172–211.

On academic achievement, see Margot I. Jackson, "Early Childhood WIC Participation, Cognitive Development, and Academic Achievement," *Social Science & Medicine* 126 (February 2015): 145–153; Dahl and Lochner, "The Impact of Family Income on Child Achievement"; Duncan, Morris, and Rodrigues, "Does Money Really Matter?"

27. Public Agenda, *Teaching Interrupted: Do Discipline Policies in Today's Public Schools Foster the Common Good?* (New York: Public Agenda, with support from Common Good, 2004), https://eric.ed.gov/?id=ED485312; NPR, "The National Public Radio / Kaiser Family Foundation / Kennedy School of Government Education Survey," August 1999, https://kaiserfamilyfoundation.files.wordpress.com/1999/08/npr003-release-topline.pdf; both cited in Scott E. Carrell and Mark L. Hoekstra, "Externalities in the Classroom: How Children Exposed to Domestic Violence Affect Everyone's Kids," *American Economic Journal: Applied Economics* 2, no. 1 (2010): 211–228, 211.

28. Bonnie E. Carlson, "Children Exposed to Intimate Partner Violence: Research Findings and Implications for Intervention," *Trauma, Violence, & Abuse* 1, no. 4 (2000): 325. Also see citations in Scott E. Carrell, Mark Hoekstra, and Elira Kuka, "The Long-Run Effects of Disruptive Peers," *American Economic Review* 108, no. 11 (November 2018): 3377–3415.

29. Carrell and Hoekstra, "Externalities in the Classroom"; Scott E. Carrell and Mark Hoekstra, "Family Business or Social Problem? The Cost of Unreported Domestic Violence," *Journal of Policy Analysis and Management* 31, no. 4 (Fall 2012): 861–875; Carrell and Hoekstra, "Long-Run Effects of Disruptive Peers." In "Family Business or Social Problem?,"

Carrell and Hoekstra show that parents typically request restraining orders after many years of experience with domestic violence, suggesting that children with any restraining order in their family's future are much more likely to be experiencing severe stress at home. For similar findings on exposure to classmates with attention-deficit disorder, see Anna Aizer, *Peer Effects and Human Capital Accumulation: The Externalities of ADD*, NBER Working Paper no. 14354 (Cambridge, MA: National Bureau of Economic Research, 2008).

30. "Idylwild Elementary School: Teachers and Staff," GreatSchools, accessed July 3, 2020, https://www.greatschools.org/florida/gainesville/24-Idylwild-Elementary-School/#Teachers_staff.

31. Steve Carrell, interviewed by the author, July 18, 2018; Simone Balestra, Beatrix Eugster, and Helge Liebert, "Peers with Special Needs: Effects and Policies," *Review of Economics and Statistics* (August 10, 2020): 1–42.

32. For example, in "Children Exposed to Intimate Partner Violence" (323), Carlson suggests that approximately one-third of children may experience interparental violence at some point during childhood. That is six times the share of children in families requesting restraining orders in Alachua.

33. Stephen Billings and his colleagues in Charlotte, NC, and Jason Cook in Seattle show adverse impacts on peers of adding more low-income students to a school. They find 10 percentage points of additional low-income students reduce test scores by about 0.02 to 0.05sd. Billings and his colleagues found similar impacts from minority share and low-income share. See Stephen B. Billings, David J. Deming, and Jonah Rockoff, "School Segregation, Educational Attainment, and Crime: Evidence from the End of Busing in Charlotte-Mecklenburg," *Quarterly Journal of Economics* 129, no. 1 (2014): 435–476; Jason B. Cook, *Race-Blind Admissions, School Segregation, and Student Outcomes: Evidence from Race-Blind Magnet School Lotteries*, SSRN Working Paper, April 2, 2021, https://papers.ssrn.com/sol3/papers.cfm?abstract_id=3818304.

I convert test score impacts to earnings based on Chetty, Friedman, and Rockoff, "Measuring the Impacts of Teachers II." They find $7,000 of lifetime earnings per student for each 0.1sd increase in test scores for one year. With the lower estimate of a 0.02sd impact on test scores, the impact of shifting a classroom from 0 percent low-income students to 100 percent low-income students is 10 * (.02sd/10pp) * ($7,000/0.1sd) * 20 kids/class = $280,000.

Earlier studies found that school integration efforts benefited Black students and did not have adverse impacts on white students. However, as Rucker Johnson describes, school integration efforts also entailed infusions of additional funding and support into school districts to shield white families from potential spillovers and prevent mass white flight from public-school districts. The lack of negative impacts on white families are therefore consistent with Billings and his colleagues' finding that additional school resources and support can alleviate some of the adverse impacts of exposure to less-advantaged peers. Evidence from Boston's Metco program also suggests small adverse impacts of exposure to lower-achieving minority students, but this study examines exposure to a small subset of minority families that actively sought out the opportunity to send their children out of Boston into predominantly white suburban public schools. See Rucker Johnson, *Long-Run Impacts of School Desegregation & School Quality on Adult Attainments*, NBER Working Paper no. 16664 (Cambridge, MA: National Bureau of Economic Research, 2011, rev. 2015); Jonathan Guryan, "Desegregation and Black Dropout Rates," *American Economic Review* 94, no. 4 (2004): 919–943; Joshua D. Angrist and Kevin Lang, "Does School Integration Generate Peer Effects? Evidence from Boston's Metco Program," *American Economic Review* 94, no. 5 (2004): 1613–1634.

The impacts of having low-income and minority peers are about half as large as the impacts of having peers with very low academic achievement. These studies tend to find that 10 percentage points of additional low-achieving peers reduce scores by about 0.1sd. This is consistent with the fact that many low-income and minority children are not low achieving and would thus not be expected to have adverse impacts on classmates. See Scott A. Imberman, Adriana D. Kugler, and Bruce I. Sacerdote, "Katrina's Children: Evidence on the Structure of Peer Effects from Hurricane Evacuees," *American Economic Review* 102, no. 5 (2012): 2048–2082; Victor Lavy, M. Daniele Paserman, and Analia Schlosser, "Inside the Black Box of Ability Peer Effects: Evidence from Variation in the Proportion of Low Achievers in the Classroom," *Economic Journal* 122, no. 559 (March 1, 2012): 208–237.

On "ten times more children in poor or near-poor families," see Kevin Drum, "Half of All Public School Kids in Poverty? Be Careful," *Mother Jones*, January 17, 2015.

34. See introduction, note 30, and Johnston, *Preferences, Selection, and the Structure of Teacher Compensation*.

35. The benefits of economic diversity for more advantaged children, although less tangible, may be very real in terms of greater empathy, compassion, and prosocial behavior in adulthood. See Gautam Rao, "Familiarity Does Not Breed Contempt: Generosity, Discrimination, and Diversity in Delhi Schools," *American Economic Review* 109, no. 3 (March 2019): 774–809.

CHAPTER 5

1. Dionissi Aliprantis, Daniel R. Carroll, and Eric R. Young, *The Dynamics of the Racial Wealth Gap*, Working Paper no. 19-18 (Cleveland: Federal Reserve Bank of Cleveland, 2020), 33; Robert Barsky, John Bound, Kerwin Ko' Charles, and Joseph P. Lupton, "Accounting for the Black–White Wealth Gap," *Journal of the American Statistical Association* 97, no. 459 (September 1, 2002): 663–673; Hero Ashman and Seth Neumuller, "Can Income Differences Explain the Racial Wealth Gap? A Quantitative Analysis," *Review of Economic Dynamics* 35 (January 1, 2020): 220–239. Note that Ashman and Neumuller, despite their finding that inheritances matter, agree with Aliprantis, Carroll, and Young that closing income gaps would close wealth gaps.

2. This section draws heavily on Heather Andrea Williams, *Self-Taught: African American Education in Slavery and Freedom* (Chapel Hill: University of North Carolina Press, 2007).

3. Williams, *Self-Taught*, 13.

4. Williams, *Self-Taught*, 18.

5. Williams, *Self-Taught*, 20–21.

6. Williams, *Self-Taught*, 23, 11.

7. Williams, *Self-Taught*, 51.

8. The "end" of the Civil War in the South gave way to extrajudicial killings of Union soldiers and African Americans, other forms of slavery, and overall restoration of Confederate society. The North quickly stopped requiring Southern leaders to swear allegiance to the United States. See Richard White, *The Republic for Which It Stands: The United States during Reconstruction and the Gilded Age, 1865–1896* (New York: Oxford University Press, 2017); Douglas A. Blackmon, *Slavery by Another Name: The Re-enslavement of Black Americans from the Civil War to World War II* (New York: Anchor, 2009).

9. Booker T. Washington, *Up from Slavery: An Autobiography* (Garden City, NY: Doubleday, 1901), 12.

10. Quoted in Robert A. Margo, *Race and Schooling in the South, 1880–1950: An Economic History* (Chicago: University of Chicago Press, 1990).

11. Margo, *Race and Schooling in the South*; David Card and Alan B. Krueger, "School Quality and Black–White Relative Earnings: A Direct Assessment," *Quarterly Journal of Economics* 107, no. 1 (1992): 151–200. On Black–white incarceration gaps back to 1880, see Katherine Eriksson, "Education and Incarceration in the Jim Crow South: Evidence from Rosenwald Schools," *Journal of Human Resources* 55, no. 1 (2020): 43–75. On long-term origins of Black–white single parenthood gaps, see Steve Ruggles, "The Origins of African-American Family Structure," *American Sociological Review* 59, no. 1 (February 1994): 136–151.

12. James Edward Blackwell, *Mainstreaming Outsiders: The Production of Black Professionals*, 2nd ed. (Dix Hills, NY: General Hall, 1987); Catherine J. Weinberger, *Engineering Educational Opportunity: Impacts of 1970s and 1980s Policies to Increase the Share of Black College Graduates with Major in Engineering or Computer Science*, NBER Working Paper no. 23703 (Cambridge, MA: National Bureau of Economic Research, August 2017).

13. Mark V. Tushnet, *The NAACP's Legal Strategy against Segregated Education: 1925–1950* (Chapel Hill: University of North Carolina Press, 2004); Card and Krueger, "School Quality and Black–White Relative Earnings."

14. I focus on earnings by men here because they are easier to interpret as a barometer of economic opportunity. Given prevailing social norms around childcare and work, higher earnings by women reflect a complex mix of greater economic opportunity and reduced access to economically supportive domestic partnerships. See Patrick Bayer and Kerwin Kofi Charles, "Divergent Paths: A New Perspective on Earnings Differences between Black and White Men since 1940," *Quarterly Journal of Economics* 133, no. 3 (2018): 1459–1501; Chetty et al., "Race and Economic Opportunity in the United States"; Neal, "The Measured Black–White Wage Gap among Women."

15. Bayer and Charles, "Divergent Paths"; David H. Autor, Lawrence F. Katz, and Melissa S. Kearney, "Trends in U.S. Wage Inequality: Revising the Revisionists," *Review of Economics and Statistics* 90, no. 2 (May 2008): 300–323; Ellora Derenoncourt and Claire Montialoux, "Minimum Wages and Racial Inequality," *Quarterly Journal of Economics* 136, no. 1 (2021): 169–228.

16. On rising incarceration rates, see Bruce Western and Christopher Wildeman, "The Black Family and Mass Incarceration," *ANNALS of the American Academy of Political and Social Science* 621, no. 1 (2009): 221–242; Derek Neal and Armin Rick, *The Prison Boom and the Lack of Black Progress after Smith and Welch*, NBER Working Paper no. 20283 (Cambridge, MA: National Bureau of Economic Research, 2014). On examples of criminal justice systems perpetuating slavery before mass incarceration, see Blackmon, *Slavery by Another Name*. On broad context and causes of mass incarceration, see Western and Wildeman, "The Black Family and Mass Incarceration," and Michelle Alexander, *The New Jim Crow: Mass Incarceration in the Age of Colorblindness* (New York: New Press, 2010). On ever-incarcerated rates by race, see Thomas P. Bonczar and Allen J. Beck, *Lifetime Likelihood of Going to State or Federal Prison*, US Bureau of Justice Statistics Special Report (Washington, DC: US Department of Justice, Office of Justice Programs, March 1997). On employment and currently incarcerated rates by race and parental income, see Chetty et al., "Race and Economic Opportunity in the United States." On long-term trends in Black institutionalization (in practice, incarceration) by age group, see Neal and Rick, *The Prison Boom*, table 1.

17. On sheriffs, see George Bulman, "Law Enforcement Leaders and the Racial Composition of Arrests," *Economic Inquiry* 57, no. 4 (2019): 1842–1858. On police use of force, see Roland G. Fryer Jr., "An Empirical Analysis of Racial Differences in Police Use of Force," *Journal of Political Economy* 127, no. 3 (June 2019): 52; Bocar A. Ba, Dean Knox, Jonathan Mummolo, and Roman Rivera, "The Role of Officer Race and Gender in Police–Civilian Interactions in Chicago," *Science* 371, no. 6530 (February 12, 2021): 696–702. On searches, see Kate Antonovics and Brian G. Knight, "A New Look at Racial Profiling: Evidence from the Boston Police Department," *Review of Economics and Statistics* 91, no. 1 (February 2009): 163–177. On fines, see Felipe Goncalves and Steven Mello, "A Few Bad Apples? Racial Bias in Policing," *American Economic Review* 111, no. 5 (May 2021): 1406–1441. On charges and sentencing, see Crystal S. Yang, "Free at Last? Judicial Discretion and Racial Disparities in Federal Sentencing," *Journal of Legal Studies* 44, no. 1 (January 2015): 75–111; M. Marit Rehavi and Sonja B. Starr, "Racial Disparity in Federal Criminal Sentences," *Journal of Political Economy* 122, no. 6 (December 2014): 1320–1354. On bail decisions, see David Arnold, Will Dobbie, and Crystal S. Yang, "Racial Bias in Bail Decisions," *Quarterly Journal of Economics* 133, no. 4 (November 1, 2018): 1885–1932. On capital sentencing, see Alberto Alesina and Eliana La Ferrara, "A Test of Racial Bias in Capital Sentencing," *American Economic Review* 104, no. 11 (November 2014): 3397–3433. On convictions, see Shamena Anwar, Patrick Bayer, and Randi Hjalmarsson, "The Impact of Jury Race in Criminal Trials," *Quarterly Journal of Economics* 127, no. 2 (May 2012): 1017–1055. On incarcerations, see David S. Abrams, Marianne Bertrand, and Sendhil

Mullainathan, "Do Judges Vary in Their Treatment of Race?," *Journal of Legal Studies* 41, no. 2 (June 2012): 347–383.

18. Price V. Fishback, Jessica LaVoice, Allison Shertzer, and Randall Walsh, *Race, Risk, and the Emergence of Federal Redlining*, NBER Working Paper no. 28146 (Cambridge, MA: National Bureau of Economic Research, November 30, 2020). On zoning, see Allison Shertzer, Tate Twinam, and Randall P. Walsh, "Race, Ethnicity, and Discriminatory Zoning," *American Economic Journal: Applied Economics* 8, no. 3 (2016): 217–246; Prottoy Akbar, Sijie Li, Allison Shertzer, and Randall P. Walsh, *Racial Segregation in Housing Markets and the Erosion of Black Wealth*, NBER Working Paper no. 25805 (Cambridge, MA: National Bureau of Economic Research, May 2019); Patrick Bayer, Fernando Ferreira, and Stephen L. Ross, "What Drives Racial and Ethnic Differences in High-Cost Mortgages? The Role of High-Risk Lenders," *Review of Financial Studies* 31, no. 1 (January 1, 2018): 175–205; Peter Christensen and Christopher Timmins, *Sorting or Steering: Experimental Evidence on the Economic Effects of Housing Discrimination*, NBER Working Paper no. 24826 (Cambridge, MA: National Bureau of Economic Research, 2018); Margo, *Race and Schooling in the South, 1880–1950*; Robert D. Bullard and Glenn Johnson, eds., *Highway Robbery: Transportation Racism & New Routes to Equity* (Boston: South End Press, 2004); Robert D. Bullard, *Dumping on Dixie: Race, Class, and Environmental Quality*, 3rd ed. (Boulder, CO: Routledge, 2000).

19. On differences in neighborhoods where Black and white children grow up today, see Chetty et al., "Race and Economic Opportunity in the United States."

20. Melinda C. Miller, "'The Righteous and Reasonable Ambition to Become a Landholder': Land and Racial Inequality in the Postbellum South," *Review of Economics and Statistics* 102, no. 2 (June 26, 2019): 381–394; Walter L. Fleming, "The Freedmen's Savings Bank," *Yale Review*, May–August 1906, 48; Marcella Alsan and Marianne Wanamaker, "Tuskegee and the Health of Black Men," *Quarterly Journal of Economics* 133, no. 1 (February 2018): 407–455; Alex Albright, Jeremy Cook, James Feigenbaum, Laura Kincaide, Jason Long, and Nathan Nunn, "After the Burning: The Economic Effects of the 1921 Tulsa Race Massacre," working paper, Harvard University, 2021, 63, https://scholar.harvard.edu/files/nunn/files/tulsa.pdf; Orley Ashenfelter, "Racial Discrimination and Trade Unionism," *Journal of Political Economy* 80, no. 3, part 1 (May 1, 1972): 435–464; Ira Katznelson, *Fear Itself: The New Deal and the Origins of Our Time* (New York: Liveright, 2013).

21. Michelle Singletary, "Stop Telling Black People We Could Close the Wealth Gap If We Valued Education More," *Washington Post*, September 25, 2020. For a description of buying homes "on contract," see Ta-Nehisi Coates, "The Case for Reparations," *Atlantic*, June 2014. On loopholes in land inherited as "heirs' property," see Lizzie Presser, "Their Family Bought Land One Generation after Slavery: The Reels Brothers Spent Eight Years in Jail for Refusing to Leave It," ProPublica with the *New Yorker*, July 15, 2019, https://features.propublica.org/black-land-loss/heirs-property-rights-why-black-families-lose-land-south/.

22. Damon Young, "Racism Makes Me Question Everything. I Got the Vaccine Anyway," *New York Times*, April 9, 2021.

23. Peter Ganong, Damon Jones, Pascal Noel, Diana Farrell, Fiona Greig, and Chris Wheat, *Wealth, Race, and Consumption Smoothing of Typical Income Shocks*, NBER Working Paper 27552 (Cambridge, MA: National Bureau of Economic Research, 2020).

24. Ronald F. Ferguson, "Why America's Black–White School Achievement Gap Persists," in *Ethnicity, Social Mobility, and Public Policy*, ed. Glenn C. Loury, Tariq Modood, and Steven M. Teles (Cambridge: Cambridge University Press, 2005), 309–341, 316.

25. Jeanne Brooks-Gunn and Lisa B. Markman, "The Contribution of Parenting to Ethnic and Racial Gaps in School Readiness," *Future of Children* 15, no. 1 (2005): 139–168.

26. Broader measures of parental skill-building resources can account for at least two-thirds of early Black–white gaps in academic achievement. See Meredith Phillips, Jeanne Brooks-Gunn, Greg J. Duncan, Pamela Klebanov, and Jonathan Crane, "Family Background, Parenting Practices, and the Black–White Test Score Gap," in *The Black–White Test Score Gap*, ed. Jencks and Phillips, 103–145; Owen Thompson, "The Determinants of Racial Differences in Parenting Practices," *Journal of Political Economy* 126, no. 1 (February 2018): 438–449; Petra E. Todd and Kenneth I. Wolpin, "The Production of Cognitive Achievement in Children: Home, School, and Racial Test Score Gaps," *Journal of Human Capital* 1, no. 1 (2007): 91–136; Ferguson, "Why America's Black–White School Achievement Gap Persists"; Brooks-Gunn and Markman, "The Contribution of Parenting to Ethnic and Racial Gaps in School Readiness." These gaps are similar to those prevailing between rich and poor parents generally: see Kalil and Ryan, "Parenting Practices and Socioeconomic Gaps."

I predict the impacts of a 0.5sd gap in parental skill building on children's income in two back-of-the-envelope ways. One is based on impacts produced by adopting parents, as discussed in Sacerdote, "How Large Are the Effects from Changes in Family Environment?," table 7, adjusted for restricted range. Another way is based on teachers, as described in Chetty, Friedman, and Rockoff, "Measuring the Impacts of Teachers II," assuming that parents have twice the impact of individual teachers on children's skill development and that impacts of teachers accumulate linearly over time. Both approaches confirm that observed gaps in parental skill building could quite easily account for a large share of racial income gaps. These calculations are speculative and merely establish plausibility.

27. For example, see Kerwin Kofi Charles and Jonathan Guryan, "Prejudice and Wages: An Empirical Assessment of Becker's *The Economics of Discrimination*," *Journal of Political Economy* 116, no. 5 (2008): 773–809. However, much uncertainty remains around the share of racial disparities accounted for by discrimination in these systems. See Kevin Lang and Ariella Kahn-Lang Spitzer, "Race Discrimination: An Economic Perspective," *Journal of Economic Perspectives* 34, no. 2 (May 1, 2020): 68–89.

28. Charles and Guryan, "Prejudice and Wages"; Derek A. Neal and William R. Johnson, "The Role of Premarket Factors in Black–White Wage Differences," *Journal of Political Economy* 104, no. 5 (1996): 869–895; Johnson and Neal, "Basic Skills and the Black–White Earnings Gap"; Marianne Bertrand and Sendhil Mullainathan, "Are Emily and Greg More Employable Than Lakisha and Jamal? A Field Experiment on Labor Market

Discrimination," *American Economic Review* 94, no. 4 (2004): 991–1013; Devah Pager, Bruce Western, and Bart Bonikowski, "Discrimination in a Low-Wage Labor Market: A Field Experiment," *American Sociological Review* 74, no. 5 (October 2009): 777–799; Patrick Kline and Christopher Walters, "Reasonable Doubt: Experimental Detection of Job-Level Employment Discrimination," *Econometrica* 89, no. 2 (2021): 765–792; Laura Giuliano, David I. Levine, and Jonathan Leonard, "Racial Bias in the Manager–Employee Relationship," *Journal of Human Resources* 46, no. 1 (Winter 2011): 26–52; Dylan Glover, Amanda Pallais, and William Pariente, "Discrimination as a Self-Fulfilling Prophecy: Evidence from French Grocery Stores," *Quarterly Journal of Economics* 132, no. 3 (August 1, 2017): 1219–1260.

29. On one-in-four Black workers with a college degree, see US Census Bureau, "Educational Attainment in the United States," table 1.4, last rev. April 17, 2020, https://www.census .gov/data/tables/2018/demo/education-attainment/cps-detailed-tables.html. Just looking at discrimination in callback rates for résumés sent to employers at random, we will find that Black college graduates face about a quarter of the disadvantage experienced by noncollege graduates; compare Bertrand and Mullainathan, "Are Emily and Greg More Employable," with John M. Nunley, Adam Pugh, Nicholas Romero, and R. Alan Seals, "Racial Discrimination in the Labor Market for Recent College Graduates: Evidence from a Field Experiment," *B.E. Journal of Economic Analysis & Policy* 15, no. 3 (July 1, 2015): 1093–1125. Many comparisons of Black and white college graduates reach misleading conclusions by failing to account for large differences in college quality and other determinants of skill. On this point, see C. J. Libassi, *The Neglected College Race Gap: Racial Disparities among College Completers* (Washington, DC: Center for American Progress, 2018). On Black college graduates earning higher pay than similarly skilled white college graduates, see Peter Arcidiacono, Patrick Bayer, and Aurel Hizmo, "Beyond Signaling and Human Capital: Education and the Revelation of Ability," *American Economic Journal: Applied Economics* 2, no. 4 (2010): 76–104 and citations therein; Derek Neal, "Why Has Black–White Skill Convergence Stopped?," in *Handbook of the Economics of Education*, vol. 1, ed. Eric A. Hanushek and Finis Welch (Amsterdam: Elsevier, 2006), 511–576. Although a focus on hourly wages can miss discrimination in employment and hence earnings, this is more of a problem for non-college-educated workers due to their much higher baseline unemployment. For example, compare Johnson and Neal, "Basic Skills and the Black–White Earnings Gap," on earnings, with Neal and Johnson, "Role of Premarket Factors in Black–White Wage Differences," on wages.

   On zero or small Black–white earnings gaps in the specific professions listed in the text, see Dan P. Ly, Seth A. Seabury, and Anupam B. Jena, "Differences in Incomes of Physicians in the United States by Race and Sex: Observational Study," *BMJ* 353 (2016): 1–7; Heather Antecol, Deborah A. Cobb-Clark, and Eric Helland, "Bias in the Legal Profession: Self-Assessed versus Statistical Measures of Discrimination," *Journal of Legal Studies* 43, no. 2 (June 2014): 323–357; Jean Moore and Tracey Continelli, "Racial/Ethnic Pay Disparities among Registered Nurses (RNs) in U.S. Hospitals: An Econometric Regression Decomposition," *Health Services Research* 51, no. 2 (2016): 511–529; Seong Soo Oh and Gregory B.

Lewis, "Stemming Inequality? Employment and Pay of Female and Minority Scientists and Engineers," *Social Science Journal* 48, no. 2 (2011): 397–403.

30. On perceiving prejudice even in the absence of racial pay gaps, see Antecol, Cobb-Clark, and Helland, "Bias in the Legal Profession." On greater educational aspirations among Blacks, see Angel L. Harris, *Kids Don't Want to Fail: Oppositional Culture and the Black–White Achievement Gap* (Cambridge, MA: Harvard University Press, 2011); Barbara Schneider and Guan Saw, "Racial and Ethnic Gaps in Postsecondary Aspirations and Enrollment," *RSF: The Russell Sage Foundation Journal of the Social Sciences* 2, no. 5 (September 2016), https://muse.jhu.edu/article/633737. On Blacks obtaining greater educational attainment than similarly skilled whites, see Arcidiacono, Bayer, and Hizmo, "Beyond Signaling and Human Capital."

31. This theory has been articulated famously in Gary Becker, *The Economics of Discrimination*, 2nd ed. (Chicago: University of Chicago Press, 1957). So far, it has been tested most directly at a national level in Charles and Guryan, "Prejudice and Wages."

32. Christopher L. Foote, Warren C. Whatley, and Gavin Wright, "Arbitraging a Discriminatory Labor Market: Black Workers at the Ford Motor Company, 1918–1947," *Journal of Labor Economics* 21, no. 3 (2003): 493–532.

33. Robert Higgs, "Did Southern Farmers Discriminate?," *Agricultural History* 46, no. 2 (April 1972): 325–328; Robert Higgs, "Firm-Specific Evidence on Racial Wage Differentials and Workforce Segregation," *American Economic Review* 67, no. 2 (March 1977): 236–245; Robert Higgs, "Racial Wage Differentials in Agriculture: Evidence from North Carolina in 1887," *Agricultural History* 52, no. 2 (April 1978): 308–311; Celeste K. Carruthers and Marianne H. Wanamaker, "Separate and Unequal in the Labor Market: Human Capital and the Jim Crow Wage Gap," *Journal of Labor Economics* 35, no. 3 (July 2017): 655–696.

34. The Black artist and civil rights activist James Weldon Johnson once spent several days on a ship overhearing the banter of white workers "of the artisan class—engineers, machinists, plumbers, electrical workers, and helpers. . . . One expression that they constantly used brought to me more vividly than anything else ever had a realization of the Negro's economic and industrial plight. . . . [T]he expression which I heard at least a hundred times was, 'Never let a n----- pick up a tool.' 'Never let a n----- pick up a tool.' 'Never let a n----- pick up a tool'" (*Along This Way: The Autobiography of James Weldon Johnson* [New York: Viking, 1933], 335).

35. Frederick Douglass made a version of this argument in 1886, writing that white people's "malignant resistance is augmented as [the Black race] approaches the plane occupied by the white race, and yet I think that that resistance will gradually yield to the pressure of wealth, education, and high character" (*The Portable Frederick Douglass*, ed. John Stauffer and Henry Louis Gates [New York: Penguin Books, 2016], 514). Corrosion of stereotypes maps into the economic theory known as "statistical discrimination" as well as more recent behavioral theories about how stereotypes both reflect, magnify, and misperceive underlying group differences. See Pedro Bordalo, Katherine Coffman, Nicola Gennaioli, and

Andrei Shleifer, "Stereotypes," *Quarterly Journal of Economics* 131, no. 4 (2016): 1753–1794; J. Aislinn Bohren, Kareem Haggag, Alex Imas, and Devin G. Pope, "Inaccurate Statistical Discrimination," Working Paper no. 2019-86, Becker Friedman Institute for Economics, University of Chicago, 2019.

On the positive impacts of diversity in college-roommate pairings on tolerance and future diversity of social networks, see Johanne Boisjoly, Greg J. Duncan, Michael Kremer, Dan M. Levy, and Jacque Eccles, "Empathy or Antipathy? The Impact of Diversity," *American Economic Review* 96, no. 5 (December 2006): 1890–1905; Scott E. Carrell, Mark Hoekstra, and James E. West, "The Impact of College Diversity on Behavior toward Minorities," *American Economic Journal: Economic Policy* 11, no. 4 (November 2019): 159–182. Also see Seth K. Goldman and Daniel J. Hopkins, "Past Place, Present Prejudice: The Impact of Adolescent Racial Context on White Racial Attitudes," *Journal of Politics* 82, no. 2 (September 27, 2019): 529–542. On the "contact hypothesis" more generally, see Elizabeth Levy Paluck, Seth A. Green, and Donald P. Green, "The Contact Hypothesis Reevaluated," *Behavioural Public Policy* 3, no. 2 (November 2019): 129–158.

For research on other origins and moderators of prejudice, see M. Bertrand and E. Duflo, "Field Experiments on Discrimination," in *Handbook of Economic Field Experiments*, ed. Abhijit Vinayak Banerjee and Esther Duflo, vol. 1 of *Handbook of Field Experiments* (Amsterdam: North-Holland, 2017), 309–393. On the role of leadership as amplified by media, see Karsten Muller and Carlo Schwarz, "From Hashtag to Hate Crime: Twitter and Anti-minority Sentiment," SSRN Working Paper, July 24, 2020, https://ssrn.com/abstract=3149103, 93. On legal reforms, see Brian Wheaton, "Laws, Beliefs, and Backlash," working paper, Harvard University, 2020.

36. Brian Ray quoted in Douglas S. Massey and Nancy A. Denton, "Review of American Apartheid: Segregation and the Making of the Underclass," *Canadian Journal of Urban Research* 4, no. 2 (1995): 340–342. The unraveling of deliberate integration efforts can be seen in Rucker Johnson, *Children of the Dream: Why School Integration Works* (New York: Basic Books, 2019). On the role of decentralized market forces in preserving de facto segregation, see David M. Cutler, Edward L. Glaeser, and Jacob L. Vigdor, "The Rise and Decline of the American Ghetto," *Journal of Political Economy* 107, no. 3 (1999): 455–506.

37. "High Schools in New York City Public Schools District," *US News & World Report*, accessed December 1, 2020, https://www.usnews.com/education/best-high-schools/new-york/districts/new-york-city-public-schools-100001.

38. Thomas S. Dee, "Teachers, Race, and Student Achievement in a Randomized Experiment," *Review of Economics and Statistics* 86, no. 1 (2004): 195–210; Thomas S. Dee, "A Teacher Like Me: Does Race, Ethnicity, or Gender Matter?," *American Economic Review* 95, no. 2 (2005): 158–165; Amine Ouazad, "Assessed by a Teacher Like Me: Race and Teacher Assessments," *Education Finance and Policy* 9, no. 3 (July 1, 2014): 334–372; Seth Gershenson, Cassandra M. D. Hart, Joshua Hyman, Constance Lindsay, and Nicholas W. Papageorge, *The Long-Run Impacts of Same-Race Teachers*, NBER Working Paper no. 25254 (Cambridge, MA: National Bureau of Economic Research, November 2018); Alsan and

Wanamaker, "Tuskegee and the Health of Black Men"; Brad N. Greenwood, Rachel R. Hardeman, Laura Huang, and Aaron Sojourner, "Physician–Patient Racial Concordance and Disparities in Birthing Mortality for Newborns," *Proceedings of the National Academy of Sciences* 117, no. 35 (September 1, 2020): 21194–21200.

39. Demaree Bess, "California's Amazing Japanese," *Saturday Evening Post* 227 (1955), cited in Jaime Arellano-Bover, "Displacement, Diversity, and Mobility: Career Impacts of Japanese American Internment," working paper, Yale University, 2020, 66; Naomi Hirahara and Heather C. Lindquist, *Life after Manzanar* (Berkeley, CA: Heyday, 2018), 147; Christopher Su, "An Ambitious Social Experiment: Education in Japanese-American Internment Camps, 1942–1945," undergraduate thesis, MIT, 2011, https://dspace.mit.edu/bitstream/handle/1721.1/65525/746805717-MIT.pdf?sequence=2&isAllowed=y.

40. Teachers quoted in Pamela Grundy, *Color and Character: West Charlotte High and the American Struggle over Educational Equality* (Chapel Hill: University of North Carolina Press, 2017), as quoted in Johnson, *Children of the Dream*, 175.

41. Taylor Branch, *Parting the Waters: America in the King Years, 1954–63* (New York: Simon & Schuster, 1989), 52.

42. This section draws heavily on Nathaniel Hilger, "Upward Mobility and Discrimination: The Case of Asian Americans," NBER Working Paper no. 22748 (Cambridge, MA: National Bureau of Economic Research, October 2016), https://doi.org/10.3386/w22748.

43. James Robert Flynn, *Asian Americans: Achievement beyond IQ* (London: Psychology Press, 1991); Malcolm Gladwell, *Outliers: The Story of Success* (New York: Back Bay Books, 2011).

44. Patricia Cloud and David W. Galenson, "Chinese Immigration and Contract Labor in the Late Nineteenth Century," *Explorations in Economic History* 24, no. 1 (January 1987): 22–42; Patricia Cloud and David W. Galenson, "Chinese Immigration: Reply to Charles McClain," *Explorations in Economic History* 28, no. 2 (April 1991): 239–247.

45. I do not mean to imply that Chinese and Japanese Americans are equivalent to each other or to later Asian American immigrants from diverse countries such as Vietnam, Korea, or Philippines, any more than my use of the terms "white" or "Black" implies equivalence of subgroups from diverse regions and traditions in Europe and Africa.

46. For example, Kevin Kenny states that prejudice against Irish Americans "never amounted to racial subjugation worthy of the name, that is a system of discrimination enshrined in law such as that inflicted on African Americans or Asian Americans" ("Diaspora and Irish Migration History," *Irish Economic and Social History* 33, no. 1 [September 1, 2006]: 50). Likewise, Hasia Diner states that "as women and men considered among the privileged by virtue of their whiteness, [Jews] enjoyed relative tolerance," experiencing "relatively full political and civil rights" from the end of the eighteenth century (*The Jews of the United States, 1654 to 2000* [Berkeley: University of California Press, 2006], 3, 25–26).

47. US Census Bureau, "The '72-Year Rule,'" accessed September 13, 2021, https://www.census.gov/history/www/genealogy/decennial_census_records/the_72_year_rule_1.html.

48. Newell G. Bringhurst, "The Ku Klux Klan in a Central California Community: Tulare County during the 1920s and 1930s," *Southern California Quarterly* 82, no. 4 (Winter 2000): 365–396.

49. Of course, segregation often takes place informally, so laws can't tell the full story. In practice, the vast majority of Asian American children attended racially integrated schools. Moreover, as far as can be gathered from limited data, schools with greater concentrations of Black, Hispanic, and Asian American children typically received per pupil funding similar to that of majority-white schools. Most parts of California never developed the strictly segregated, two-tiered public-education system that emerged in the South. See Hilger, "Upward Mobility and Discrimination."

50. The earliest cohorts for which I observe high upward mobility were born in years from 1922 to 1940.

51. See discussion of these data in Hilger, "Upward Mobility and Discrimination," Data Appendix, and original description in Joseph P. Ferrie, Karen Rolf, and Werner Troesken, "Cognitive Disparities, Lead Plumbing, and Water Chemistry: Prior Exposure to Water-Borne Lead and Intelligence Test Scores among World War Two U.S. Army Enlistees," *Economics & Human Biology* 10, no. 1 (January 2012): 98–111.

52. Most people are willing to break laws for personal gain when expected penalties are slim, as we know from research on tax evasion by small business owners, employers of domestic labor, and the wealthy. See Erik Hurst and Benjamin Wild Pugsley, "What Do Small Businesses Do?," *Brookings Papers on Economic Activity* 2011, no. 2 (April 28, 2012): 73–118; Catherine B. Haskins, "Household Employer Payroll Tax Evasion: An Exploration Based on IRS Data and on Interviews with Employers and Domestic Workers," PhD diss., University of Massachusetts, Amherst, 2010; Annette Alstadsaeter, Niels Johannesen, and Gabriel Zucman, "Tax Evasion and Inequality," *American Economic Review* 109, no. 6 (June 2019): 2073–2103.

53. Chinese Railroad Workers in North America Project, "Oral History Interviews," Stanford University, accessed September 13, 2021, https://web.stanford.edu/group/chineserailroad/cgi-bin/website/oral-history/.

54. Dennis Abrams, *Maxine Hong Kingston* (New York: Chelsea House, 2009).

55. James J. Heckman and Brook S. Payner, "Determining the Impact of Federal Antidiscrimination Policy on the Economic Status of Blacks: A Study of South Carolina," *American Economic Review* 79, no. 1 (March 1, 1989): 138–177.

56. See Andrés Reséndez, *The Other Slavery: The Uncovered Story of Indian Enslavement in America* (Boston: Mariner Books, 2016), on slavery of Native Americans, a group that intermingles with the families of many people currently identifying as Latino or Hispanic; see, for example, Simon Romero, "Indian Slavery Once Thrived in New Mexico: Latinos Are Finding Family Ties to It," *New York Times*, January 28, 2018.

57. Lewis Meriam, *The Problem of Indian Administration* (Washington, DC: Institute for Government Research; New York: Rockefeller Foundation, 1928); US Senate, Committee on

Labor and Public Welfare, Special Subcommittee on Indian Education, *Indian Education: A National Tragedy—a National Challenge (The Kennedy Report)* (Washington, DC: US Government Printing Office, 1969), https://eric.ed.gov/?id=ED034625; Donald Warne and Linda Bane Frizzell, "American Indian Health Policy: Historical Trends and Contemporary Issues," *American Journal of Public Health* 104, no. S3 (April 22, 2014): S263–S267.

58. Paul Schuster Taylor, *Mexican Labor in the United States Imperial Valley* (Berkeley: University of California Press, 1928); Charles Wollenberg, *All Deliberate Speed: Segregation and Exclusion in California Schools, 1855–1975* (Berkeley: University of California Press, 1978); David Torres-Rouff, "Becoming Mexican: Segregated Schools and Social Scientists in Southern California, 1913–1946," *Southern California Quarterly* 94, no. 1 (2012): 91–127.

59. Michael Hurst, "The Determinants of Earnings Differentials for Indigenous Americans: Human Capital, Location, or Discrimination?," *Quarterly Review of Economics and Finance* 37, no. 4 (1997): 787–807; Stephen J. Trejo, "Why Do Mexican Americans Earn Low Wages?," *Journal of Political Economy* 105, no. 6 (1997): 1235–1268.

CHAPTER 6

1. J. Bradford Delong and Konstantin Magin, "The U.S. Equity Return Premium: Past, Present, and Future," *Journal of Economic Perspectives* 23, no. 1 (2009): 193–208; Paul Gomme, B. Ravikumar, and Peter Rupert, "The Return to Capital and the Business Cycle," *Review of Economic Dynamics* 14, no. 2 (April 1, 2011): 262–278; Francesco Caselli and James Feyrer, "The Marginal Product of Capital," *Quarterly Journal of Economics* 122, no. 2 (May 2007): 535–568; Andrea Frazzini, David Kabiller, and Lasse Heje Pedersen, "Buffett's Alpha," *Financial Analysts Journal* 74, no. 4 (2018): 35–55.

2. Eugene F. Fama and Kenneth R. French, "Luck versus Skill in the Cross-Section of Mutual Fund Returns," *Journal of Finance* 65, no. 5 (2010): 1915–1947; Jonathan B. Berk and Jules H. van Binsbergen, "Measuring Skill in the Mutual Fund Industry," *Journal of Financial Economics* 118, no. 1 (October 2015): 1–20.

3. Robert E. Hall and Susan E. Woodward, "The Burden of the Nondiversifiable Risk of Entrepreneurship," *American Economic Review* 100, no. 3 (2010): 1163–1194; William R. Kerr, Ramana Nanda, and Matthew Rhodes-Kropf, "Entrepreneurship as Experimentation," *Journal of Economic Perspectives* 28, no. 3 (2014): 25–48.

4. Some studies discuss other approaches to quantifying the net benefits of policies. I stick with the rate of return here because it eases comparison to other kinds of financial investments. See, for example, Nathaniel Hendren and Ben Sprung-Keyser, "A Unified Welfare Analysis of Government Policies," *Quarterly Journal of Economics* 135, no. 3 (August 1, 2020): 1209–1318; Amy Finkelstein and Nathaniel Hendren, "Welfare Analysis Meets Causal Inference," *Journal of Economic Perspectives* 34, no. 4 (November 1, 2020): 146–167.

5. Mainstream politicians have proposed this approach. See Sarah Kliff, "An Exclusive Look at Cory Booker's Plan to Fight Wealth Inequality: Give Poor Kids Money," *Vox*, October

22, 2018, https://www.vox.com/policy-and-politics/2018/10/22/17999558/cory-booker-baby-bonds; Steve Holt, "Can Baby Bonds Help Shrink the Wealth Gap?," Bloomberg CityLab, July 11, 2017, https://www.bloomberg.com/news/articles/2017-07-11/can-baby-bonds-help-shrink-the-wealth-gap.

6. In "Where Is the Best Place to Invest $102,000," Adam Looney and Michael Greenstone estimate the return on investment in college from earnings impacts alone. And in Michael Greenstone and Adam Looney, *Is Starting College and Not Finishing Really That Bad?* (Washington DC: The Hamilton Project/Brookings Institution, 2013), they conclude that the return on investment in additional years in college without obtaining a degree is also large. On college major choices, see Cristobal de Brey, Thomas L. Snyder, Anlan Zhang, and Sally A. Dillow, *Digest of Education Statistics, 2019* (Washington, DC: National Center for Education Statistics, 2019), table 322.10, "Bachelor's degrees Conferred by Postsecondary Institutions, by Field of Study: Selected Years, 1970–71 through 2017–18," https://nces.ed.gov/programs/digest/d19/tables/dt19_322.10.asp.

7. David Card, "Estimating the Return to Schooling: Progress on Some Persistent Econometric Problems," *Econometrica* 69, no. 5 (2001): 1127–1160; Zimmerman, "The Returns to College Admission"; Manudeep Bhuller, Magne Mogstad, and Kjell G. Salvanes, "Life-Cycle Earnings, Education Premiums, and Internal Rates of Return," *Journal of Labor Economics* 35, no. 4 (April 6, 2017): 993–1030; Philip Oreopoulos and Kjell G. Salvanes, "Priceless: The Nonpecuniary Benefits of Schooling," *Journal of Economic Perspectives* 25, no. 1 (January 1, 2011): 159–184; Enrico Moretti, "Chapter 51—Human Capital Externalities in Cities," in *Handbook of Regional and Urban Economics*, vol. 4: *Cities and Geography*, ed. J. Vernon Henderson and Jacques-François Thisse (Amsterdam: Elsevier, 2004), 2243–2291; Fabian Lange and Robert Topel, "The Social Value of Education and Human Capital," in *Handbook of the Economics of Education*, ed. Hanushek and Welch, 1:459–509.

8. Zimmerman, "The Returns to College Admission for Academically Marginal Students"; Smith, Goodman, and Hurwitz, *The Economic Impact of Access to Public Four-Year Colleges*, and studies cited therein.

9. Bettinger et al., "Role of Application Assistance and Information in College Decisions." The social ROI on nudges that increase investment in college is approximately the ROI on college itself because the costs of the nudges are typically trivial compared to both the costs and the benefits of the additional college investments they facilitate.

10. Scott Carrell and Bruce Sacerdote, "Why Do College-Going Interventions Work?," *American Economic Journal: Applied Economics* 9, no. 3 (2017): 124–151.

11. Dynarski et al., "Closing the Gap"; Bulman, "The Effect of Access to College Assessments on Enrollment and Attainment"; Caroline Hoxby and Sarah Turner, "Expanding College Opportunities for High-Achieving, Low Income Students," SIEPR Discussion Paper no. 12-014, 2012; Michael Hurwitz, Jonathan Smith, Sunny Niu, and Jessica Howell, "The Maine Question: How Is 4-Year College Enrollment Affected by Mandatory College Entrance Exams?," *Educational Evaluation and Policy Analysis* 37, no. 1 (March 1, 2015):

138–159; Joshua Hyman, "ACT for All: The Effect of Mandatory College Entrance Exams on Postsecondary Attainment and Choice," *Education Finance and Policy* 12, no. 3 (July 1, 2017): 281–311; Amanda Pallais, "Small Differences That Matter: Mistakes in Applying to College," *Journal of Labor Economics* 33, no. 2 (2015): 28.

12. Robert Lerman, *Expanding Apprenticeship Opportunities in the United States* (Washington, DC: Brookings Institution, 2014); Robert I. Lerman, "Expanding Apprenticeship in the United States: Barriers and Opportunities," in *Contemporary Apprenticeship: International Perspectives on an Evolving Model of Learning*, ed. Alison Fuller and Lorna Unwin (New York: Routledge, 2013), 105–124. See also the *Registered Apprenticeship National Results Fiscal Year* reports for the number of new apprentices by year, available at "Data and Statistics," US Department of Labor, https://www.dol.gov/agencies/eta/apprenticeship/about /statistics/2020.

13. Frances A. Campbell, Elizabeth P. Pungello, Margaret Burchinal, Kirsten Kainz, Yi Pan, Barbara H. Wasik, Oscar A. Barbarin, et al., "Adult Outcomes as a Function of an Early Childhood Educational Program: An Abecedarian Project Follow-Up," *Developmental Psychology* 48, no. 4 (2012): 1033–1043. For children born in the 1970s, college typically lasted five years and raised earnings by 60 percent. See Claudia Goldin and Lawrence F. Katz, *The Race between Education and Technology: The Evolution of US Educational Wage Differentials, 1890 to 2005*, NBER Working Paper no. 12984 (Cambridge, MA: National Bureau of Economic Research, 2007).

14. The formula to obtain the ROI in the example is: cost * (ROI ^ years_of_delay) = benefit, implying ROI = (benefit / cost)^(1/years_of_delay). The actual calculation in the cited research is this exact intuition but accounts for the gradual accumulation of benefits over a long period of time.

15. James J. Heckman, Seong Hyeok Moon, Rodrigo Pinto, Peter A. Savelyev, and Adam Yavitz, "The Rate of Return to the HighScope Perry Preschool Program," *Journal of Public Economics* 94, no. 1–2 (February 2010): 114–128; Jorge Luis García, James J. Heckman, Duncan Ermini Leaf, and María José Prados, "Quantifying the Life-Cycle Benefits of an Influential Early-Childhood Program," *Journal of Political Economy* 128, no. 7 (July 2020): 2502–2541. In *From Preschool to Prosperity: The Economic Payoff to Early Childhood Education* (Kalamazoo, MI: W. E. Upjohn Institute, 2014), Timothy Bartik provides related estimates for large-scale public-preschool programs.

16. "Over $900,000" comes from the calculation $80,000 * 1.13^20 = $922,000.

17. See chapter 1, note 9, on larger impacts for disadvantaged children. On low rates of center-based early education participation by low-income children, see Lynda Laughlin, *Who's Minding the Kids? Child Care Arrangements: Spring 2011* (Washington, DC: US Census Bureau, 2013), https://www.census.gov/prod/2013pubs/p70-135.pdf. For infants and toddlers, see "Percentage of All Infants and Toddlers by Primary Care Arrangement in the Past Week (2012)," Child Trends, September 4, 2019, https://www.childtrends.org/blog /nearly-30-percent-of-infants-and-toddlers-attend-home-based-child-care-as-their

-primary-arrangement#:~:text=11.9%20percent%20of%20infants%20and,care%20
and%20parental%20care%20overall.

18. Ninety percent of Head Start providers are formal centers. See Office of Head Start, "Services Snapshot: National All Programs (2017–2018)," https://eclkc.ohs.acf.hhs.gov/sites/default /files/pdf/no-search/service-snapshot-all-programs-2017-2018.pdf. On eligibility and eligibility duration, see Head Start, "1302.12 Determining, Verifying, and Documenting Eligibility," in *Head Start Policy & Regulations*, accessed September 13, 2021, https://eclkc.ohs.acf .hhs.gov/policy/45-cfr-chap-xiii/1302-12-determining-verifying-documenting-eligibility.

19. David Bank and Jenny Griffin, "For-Profit Head Start Programs Pay Off for Children, but Investors Have to Wait," Aspen Institute, January 29, 2015, https://www.aspeninstitute .org/blog-posts/profit-head-start-programs-pay-children-investors-have-wait/. On efficacy of for-profit schools in the college context, see Stephanie Riegg Cellini and Nicholas Turner, "Gainfully Employed? Assessing the Employment and Earnings of For-Profit College Students Using Administrative Data," *Journal of Human Resources* 54, no. 2 (March 31, 2019): 342–370.

20. On participation, hours, and quality, see W. Steven Barnett and Allison H. Friedman-Krauss, "State(s) of Head Start," National Institute for Early Education Research, 2016. On hours, also see Office of Head Start, "Services Snapshot: National All Programs (2017–2018)." The Program Performance Standards are available at https://eclkc.ohs.acf.hhs.gov /policy/45-cfr-chap-xiii. For evidence that wraparound services may not drive improvements compared to other center-based care, see Kline and Walters, "Evaluating Public Programs with Close Substitutes"; Feller et al., "Compared to What?" For one thoughtful proposal for reforming Head Start, see Sara Mead and Ashley LiBetti Mitchel, "Reforming Head Start for the 21st Century: A Policy Prescription," in *Challenging Assumptions about Behavioral Policy*, vol. 1, no. 1, ed. Craig R. Fox and Sim B. Sitkin (Washington, DC: Brookings Institution, 2016), 19–28.

21. Head Start spends about 60 percent as much per child as model programs such as Perry Preschool. See Janet Currie, "Early Childhood Education Programs," *Journal of Economic Perspectives* 15, no. 2 (2001): 213–238. For an in-depth overview of Head Start in comparison to Perry Preschool, see Zigler and Styfco, "Is the Perry Preschool Better than Head Start?" On the costs of state preschool programs, see Mariana Zerpa, "Short and Medium Run Impacts of Preschool Education." On the costs of Head Start, see W. Steven Barnett, Pew Charitable Trusts, and National Institute for Early Education Research, *The State of Preschool 2006: State Preschool Yearbook* (New Brunswick, NJ: National Institute for Early Education Research, 2006). I have added 20 percent to the stated cost of Head Start given in this source because it does not include the 20 percent nonfederal share of program costs.

22. I focus ROI calculations on results from Head Start rather than from Early Head Start because Head Start is a larger and older program and, as such, has been analyzed more thoroughly. Mike Puma, Stephen Bell, Ronna Cook, Camilla Heid, Pam Broene, Frank Jenkins, Andrew Mashburn, and Jason Downer, *Third Grade Follow-Up to the Head Start Impact Study: Final Report*, OPRE Report 2012-45 (Washington, DC: Administration for

Children & Families, US Department of Health and Human Services, 2012), https://eric
.ed.gov/?id=ED539264. On earnings as predicted based on test scores, see Kline and Walters, "Evaluating Public Programs with Close Substitutes." On health and crime, see Carneiro and Ginja, "Long-Term Impacts of Compensatory Preschool." On long-term ROI
possibly approaching or exceeding 20 percent, see Bailey, Timpe, and Sun, "Prep School for
Poor Kids." Many prior scholars have misinterpreted the Head Start Impact Study to imply
that the program has minimal benefits. The papers cited here explain why that implication
is misleading. On the large positive impacts of Early Head Start, see Love et al., "The Effectiveness of Early Head Start."

23. As a voucher program, CCDF stands out by providing unusually weak guardrails on provider quality. On K12 voucher program regulations, see Yujie Sude, Corey A. DeAngelis,
and Patrick J. Wolf, "Supplying Choice: An Analysis of School Participation Decisions in
Voucher Programs in Washington, DC, Indiana, and Louisiana," *Journal of School Choice*
12, no. 1 (January 2, 2018): 8–33; Atila Abdulkadiroğlu, Parag A. Pathak, and Christopher
R. Walters, "Free to Choose: Can School Choice Reduce Student Achievement?," *American
Economic Journal: Applied Economics* 10, no. 1 (2018): 175–206, sec. 4.

    Although most Head Start centers offer more than six hours of care per day, they offer
fewer hours per day, week, and year than the childcare centers chosen by CCDF participants, which typically offer about eight hours per day, five days a week. For hours offered
by Head Start providers, see Office of Head Start, "Services Snapshot: National All Programs (2017–2018)." For typical hours for CCDF participants, I use calculations based on
approximately 21.75 workdays per month and total hours of care per month documented
in Office of Child Care, "FY 2018 Preliminary Data Table 14—Average Monthly Hours
for Children in Care by Age Group and Care Type," December 3, 2019, https://www
.acf.hhs.gov/occ/data/fy-2018-preliminary-data-table-14-average-monthly-hours-children
-care-age-group-and-care.

    Both Head Start and CCDF also primarily serve working parents. Sixty-three percent
of Head Start families work, and about 74 percent of CCDF participants report using
the program to support their employment. On Head Start, see Stephanie Schmit, *Head
Start Participants, Programs, Families, and Staff in 2011* (Washington, DC: Center for
Law and Social Policy, November 2012), https://nieer.org/wp-content/uploads/2013/06
/HSpreschool-PIR-2011-Fact-Sheet.pdf. On CCDF participants, see Office of Child Care,
"FY 2018 Preliminary Data Table 10—Reasons for Receiving Care, Average Monthly
Percentage of Families," December 3, 2019, https://www.acf.hhs.gov/occ/data/fy-2018
-preliminary-data-table-10-reasons-receiving-care-average-monthly-percentage.

    Some researchers resist comparisons between Head Start and CCDF because, they
argue, CCDF's goal has been to support parental employment rather than to provide early
education for children. However, from its inception CCDF has allocated part of block grant
funding to improvements in childcare quality; see chapter 9 on the legislative history of child
care in US House of Representatives, Committee on Ways and Means, *Green Book* (Washington, DC: US Government Printing Office, 2012). This pursuit of higher quality has also
materialized in the Quality Rating and Improvement Systems for CCDF subsidy recipients

going back to the late 1990s. See National Center on Early Childhood Quality Assurance, "History of QRIS Growth over Time," QRIS Compendium 2016 Fact Sheets, 2017.

Some researchers have also pointed out that CCDF recipients often apply for WIC benefits simultaneously. However, most of the large difference in WIC receipt across CCDF and Head Start participants likely reflects the fact that Head Start children are simply older. WIC participation is about 90 percent for CCDF participants (Chris M. Herbst and Erdal Tekin, *Child Care Subsidies and Child Development*, IZA Discussion Paper no. 3836 [Bonn: Institute of Labor Economics, n.d.], 52), compared to about 50 percent for Head Start participants (Schmit, *Head Start Participants, Programs, Families, and Staff in 2011*). This age difference between children served by the two programs is not driving the different impacts, however. Early Head Start also has large positive impacts: see Love et al., "The Effectiveness of Early Head Start."

24. On CCDF red tape, see Gina Adams and Hannah Matthews, "Confronting the Child Care Eligibility Maze: Simplifying and Aligning with Other Work Supports," Work Support Strategies: Streamlining Access, Strengthening Families, Urban Institute, 2013. On policies shaping the red tape, see the Urban Institute CCDF Policies Database—for example, "Key Cross-State Variations in CCDF Policies as of October 1, 2018," November 2019, https://www.urban.org/sites/default/files/publication/101629/key_cross-state_variations_in_ccdf_policies_as_of_october_1_2018_1.pdf. On the share of eligible families receiving subsidies, see US Government Accountability Office (GAO), *Child Care and Development Fund: Subsidy Receipt and Plans for New Funds*, GAO-19-222R, GAO@100 (Washington, DC: US GAO, 2019), https://www.gao.gov/products/GAO-19-222R. On awareness of subsidies, see Anne B. Shlay, Marsha Weinraub, Michelle Harmon, and Henry Tran, "Barriers to Subsidies: Why Low-Income Families Do Not Use Child Care Subsidies," *Social Science Research* 33, no. 1 (2004): 134–157; Chris M. Herbst, "Who Are the Eligible Nonrecipients of Child Care Subsidies?," *Children and Youth Services Review* 30, no. 9 (2008): 1037–1054.

States have been reducing some of the red tape around CCDF, but this process has a long way to go. See Gina Adams and Julia R. Henly, "Child Care Subsidies: Supporting Work and Child Development for Healthy Families," Health Policy Brief, HealthAffairs, April 13, 2020. In an interview, Sandee Blechman and Chacy Oh at the San Francisco Children's Council explained why many childcare providers decline to accept CCDF subsidies (interviewed by the author, June 1, 2017).

25. T. J. Sabol and colleagues show how QRIS systems often provide information that fails to capture childcare quality. See T. J. Sabol, S. L. Soliday Hong, R. C. Pianta, and M. R. Burchinal, "Can Rating Pre-K Programs Predict Children's Learning? Supplementary Materials," *Science* 341, no. 6148 (2013): 845–846.

26. See, for example, James Gordon, Chris Herbst, and Erdal Tekin, *Who's Minding the Kids? Experimental Evidence on the Demand for Child Care Quality*, NBER Working Paper no. 25335 (Cambridge, MA: National Bureau of Economic Research, 2018, rev. 2020), and references therein.

27. Chris M. Herbst and Erdal Tekin, "The Impact of Child-Care Subsidies on Child Development: Evidence from Geographic Variation in the Distance to Social Service Agencies," *Journal of Policy Analysis and Management* 35, no. 1 (2016): 94–116. On adverse effects of school voucher programs that expose parents to low-quality options, see Abdulkadiroğlu, Pathak, and Walters, "Free to Choose." Negative impacts of voucher programs on academic outcomes have also been found in Ohio and Indiana. See David Figlio and Krzysztof Karbownik, *Evaluation of Ohio's EdChoice Scholarship Program: Selection, Competition, and Performance Effects* (Columbus, OH: Thomas B. Fordham Institute, 2016); R. Joseph Waddington and Mark Berends, "Impact of the Indiana Choice Scholarship Program: Achievement Effects for Students in Upper Elementary and Middle School," *Journal of Policy Analysis and Management* 37, no. 4 (2018): 783–808. On adverse impacts of lower-quality early education programs in other countries, see studies of Quebec and Bologna discussed in note 9 of chapter 1.

28. Momoko Hayakawa and Arthur Reynolds, "Strategies for Scaling Up: Promoting Parent Involvement through Family-School-Community Partnerships," *Voices in Urban Education* 44 (2016): 45, 51; see also Arthur J. Reynolds, Judy A. Temple, Suh-Ruu Ou, Irma A. Arteaga, and Barry A. B. White, "School-Based Early Childhood Education and Age-28 Well-Being: Effects by Timing, Dosage, and Subgroups," *Science* 333, no. 6040 (July 15, 2011): 360–364.

29. Rob Waters, "A Conversation with Tony D: How 'Becoming a Man' Got to the White House," *Forbes*, March 9, 2016, https://www.forbes.com/sites/robwaters/2016/03/09/a-conversation-with-tony-d-how-becoming-a-man-got-to-the-white-house.

30. Sara B. Heller, "Summer Jobs Reduce Violence among Disadvantaged Youth," *Science* 346, no. 6214 (December 5, 2014): 1219–1223; Sara B. Heller, Anuj K. Shah, Jonathan Guryan, Jens Ludwig, Sendhil Mullainathan, and Harold A. Pollack, "Thinking, Fast and Slow? Some Field Experiments to Reduce Crime and Dropout in Chicago," *Quarterly Journal of Economics* 132, no. 1 (2017): 1–54.

31. Quoted in Margaret K. Nelson, *Parenting out of Control: Anxious Parents in Uncertain Times* (New York: New York University Press, 2012), 32.

32. Melissa S. Kearney and Phillip B. Levine, "Why Is the Teen Birth Rate in the United States so High and Why Does It Matter?," *Journal of Economic Perspectives* 26, no. 2 (2012): 141–166.

33. A federally funded, large-scale, randomized controlled trial found exactly zero impact of four highly regarded abstinence-only sex education programs. See Melissa S. Kearney, "Teen Pregnancy Prevention," in *Targeting Investments in Children: Fighting Poverty When Resources Are Limited*, ed. Phillip B. Levine and David J. Zimmerman, a National Bureau of Economic Research Conference Report (Chicago: University of Chicago Press, 2010); Melissa S. Kearney and Phillip B. Levine, "Media Influences on Social Outcomes: The Impact of MTV's *16 and Pregnant* on Teen Childbearing," *American Economic Review* 105, no. 12 (December 2015): 3597–3632.

34. Kathryn Edit and Maria Kelafas, *Promises I Can Keep: Why Poor Women Put Motherhood before Marriage* (Berkeley: University of California Press, 2005), 10.

35. David S. Lee and Justin McCrary, "The Deterrence Effect of Prison: Dynamic Theory and Evidence," working paper, 2016, figure A.1, https://eml.berkeley.edu/~jmccrary/lee_and_mccrary2009.pdf.

36. Neal Hazel, *Cross-National Comparison of Youth Justice* (London: Youth Justice Board/ Bwrdd Cyfiawnder Ieuenctid, 2008), 59, table 8.1.

37. Table 8: "Per Pupil Amounts for Current Spending of Public Elementary-Secondary School Systems by State: Fiscal Year 2018," in "Summary Tables" in US Census Bureau, "2018 Public Elementary-Secondary Education Finance Data," last rev. April 14, 2020, https:// www.census.gov/data/tables/2018/econ/school-finances/secondary-education-finance .html.

38. Alexander, *The New Jim Crow*.

39. Justin McCrary and David S. Lee, "The Deterrence Effect of Prison: Dynamic Theory and Evidence," working paper, Berkeley Program in Law and Economics, 2009.

40. Michael Mueller-Smith, "The Criminal and Labor Market Consequences of Incarceration," working paper, Department of Economics, University of Michigan, August 18, 2015, https://sites.lsa.umich.edu/mgms/wp-content/uploads/sites/283/2015/09/incar.pdf; Jeffrey R. Kling, "Incarceration Length, Employment, and Earnings," *American Economic Review* 96, no. 3 (2006): 863–876; Jeffrey Grogger, "The Effect of Arrests on the Employment and Earnings of Young Men," *Quarterly Journal of Economics* (February 1995): 51–71; Harry J. Holzer, "Collateral Costs: The Effects of Incarceration on the Employment and Earnings of Young Workers," in *Do Prisons Make Us Safer? The Benefits and Costs of the Prison Boom*, ed. Steven Raphael and Michael A. Stoll (New York: Russell Sage Foundation, 2009), 239–268; Magnus Lofstrom and Steven Raphael, "Crime, the Criminal Justice System, and Socioeconomic Inequality," *Journal of Economic Perspectives* 30, no. 2 (May 2016): 103–126.

41. Dobkin et al., "The Economic Consequences of Hospital Admissions"; Til von Wachter, Jae Song, and Joyce Manchester, "Long-Term Earnings Losses due to Mass Layoffs during the 1982 Recession: An Analysis Using U.S. Administrative Data from 1974 to 2004," working paper, 2009, http://www.econ.ucla.edu/tvwachter/papers/mass_layoffs_1982.pdf.

42. Patrick Bayer, Randi Hjalmarsson, and David Pozen, "Building Criminal Capital behind Bars: Peer Effects in Juvenile Corrections," *Quarterly Journal of Economics* 124, no. 1 (2009): 105–147; Aizer and Doyle, "Juvenile Incarceration, Human Capital, and Future Crime."

43. David Sims offers a good example of how underfunding can corrupt reforms inspired by smaller-scale experiments. See David Sims, "A Strategic Response to Class Size Reduction: Combination Classes and Student Achievement Abstract," *Journal of Policy Analysis and Management* 27, no. 3 (2008): 457–478; David P. Sims, "Crowding Peter to Educate Paul: Lessons from a Class Size Reduction Externality," *Economics of Education Review* 28, no. 4 (August 2009): 465–473.

44. White House, "The American Families Plan," April 2021, https://www.whitehouse.gov
/wp-content/uploads/2021/04/American-Families-Plan-Fact-Sheet-FINAL.pdf.

45. The best studies suggest that for the first 12 to 18 weeks of leave, positive impacts on chil-
dren's future earnings alone would more than pay for the program. See Maya Rossin-Slater,
"Easing the Burden: Why Paid Family Leave Policies Are Gaining Steam," SIEPR Policy
Brief, 2018, https://siepr.stanford.edu/research/publications/paid-family-leave-policies.

The WIC program could replicate its successful competitive bidding process for infant
formula to buy diapers at large discounts on parents' behalf. See Steven Carlson, Robert
Greenstein, and Zoë Neuberger, *WIC's Competitive Bidding Process for Infant Formula Is
Highly Cost-Effective* (Washington, DC: Center for Budget and Policy Priorities, 2017).

Quality childcare is essential to avoid the adverse impacts that have emerged for
middle-class parents in low-quality childcare systems. See Baker, Gruber, and Milligan,
"Universal Child Care, Maternal Labor Supply, and Family Well-Being"; Baker, Gruber,
and Milligan, "The Long-Run Impacts of a Universal Child Care Program."

46. On evidence that well-designed summer programs can benefit students, see Andrew
McEachin, Catherine Augustine, and Jennifer McCombs, "Best Practices in Summer Programming," in *The Summer Slide*, ed. Alexander et al., Kindle Edition, location 4294–4639.
For a recent evaluation of an extended school day devoted to additional literacy instruction
that showed potential, see David Figlio, Kristian L. Holden, and Umut Ozek, "Do Students
Benefit from Longer School Days? Regression Discontinuity Evidence from Florida's Additional Hour of Literacy Instruction," *Economics of Education Review* 67 (December 1, 2018):
171–183. For an example of schools using extended time in more and less effective ways,
see Andrés Barrios-Fernández and Giulia Bovini, "It's Time to Learn: School Institutions
and Returns to Instruction Time," *Economics of Education Review* 80 (February 1, 2021):
102068. For a cautionary tale of adverse impacts of low-quality after-school programs, see
Ailin He and Nagham Sayour, "After-School Care, Child Care Arrangements, and Child
Development," *Journal of Human Capital* 14, no. 4 (October 29, 2020): 617–652, https://
doi.org/10.1086/711950. Also see survey results documenting fatigue and alienation in
one extended-learning program in Tennessee: Robyn J. Beard, "Extended-Time and Its
Influence on Academic Achievement and Growth for African American Students in High-
Minority, High-Poverty Schools: A Case Study," PhD diss., Union University, 2020.

On community schooling, see John Rogers, *Community Schools: Lessons from the Past
and Present* (Los Angeles: University of California Institute for Democracy, Education, and
Access, 1998), https://sedn.senate.ca.gov/sites/sedn.senate.ca.gov/files/rogers_community
_schools_lessons_1998.pdf; William R. Johnston, John Engberg, Isaac M. Opper, Lisa
Sontag-Padilla, and Lea Xenakis, *Illustrating the Promise of Community Schools: An Assessment of the Impact of the New York City Community Schools Initiative* (New York: RAND,
New York City Mayor's Office for Economic Opportunity, 2020).

47. On financial aid amount and structure, see, for example, Dynarski et al., "Closing the
Gap." On college support programs, see Rachel Fulcher Dawson, Melissa S. Kearney, and
James X. Sullivan, *Comprehensive Approaches to Increasing Student Completion in Higher*

Education: A Survey of the Landscape, NBER Working Paper no. 28046 (Cambridge, MA: National Bureau of Economic Research, 2020). On vocational training programs, see, for example, David Fein and Jill Hamadyk, *Bridging the Opportunity Divide for Low-Income Youth: Implementation and Early Impacts of the Year Up Program*, OPRE Report (Washington, DC: Office of Planning, Research, and Evaluation, Administration for Children and Families, US Department of Health and Human Services, May 1, 2018); Heller, "Summer Jobs Reduce Violence"; Debbie Reed, Albert Yung-Hsu Liu, Rebecca Kleinman, Annalisa Mastri, Davin Reed, Samina Sattar, and Jessica Ziegler, *An Effectiveness Assessment and Cost–Benefit Analysis of Registered Apprenticeship in 10 States* (Oakland, CA: Mathematica Policy Research, 2012).

48. "State Health Facts: Medicaid-to-Medicare Fee Index, Timeframe: 2016," Kaiser Family Foundation, https://www.kff.org/medicaid/state-indicator/medicaid-to-medicare-fee-index. See also Stephen Zuckerman, Laura Skopec, and Marni Epstein, *Medicaid Physician Fees after the ACA Primary Care Fee Bump* (Washington, DC: Urban Institute, March 2017), http://www.urban.org/sites/default/files/publication/88836/2001180-medicaid-physician -fees-after-the-aca-primary-care-fee-bump_0.pdf; Kayla Holgash and Martha Heberlein, "Physician Acceptance of New Medicaid Patients: What Matters and What Doesn't," *Health Affairs Blog*, April 10, 2019, https://www.healthaffairs.org/do/10.1377/hblog2019 0401.678690/full/.

CHAPTER 7

1. Neal Lane and Harold Varmus, *Investing in Our Future: A National Research Initiative for America's Children for the 21st Century* (Washington, DC: National Science and Technology Council Committee on Fundamental Science, Committee on Health, Safety, and Food, 1997). On the role of public and private funding in R&D, see Jonathan Gruber and Simon Johnson, *Jump-Starting America: How Breakthrough Science Can Revive Economic Growth and the American Dream* (New York: PublicAffairs, 2019) and Mariana Mazzucato, *The Entrepreneurial State: Debunking Public vs. Private Sector Myths* (New York: PublicAffairs, 2015).

2. Lane and Varmus, *Investing in Our Future*.

3. Thomas A. Husted and Lawrence W. Kenny, "The Effect of the Expansion of the Voting Franchise on the Size of Government," *Journal of Political Economy* 105, no. 1 (February 1997): 54–82; Grant Miller, "Women's Suffrage, Political Responsiveness, and Child Survival in American History," *Quarterly Journal of Economics* 123, no. 3 (August 2008): 1287–1327; Margo, *Race and Schooling in the South*; Elizabeth U. Cascio and Ebonya Washington, "Valuing the Vote: The Redistribution of Voting Rights and State Funds Following the Voting Rights Act of 1965," *Quarterly Journal of Economics* 129, no. 1 (February 2014): 379–433; Graziella Bertocchi, Arcangelo Dimico, Francesco Lancia, and Alessia Russo, "Youth Enfranchisement, Political Responsiveness, and Education Expenditure: Evidence from the US," *American Economic Journal: Economic Policy* 12, no. 3 (August 2020): 76–106.

4.   Michael P. McDonald, "Voter Turnout Demographics," United States Elections Project, accessed May 18, 2021, http://www.electproject.org/home/voter-turnout/demographics.

5.   Author's calculations based on data from the Center for Responsive Politics at OpenSecrets .org, summing lobbying expenditures by organizations related to child and elderly interests (elderly almost entirely accounted for by AARP).

6.   Author's calculations based on Julia B. Isaacs, Cary Lou, Heather Hahn, Ashley Hong, Caleb Quakenbush, and C. Eugene Steuerle, *Kids' Share 2018: Report on Federal Expenditures on Children through 2017 and Future Projections* (Washington, DC: Urban Institute, 2018); Lino et al., *Expenditures on Children by Families, 2015*; and other sources to capture private spending. I avoid double-counting public-income transfers in private spending when comparing total spending per child and per elderly person. This is important primarily because Social Security is a major federal expense and a major share of private elderly expenditure. I estimate total spending per child at $24,772 and per elderly person at $36,989 in 2018.

7.   "Major Payment Reform Program for Cancer Drugs Falls Short," *Penn Medicine News*, May 6, 2019, https://www.pennmedicine.org/news/news-releases/2019/may/major-payment -reform-program-for-cancer-drugs-falls-short.

8.   Martha J. Bailey and Andrew Goodman-Bacon, "The War on Poverty's Experiment in Public Medicine: Community Health Centers and the Mortality of Older Americans," *American Economic Review* 105, no. 3 (March 2015): 1067–1104.

9.   First Five Years Fund, "2021 Policy Poll: Fact Sheet," January 29, 2021, https://www.ffyf .org/2021-policy-poll-fact-sheet/.

10. Thomas Piketty, Emmanuel Saez, and Gabriel Zucman, "Distributional National Accounts: Methods and Estimates for the United States," *Quarterly Journal of Economics* 133, no. 2 (May 1, 2018): 553–609.

11. Jobs estimated using an aggregate GDP/employment ratio.

12. Amy Joyce and Caitlin Gibson, "Consumed by Competition, Parents Fuel a College Admissions Game That Few Can Play," *Washington Post*, March 13, 2019.

13. Stacy B. Dale and Alan B. Krueger, "Estimating the Effects of College Characteristics over the Career Using Administrative Earnings Data," *Journal of Human Resources* 49, no. 2 (Spring 2014): 323–358; Stacy Berg Dale and Alan B. Krueger, "Estimating the Payoff to Attending a More Selective College: An Application of Selection on Observables and Unobservables," *Quarterly Journal of Economics* 117, no. 4 (November 2002): 1491–1527; Jack Mountjoy and Brent Hickman, *The Returns to College(s): Estimating Value-Added and Match Effects in Higher Education*, Becker Friedman Institute for Economics Working Paper no. 2020-08 (Chicago: University of Chicago, 2020).

14. Gruber and Johnson, *Jump-Starting America*; Mazzucato, *The Entrepreneurial State*.

15. Marie Jahoda, Paul Lazarsfeld, and Hans Zeisel, *Marienthal: The Sociography of an Unemployed Community* (1933; reprint, New York: Aldine-Atherton, 1971); Daniel Nelson,

Unemployment Insurance: The American Experience, 1915–1935 (Madison: University of Wisconsin Press, 1969); John Bound, "The Health and Earnings of Rejected Disability Insurance Applicants," *American Economic Review* 79, no. 3 (1989): 482–503; Gary V. Engelhardt and Jonathan Gruber, "Social Security and the Evolution of Elderly Poverty," in *Public Policy and the Income Distribution*, ed. Alan Auerbach, David Card, and John Quigley (New York: Russell Sage Foundation, 2006), 259–287; Chetty and Finkelstein, "Social Insurance."

16. Martha J. Bailey and Nicolas J. Duquette, "How Johnson Fought the War on Poverty: The Economics and Politics of Funding at the Office of Economic Opportunity," *Journal of Economic History* 74, no. 2 (2014): 351–388. Federal revenue as a share of GDP was 18 percent in 1970, so 0.15 * 0.18 = 0.027. See "Federal Receipts as Percent of Gross Domestic Product (FYFRGDA188S)," FRED Economic Data, accessed May 18, 2021, https://fred .stlouisfed.org/series/FYFRGDA188S.

17. Republican Task Force on Poverty, Opportunity, and Upward Mobility, *A Better Way: Our Vision for a Confident America: Poverty, Opportunity, and Upward Mobility* (Washington, DC: Republican Party, June 7, 2016), https://www.ncsha.org/wp-content/uploads/Paul -Ryan-A-Better-Way-Our-Vision-for-a-Confident-America-June-2016.pdf.

18. This discussion of poverty rates draws on Bruce D. Meyer and James X. Sullivan, *Winning the War: Poverty from the Great Society to the Great Recession*, NBER Working Paper no. 18718 (Cambridge, MA: National Bureau of Economic Research, January 2013).

19. The actual problems aren't *quite* this obvious, but the essential point holds. See Jerry Hausman, "Sources of Bias and Solutions to Bias in the Consumer Price Index," *Journal of Economic Perspectives* 17, no. 1 (Winter 2003): 23–44.

20. Concerns about increases in extreme poverty have been raised in, for example, Robert Haveman, Rebecca Blank, Robert Moffitt, Timothy Smeeding, and Geoffrey Wallace, "The War on Poverty: Measurement, Trends, and Policy," *Journal of Policy Analysis and Management* 34, no. 3 (2015): 593–638; H. Luke Shaefer and Kathryn Edin, "Rising Extreme Poverty in the United States and the Response of Federal Means-Tested Transfer Programs," *Social Service Review* 87, no. 2 (June 2013): 250–268. These concerns have turned out to be statistical artifacts. See Bruce D. Meyer, Derek Wu, Victoria Mooers, and Carla Medalia, "The Use and Misuse of Income Data and Extreme Poverty in the United States," *Journal of Labor Economics* 39, no. S1 (2021): S5–S58, along with citations included therein referencing a long history of research by Bruce Meyer, James Sullivan, and others. These researchers have documented large and growing errors in survey data that dramatically distort measured levels and trends in extreme poverty.

21. Timothy Smeeding, "Poor People in Rich Nations: The United States in Comparative Perspective," *Journal of Economic Perspectives* 20, no. 1 (2006): 69–90.

22. David W. Brown, Amanda E. Kowalski, and Ithai Z. Lurie, "Long-Term Impacts of Childhood Medicaid Expansions on Outcomes in Adulthood," *Review of Economic Studies* 87, no. 2 (March 1, 2020): 792–821; Janet Currie and Jonathan Gruber, "Saving Babies: The

Efficacy and Cost of Recent Changes in the Medicaid Eligibility of Pregnant Women," *Journal of Political Economy* 104, no. 6 (December 1, 1996): 1263–1296; Janet Currie and Jonathan Gruber, "Health Insurance Eligibility, Utilization of Medical Care, and Child Health," *Quarterly Journal of Economics* 111, no. 2 (May 1996): 431–466.

Hilary Hoynes, Diane Whitmore Schanzenbach, and Douglas Almond, "Long-Run Impacts of Childhood Access to the Safety Net," *American Economic Review* 106, no. 4 (2016): 903–934; Bailey et al., *Is the Social Safety Net a Long-Term Investment?*

Jens Ludwig and Douglas L. Miller, "Does Head Start Improve Children's Life Chances? Evidence from a Regression Discontinuity Design," *Quarterly Journal of Economics* 122, no. 1 (2007): 159–208; David Deming, "Early Childhood Intervention and Life-Cycle Skill Development: Evidence from Head Start," *American Economic Journal: Applied Economics* 1, no. 3 (2009) 111–134; Kline and Walters, "Evaluating Public Programs with Close Substitutes"; Rucker C. Johnson and C. Kirabo Jackson, *Reducing Inequality through Dynamic Complementarity: Evidence from Head Start and Public School Spending*, NBER Working Paper no. 23489 (Cambridge, MA: National Bureau of Economic Research, 2017, rev. February 2018).

23. Katznelson, *Fear Itself*; Ira Katznelson, *When Affirmative Action Was White: An Untold History of Racial Inequality in Twentieth-Century America* (New York: Norton, 2006).

24. Doris Kearns Goodwin, *No Ordinary Time: Franklin & Eleanor Roosevelt, the Home Front in World War II* (New York: Touchstone, 1996).

25. Ilyana Kuziemko and Ebonya Washington, "Why Did the Democrats Lose the South? Bringing New Data to an Old Debate," *American Economic Review* 108, no. 10 (October 2018): 2830–2867.

26. Robert Caro's works have documented this and other monumental dramas of Johnson's complex, extraordinary life.

27. Bailey and Duquette, "How Johnson Fought the War on Poverty."

28. To document this and other historical quotes, I use "n-----" in place of the n-word. Nadine Cohodas, "Thurmond, James Strom," *South Carolina Encyclopedia*, June 28, 2016, updated August 16, 2016, https://www.scencyclopedia.org/sce/entries/thurmond-james-strom/.

29. Alexander P. Lamis, ed., *Southern Politics in the 1990s* (Baton Rouge: Louisiana State University Press, 1999), 8.

30. AARP was founded by Ethel Percy Andrus, a pioneering educator inspired into action after witnessing the poverty of elderly friends and colleagues who had spent their lives contributing to their communities. Christine L. Day, *AARP: America's Largest Interest Group and Its Impact (American Interest Group Politics)* (Santa Barbara, CA: Praeger, 2017).

31. In 1966, PTA membership was 12 million and the US population 200 million; in 2020, PTA membership was 3.5 million and the US population 320 million. The "12 million" figure comes from Thomas Toch, "The Plight of the PTA," *Brookings* (blog), January 7, 2001, https://www.brookings.edu/articles/the-plight-of-the-pta/; the "3.5 million" number

comes from PTA executive director Nathan Monell's page on the PTA website, accessed August 17, 2021, https://www.pta.org/home/About-National-Parent-Teacher-Association/ PTA-Leadership/Board-Officers-Members/Nathan-R-Monell-CAE, which refers to "PTA's 22,000 local units and nearly 3.5M members."

32. On PTA policy positions, see National PTA, "National PTA's 2021–2023 Public Policy Platform," accessed June 20, 2021, https://www.pta.org/home/advocacy/federal-legislation /Public-Policy-Agenda. Examples of free STEM program resources: "The Ultimate STEM Guide for Kids: 239 Cool Sites about Science, Technology, Engineering and Math," Master's in Data Science, 2U, November 22, 2019, https://www.mastersindatascience.org /resources/the-ultimate-stem-guide-for-kids-239-cool-sites-about-science-technology -engineering-and-math/.

33. AARP, "Is an AARP Membership Worth It?," accessed May 18, 2021, https://www.aarp .org/benefits-discounts/is-aarp-membership-worth-it.html#:~:text=How%20Much%20 Does%20an%20AARP,by%20choosing%20a%20multiyear%20membership.

34. Davis Guggenheim, dir., *An Inconvenient Truth* (Hollywood: Paramount Classics, 2006).

35. US Census Bureau, "America's Families and Living Arrangements: 2020."

Index

Page numbers in italics refer to tables and figures.

Asthma, 76–77, 141
Asymmetric information, 116, 140
Atwater, Lee, 207–208
Autism, 117–118

Baker, Josephine, 88
Baldwin, Bird, 28, 39
Beatty, Charles Eugene ("Chief"), 38
Becker, Gary Stanley, 257n14
Becoming a Man (BAM), 176–178
Behavior modification, 90–95, *94*, 101, 103
Ben-Shalom, Yonatan, 260n26
Bergh, Henry, 255n30
Biden, Joe, 185
Billings, Stephen, 261n33
Black Americans
  access to New Deal programs, 204
  vs. Asian Americans, income of, 152
  emancipation of, 135
  enfranchisement of, 205–206
  enslaved, skill suppression in, 134–136,
    137, 138–143, 266n26
  incarceration of, 138–140
  skill equalization for, 133, 143–149,
    267n29
  Southern, disenfranchisement after
    Reconstruction, 204–205
  terminology, 232n19
Bloom, Nick, 81
Borrowing constraints (access to money),
  120–127, 141, 257n14, 258n18
Bouchard, T. J., 244n15
Branch, Taylor, 149
Breastfeeding, 228n2
Brigham, Amariah, 35
Brooks-Gunn, Jeanne, 54
Brown, Emma: "In 23 States, Richer School
  Districts Get More Local Funding Than
  Poorer Districts," 10–11
Brown v. Board of Education, 136, 140
Bryant, Donna, 53
Buffet, Warren, 165

Bulman, George, 125–126
Burke, Barbara, 36
Burns, Augustus, 239n33
Bush, George H. W., 207
Bush, George W., 207–208
Bussey, Cyrus, 24

California, 152–155, 160–161, 271n49
California education funding, 11, 233n26
Callaghan, Timothy, 118
Campbell, Frances, 42, 44, 49–50
Caring, 2–3
Carlson, Bonnie E., 261n32
Carlton, Dolores, 68–69
Carolina Abecedarian Project, 241n50
  Carolina Infant Curriculum, 46, *47*, 48, 112
  establishment of, 44–45
  funding of, 189
  future earnings impacted by, 50, 170,
    240–241n43
  vs. home-visiting programs, 87, 251n4
  investments in, 171, 274n16
  Learning Games, 46, *47*, 48, 112
  success of, 49–51, 54, 87
Carrell, Steve, 128–130, 260–261n29
Carroll, Daniel R., 262n1
CCDF (Child Care Development Fund),
  173–174, 276–277nn23–24
Changing Destructive Adolescent Behavior
  (Parent Project), 101
Charles, Kerwin, 145
Chetty, Raj, 14, 65
Child abuse and neglect, 3, 62–63, 130, 211
Childcare
  Carolina Infant Curriculum, 46, *47*,
    48, 112 (*see also* Carolina Abecedarian
    Project)
  emergence of, 42
  measuring quality of, 174, 277n25
Child Care Aware, 211
Child Care Development Fund (CCDF),
  173–174, 276–277nn23–24

Child development. *See also* Infants
  fixed, heritable intelligence view, 28, 30,
    35–36, 238n18
  intellectual disability, 39–40, 42, 44
  orphanage studies on, 30–31
  research on, 27–28 (*see also* Iowa Child
    Welfare Research Station; NICHD;
    Preschool)
Child-Parent Centers, 174–175
Child psychologists, 90–95, *94*
Children. *See also* Infants; Teenagers
  advocacy for, 25–26, 211–213, 236n7 (*see
    also* Iowa Child Welfare Research Station;
    US Children's Bureau)
  as disenfranchised, 191–192
  health care for, 187, 193, 220
  mortality rate of, 21–22
  personal responsibility of, 178–179, 181,
    183
  psychiatric disorders in, 91
  R&D on, 189–193, 220
Children's Defense Fund, 192, 211
Children's Health Insurance Program
  (CHIP), 220
Child skill building. *See* Skill building in
  children
Child Study Association of America, 85
Child Welfare League of America, 211
Chinese Americans, 153, 156–159. *See also*
  Asian Americans
Chinese Exclusion Act (1882), 155–156, 206
Civil Rights Act (1964), 138, 160, 205–206
Civil Rights Act (1965), 138, 205–206
Civil Rights Act (1968), 206
Civil rights movement, 38, 138–140, 144,
  149, 161, 206
Civil War, 135, 263n8
CMTO (Creating Moves to Opportunity),
  69–70, 185, 217–218
College
  applying to, 73, 186, 248n43
  Black vs. white graduates of, 144, 267n29

competition for elite universities, 196
  entrance exams for, 6, 73, 247n38 (*see also*
    SAT test)
  financial aid for, 73–74, 126, 140–141,
    168–169, 186, 218–219
  guidance counseling, 217
  investments in, 167–169, 273n6, 273n9,
    274n13
  and skill building in children, 6–7, 123
  support during, 74–75, 186, 218
Confederacy, 135–136, 263n8
COVID-19 pandemic, 15, 247n38
CPI (Consumer Price Index), 201
Cravens, Hamilton, 85
Creating Moves to Opportunity (CMTO),
  69–70, 185, 217–218

Databank (IRS), 14–15, 65–67, 69–70, 72,
  123, 191
Deer, Brian, 117–118
Democratic Party, 204–207
Department of Defense, 198
Diapers, 185, 216, 280n45
Discrimination, 130. *See also* Jim Crow regime
  against Asian Americans, 19, 150, 152–
    155, 159–161, 270n46
  ban on, 19, 204–206 (*see also* Civil Rights
    Acts)
  against Black people, 138–139, 270n46 (*see
    also under* Racial inequality)
  blaming minorities for problems caused
    by, 142
  in criminal justice, 138–139
  in housing, 139, 206
  in the labor market, 144–146, 268n34
  against obese people, 78
  persistence of, 6
  segregation, 139–140, 146–148, 154–
    155, 204–206, 271n49 (*see also* School
    integration)
  skill acquisition affected by, 6
  types of, 6

child skill development by, 171–173
  cost of, 172–173, 275n21
  eligibility for, 172
  establishment of, 199–200
  expansion of, 55
  investments in, 173, 203, 275n22
  low participation in, 172
  test scores in, 50
Health care industry, size of, 2, 228n2
Healthy Families America, 86
Hearn, Ruby Puryear, 51–55. *See also* IHDP
Heckman, James, 231n11, 252–253n8
Hillis, Cora Bussey, 23–28, 31, 39–41, 114,
  188, 191, 209, 236n7
HIPPY (Home Instruction Program for
  Preschool Youngsters), 86
Hispanic Americans, 162–163
Historically Black Colleges and Universities,
  147
Hoekstra, Mark, 128, 130, 260–261n29
Holmes, Frances, 92
Holt Adoption Agency, 60–62
HOME (Home Observation Measurement
  of the Environment) assessment, 142–143
Home Instruction Program for Preschool
  Youngsters (HIPPY), 86
Hoover, Herbert, 22
Howard University, 147

Identical-twin studies, 244–245n15
IHDP (Infant Health and Development
  Program), 53–55, 96–97, 241n46,
  241nn49–50, 251n4
Ikeda, Victor, 148
Immigration Act (1965), 156, 206
"In 23 States, Richer School Districts Get
  More Local Funding Than Poorer
  Districts" (Brown), 10–11
Incarceration
  of Black people, 138–140
  of children, 182–183
  employment and earnings following,
  182–183

Income inequality
  by class, 5–7, 133, *221*, 230n9
  closing income gaps to close wealth gaps,
  133, 144, 262n1
  by gender, 263n14
  luck's role in, 229n8
  by race, 5–7, 19, 133, 138–142, *221*,
  230n9, 230–231n11
  skill building in children as reducing, 5–7,
  229–230nn8–9, 230–231n11
Inconvenient Truth, An, 212–213
Incredible Years, 96, 98
Inequality. *See also* Income inequality; Racial
  inequality
  in schools vs. families, 8–12, *9*,
  232nn17–18
  skills' role in income, 5 (*see also under*
  Racial inequality)
Infant Health and Development Program.
  See IHDP
Infants. *See also* Childcare
  development studies of (*see* Carolina
  Abecedarian Project; IHDP)
  IQ testing of, 49
  low-birthweight, 52–55, 127
  mortality of, 21–22
  preschool for, 34–35, 170
  screenings for, 40–41
Inflation, 200–201
Institute of Education Sciences (IES), 220
Intellectual disability, 39–40, 42, 44
Invest in Kids, 98
Investments
  and affordability, 194
  in the Carolina Abecedarian Project, 171,
  274n16
  in college, 167–169, 273n6, 273n9,
  274n13
  competition among investors, 166
  federally funded R&D, 198–199
  in Head Start, 173, 203, 275n22
  in preschool, 170–171, 175, 274n14
  return on investment (ROI), 165–166

Investments (cont.)
in skill building in children, 13–14, 19, 64–65, 167, 272n4
wealth generated by, 165
Iowa Child Welfare Research Station, 58
criticism of, 35–36, 38
founding of, 26–28, 188, 209
funding for, 40, 238–239n29
influence of, 36–38, 43, 63, 171–172
preschool test scores studied by, 28, *29*, 30–34, 237n11
research on cultivating economic skills, 27–28
and the Soldiers' Home orphanage, 30–32
IQ tests, 31–32, 49–50
Isen, Adam, 125–126
Isolation response, 131

Japanese Americans, 153–157. *See also* Asian Americans
Japanese Exclusion Act (Immigration Act of 1924), 206
Japanese internment camps, 147–148, 155
Jencks, Christopher, 231n11
Jersild, Arthur, 92
Jim Crow regime, 12, 36, 143, 150–151, 154, 162
Job creation, 195
Johnson, James Weldon, 268n34
Johnson, Lyndon B., 139, 199, 206–207
Johnson, Ned, 195
Johnson, Rucker, 261n33

Kalil, Ariel, 97
Kazdin, Alan, 96
Kefalas, Maria, 180–181
Kennedy, Eunice, 39–42, 188
Kennedy, John F. ("Jack"), 40, 205–206
Kennedy, Joseph, 39
Kennedy, Rosemary, 39
Kephart, Newell, 238n21

King, Martin Luther, Jr., 138–139, 205–206
Kingston, Maxine Hong, 160–161
Kirk, Samuel, 36–37, 43, 171–172
Kozol, Jonathan: *Savage Inequalities*, 10
Kraemer, Helena, 54
Ku Klux Klan, 207
Kuziemko, Ilyana, 205–206

Lareau, Annette, 68–70, 125–126
Lathrop, Julia, 21–22, 132
Laura Spelman Rockefeller Foundation, 85, 250n1
Layoffs, and college attendance, 123–126
Learning Heroes, 113
Lee-DeLauro End Diaper Need Act (2019), 216
Lenroot, Katherine, 22–23
Levitt, Eugene, 91
Lewis, Isabelle, 44–46
Literacy, 135
Lobbying, 1, 26, 192, 282n5
Looney, Adam, 273n6
Lottery wins, and college outcomes, 126
Lucas, James, 134

Management-practices research, 80–83
March on Washington, 139
Masculinity, 176
McNemar, Quinn, 35–36
Medicaid, 180, 187, 199–200, 203, 220
Medicare, 184, 187, 192–194, 199–200
Mendez v. Westminster, 163
"Mental retardation." *See* Intellectual disability
Metco, 261–262n33
Military spending, 194
Moral hazard, 257n8
Morgan, Roger, 99–103, 106, 255n29
Motta, Matthew, 118
Moving to Opportunity (MTO), 69–70
Mulhern, Christine, 248n42
Murray, Charles, 59–60

NAACP (National Association for the
    Advancement of Colored People), 136
Nannies, 227n2
National Association for the Advancement of
    Colored People (NAACP), 136
National Congress of Mothers, 26, 209
National Council of Parent Education, 85
National Diaper Bank Network, 216
National Institutes of Health, 198
National Longitudinal Survey of Youth
    (NLSY), *221*, 230n9
National Nanotechnology Initiative, 198
National Science Foundation, 60, 198
Native Americans, 155, 162–163, 271n56
Nat Turner's Rebellion (1831), 134
Nature vs. nurture, 27, 57, 242n1
Nelson, Margaret, 178
Neumuller, Seth, 262n1
Neural tube defects, 40–41
New Deal, 22, 34, 199, 203–204, 207
NFP (Nurse-Family Partnership), 88–90,
    96–97, 252–253n8, 253n11
NICHD (National Institute of Child Health
    and Human Development), 40–42, 188–
    189, 198, 220, 238n29
NLSY (National Longitudinal Survey of
    Youth), *221*, 230n9
Nurse-Family Partnership (NFP). *See* NFP
Nurture Assumption, The (Harris), 59–60

Obata, Chiura, 148
Obesity, 78–79, 187
Office of Economic Opportunity, 201
Olds, David, 87–89, 252n8. *See also* NFP
Orphan Drug Act (1983), 198
Orshansky, Mollie, 200–201
O'Shea, Wendy, 89–90
Our Children (PTA magazine), 211

Paid family leave, 185, 215–216
Parental activism, 19–20, 211–213
Parental income, 121–127, 258–259nn24–25

Parent-Child Interaction Therapy, 96
Parent education
    behavioral-modification training, 90–95,
        94, 101, 103
    court-mandated programs, 99–106
    vs. dog training and care, 102, 255n30
    early efforts, 85
    group counseling, 86
    home visits, 86–90, 97, 251n4
    nurse home-visiting programs, 87–90, 96–
        97, 252–253n8, 253n11
    one-on-one parent counseling, 86
    Parent Management Training, 90–98, *94*,
        101
    Parent Project, 99–108, 177, 191, 255n29,
        256n32
    parents' lack of interest in, 97–98
    practice trials/simulations, 95–96
Parenting
    child health management, 76–78
    child nutrition management, 78–79
    and choice of home/neighborhood, 67–71,
        246n30
    impact on children's outcomes, 59–64,
        243nn6–7, 244n13, 244–245n15
    impact on college outcomes (*see* College)
    as an industry, 1–3
    as a job, 65, 75, 82
    management skills, 82–83
    market value of, 2, 227–228n2
    sides of (*see* Caring; Skill building in
        children)
    tutoring/homework help, 71–72, 115
Parenting, key challenges to
    borrowing constraints, 120–127, 141,
        257n14, 258n18
    complexity, 111–112
    information, 115–119, 140
    learning/feedback, 112–115, *114*
    spillover effect, 127–131, 261–262n33
Parent Management Training, 90–98, *94*,
    101